Philip II of Spain

MEN IN OFFICE

General Editor:
Professor Ragnhild Hatton

PETER PIERSON

Philip II of Spain

with 34 illustrations

THAMES AND HUDSON

LONDON

To Harry de Wildt

*Printed in Great Britain by
Cox & Wyman Ltd, London, Fakenham and Reading*

Contents

Preface

'Philip II', wrote Victor Hugo in the last century, 'was a terrible thing.'
The Enlightenment found him the champion of obscurantism, and
the Romantic Age passionately assailed him as an enemy of freedom.
Outside Spain (and for Spanish liberals) he assumed a leading place
among the tyrants of history. But in the twentieth century new figures
have emerged to supplant Philip II as an archetypal tyrant in the public
imagination.

For a proper understanding of Philip II and his reign, this makes
matters easier: polemics and apologies have abandoned the field to
dispassionate investigation. We can study the man in the context of
his own values and times, which in many ways prove not dissimilar
to our own. In regard to values, then as now, we must admit to a
frequent discrepancy between what is professed and what is practised.
In the late sixteenth century, rebellion and war were endemic, engendered not only by material considerations but also by ideologies based
on religious convictions. And Europe then, like much of the world
now, was readjusting to rapidly (in a relative sense) changing conditions,
which caused serious dislocations in all aspects of life and thought.

Given the context, the study of Philip II can be rewarding for our
own age. Philip was a conservative, in that he meant to uphold the
traditional order of government, society and religion. He was ambitious
to do no more than improve the workings of government, especially
in regard to justice, to ensure that the Church in his dominions tended
its and his flock, and to hold the cost of government to the level of
his revenues. War, which he wished to avoid but could not, proved,
however, his undoing. To his mind, all his wars were defensive, for
the sake of his rights, his patrimony and his religion; though to historians, his conquest of Portugal and his war against Henry IV of
France were clearly wars of aggression.

The first part of this book is devoted to a study of Philip's childhood and education, and takes him through his apprenticeship for his kingly office, in which he was guided by his father, Emperor Charles V (Carlos I of Spain).

Upon his father's abdication, Philip began to rule his vast dominions, which came to form the first empire 'upon which the sun never set'. The government devised to rule his dominions forms a landmark in the development of the modern bureaucratic state, although its motivating assumptions most often remained medieval. Having surveyed Philip's dominions, studied the organization and functioning of his Court and analysed Philip and his relationships with those who served him, five important issues have been isolated for study in turn: (1) unity and disunity in the Iberian peninsula, (2) Italian and Mediterranean problems, (3) the revolt of the Netherlands, (4) the emergence of England as a world power and (5) the civil–religious wars of France. Whether foreign or domestic, each issue had its external and internal repercussions. Some posed problems for Philip as legacies of the past; others he handled in such a manner as to create new problems, which he left unsolved at the time of his death.

In my choice of words and phrases, I have been careful to avoid those which do not accurately describe the sixteenth-century situation, as regarded by men of those times. This is especially true in matters of Philip's foreign relations, which I believe have been distorted by many modern scholars through their employment of the vocabulary of nineteenth- and twentieth-century nation-states. Philip II thought consciously in terms of dynasty and religion, not of nation-states.

In writing this book, I want to acknowledge my debt to all others who have studied Philip II and his age, many of whom I mention in my bibliographical essay. The archival material with which I have worked is far too vast for any one scholar to encompass, and one must stand in amazement before the fact that Philip II himself looked over and annotated so many of the documents generated by his regime. I wish to thank my editor Ragnhild Hatton for her hard work with my manuscripts and her trenchant comments and advice. For criticism and help I would also like to thank John H. Elliott, Manuel Fernández Alvarez, Helmut G. Koenigsberger, Albert Lovett and Geoffrey Parker. For a wide range of reasons, my thanks too to Andrew Lossky, Elizabeth Gleason, E. Thaddeus Flood, Geoffrey Symcox, Elizabeth Israels Perry, Doña Matilda Medina, Stanley Payne, Lewis Spitz, the Fulbright programme, the Mabelle McLeod Lewis Memorial Fund, my colleagues and students at the University of Santa Clara, my parents and Mr and Mrs Henricus de Wildt.

I

Charles and Philip: The Education
of a Christian Prince

Philip II of Spain: one sees the haughty glance of Titian's youth of twenty-four, the confident stare of the young man of thirty portrayed by Anthonis Mor, the benign gaze of the mature man in his forties in the portrait by Sánchez Coello, and Pantoja de la Cruz's look of the ageing man in his sixties. In all there appears the same sense of dignity: behind the face there remained the same commanding vision.

Philip's Spain: we find it portrayed in the writings of Cervantes and Mateo Alemán, the diaries of St Teresa of Ávila, the histories by Diego Hurtado de Mendoza and Luis Cabrera de Córdoba; but we miss the brilliant visual depictions of popular life that Velázquez, Murillo and Zurbarán were to produce in the following century. Pieter Breughel, one of Philip's Flemish subjects, painted the best-known scenes of popular life in Philip's era, but only of his Netherlands. Philip was more than king of Spain, the title by which he is best known: he also ruled the seventeen provinces of the Low Countries, as well as being king of Naples, Sicily and Sardinia, duke of Milan, king of Aragon, Castile with its overseas possessions, and, in 1580, king of Portugal.

Yet it is with Spain that we associate him, and with some justification; for he saw the world through Castilian eyes, and according to his biographer and teacher, Juan Ginés de Sepúlveda, he had praise for none but Spaniards.[1] None the less he saw himself as a member, and after the death of his father the Emperor Charles V, as head of the Habsburg family, the House of Austria. He insisted that he bore equal love for all his own subjects, but his obvious preference for men of Iberian origins and his lack of ease among others made him, in the words of the Venetian ambassador Suriano, disliked by Italians, disagreeable to Flemings and hateful to Germans.[2] When he succeeded his father he withdrew as soon as he could to the Iberian peninsula. Here he lived out his life, reigning for more than forty years.

BIRTH AND EDUCATION

Philip, prince of Spain, was born on 21 May 1527 at Valladolid and two weeks later christened amid ceremonies worthy of the first-born son of Don Carlos I, king of Castile and Aragon, known better to history as the Emperor Charles V, and Isabel, infanta of Portugal, empress and queen.[3]

A month later the ceremonies were stopped short: Charles learned that his armies, gathered in Italy to fight a league of Francis I, king of France, and Pope Clement VII de' Medici, had broken from control and brutally sacked papal Rome. Though he privately blamed the pope for the misfortune, Charles did public penance. The predictions of peace and prosperity for Prince Philip, made by court astrologers who plotted his sun in Gemini, seemed thus soon eclipsed by gloomier prospects, discerned by other seers, in the torrential rains that fell the day of his birth. For Philip was not only heir to Charles's vast possessions, but also to his many and mounting problems.

Charles's possessions came to him largely through inheritance, and excited the fear and envy of his contemporaries. In defence of these possessions, and from the circumstances of his times, Charles developed a sense of mission, which he passed, along with most of his lands, to Philip. What was the nature of Charles's inheritance and mission, which became paramount factors in Philip's life?

In 1506, Charles, aged six, inherited the Low Countries and Franche-Comté (the Free County of Burgundy) upon the death of his father, Philip the Handsome. It was after him that Charles named his own son and heir. Significantly, neither Charles nor Philip were customary names for Spanish kings, but rather were derived from the line of Valois dukes of Burgundy, to whose dominions and interests Charles bound the destiny of Spain and the rest of the Catholic Monarchy.[4]

The Catholic Monarchy consisted of Castile and the realms of the crown of Aragon, Aragon in Spain and the Italian kingdoms of Sicily, Sardinia and Naples, and was brought together by the marriage of their rulers, Isabella the Catholic, queen-proprietress of Castile,[5] and Ferdinand the Catholic, king of Aragon. Charles's mother Queen Joanna became their heir through the unexpected deaths of her elder brother and sister, something Ferdinand had not reckoned with when he arranged her marriage to Philip, the only son of the Emperor Maximilian I, for the sake of the Emperor's alliance against the king of France.

When Isabella died in 1504, Joanna and her husband, now King Consort Philip I, hastened to Castile to assume its government and, in effect, divide the Catholic Monarchy. Philip attempted to set the erratic Joanna aside, claiming that she was incompetent to rule by reason of madness, but the Castilian Cortes balked at his claim.[6] In 1506 he died. Ferdinand then attempted the same manoeuvre, but with success. The highly strung Joanna, broken by Philip's death, was confined to a tower at Tordesillas, and Ferdinand served as her regent in Castile, which resumed its place in the Catholic Monarchy. To succeed Ferdinand, upon his death in 1516, Charles had to continue his mother's confinement. He persuaded the Cortes of the Spanish realms to accept him as co-ruler, that is as king, alongside his unfortunate mother, and give him full exercise of royal power so long as she remained incompetent.

In 1519, Charles's paternal grandfather Maximilian (who had given Charles's dynasty its name, 'of Austria' or Habsburg) died, leaving Charles the Austrian duchies. In the same year, Charles was elected Holy Roman Emperor, an office the Habsburgs were coming to consider their own.

From his grandparents Charles also received legacies of other than lands. He inherited an ongoing war with the king of France over dynastic claims and strategic positions, the duty to protect the Church of Rome against the new Protestant heresies, and the task of defending Christendom against its traditional foe, the Islamic world, led aggressively by the Ottoman Turks in the sixteenth century. Symbolically, these brewing troubles came to a head in the sack of Rome, in which many of them were involved, and appeared to end that fortunate age we now call the Renaissance, dashing the optimism generated by the 'new learning', new inventions such as printing and the discovery of the New World.

It was against this background that Charles developed his sense of mission, for which he believed Providence had endowed him with his extraordinary inheritance.[7] Within Christendom, he wished for peace among Christian princes, on his terms, and a solution to the issues dividing the reformers from Rome: once these goals had been realized, he hoped to resume the crusade against Islam. Charles's programme, needless to say, was widely opposed and never succeeded. His world therefore appeared increasingly grim, ever shattered by costly wars, shaken by reformers and threatened by the Turks. Embittered, yet never giving up hope, he made it one of his chief duties to prepare his son and heir to face this world and follow him in his mission.

We know little of Philip's earliest years. During nearly five of them (1529–33) Charles was absent from Spain, and thus could not supervise in person his son's upbringing or bring his fatherly presence to bear. Philip and his sisters, Maria (b. 1529) and Juana (b. 1535), were largely under the control of their mother, Isabel, a woman of regal dignity, strong character and profound religiosity. Charles, who had married her in 1526 for political reasons, had soon come to love and respect her deeply.

The Empress frequently reminded Philip that he was the son of the greatest emperor the world had ever known, and to comport himself accordingly.[8] When he did not, she could be severe, and on at least one occasion she punished him hard enough for her ladies to sob at 'such cruelty'.[9] Charles, on the other hand, seems to have been more indulgent: when he found Philip romping with some other children in the royal bedchamber, he accepted his son's excuse that the others 'had started it'; they were scolded and sent away, while Philip remained in his father's good graces.[10]

Charles, though moody, could be outgoing and affable, while Isabel was reserved, and kept her warmth for the intimate circles of family and friends. Here Philip took more after his mother than his father: in public he was dignified, even haughty, never affable; but with his family and a few friends he was capable of great tenderness and affection. Isabel, however, was not lacking in a sense of humour. Philip's first governor, Don Pedro González de Mendoza, a cleric and son of the duke of Infantado, wrote in 1535 to Charles that he and the marquis of Lombay (Francisco Borja, later superior general of the Jesuits) had led Prince Philip, mounted on a burro, through the streets of Toledo, causing the crowds to joke and the Empress, who followed, to laugh.[11] In humour as in deportment, the evidence of his later life suggests that Philip leaned to his mother's side: he laughed at antics,[12] but avoided the unbuttoned revels, popular in the Netherlands, which Charles enjoyed.

Although Philip grew up with his mother's manner and temperament, he worshipped Charles, the mighty father and emperor; and Charles, so often absent from Philip's life, when with him showered him with affection and took him into his confidence about the great affairs of the world. Above all Philip wanted to be worthy of Charles: it was against his dreams of Charles's triumphs and his nightmares of Charles's failures that Philip measured his own conduct, and if Gregorio Marañón, personal physician of Alfonso XIII of Spain and a fine amateur historian, is correct, Philip in so doing found himself inadequate.[13] Philip said too little about himself for us ever to be sure about what went on inside his mind: studying the mature king and trying to find the roots of his later conduct in his childhood and with his parents must always remain a risky business.

In 1535 Charles removed Philip from the tutelage of his mother and her ladies to begin his education in the world of men. He established a household for the prince, to whom he assigned as governor his old companion and councillor, Don Juan de Zúñiga, *comendador mayor* of Castile. The best evidence for Philip's life in these years comes from the letters of Zúñiga's wife, Doña Estefanía de Requesens, to her mother.[14] We learn from them of Philip's childhood illnesses, and of the games he played with the children of the court: on one occasion she describes Philip playing with his page, her son Don Luis de Requesens, both engrossed in building a church of playing cards. Philip's chief amusement seems to have been arranging mock tournaments, but he also followed closely his parents' interest in world affairs.

Zúñiga's prime function in Philip's upbringing concerned the prince's development in the courtly and manly arts. In this he could be severe with the prince, which Charles, who apparently could not, appreciated.[15] Under Zúñiga's guidance Philip learned to ride and hunt, and to participate in various forms of jousting, such as tilting and the graceful Moorish joust with light lances called *cañas*, which demanded good horsemanship rather than brute strength. In the gentle arts, Philip learned to act gallantly and elegantly, with proper grace and courtesy,[16] as befitted the ideal of the Renaissance prince. He played the guitar but seems not to have sung. He became fond of birds, flowers and the woods, a side of his character more representative of the Netherlands than of Spain;[17] and from Charles he also acquired a taste for the fine arts and good music.

The academic side of Philip's upbringing was the province of Master Juan Martínez Silíceo, an affable but bigoted cleric of humble origins. Silíceo had studied philosophy and theology in Spain and at Paris, and was called from a chair at Salamanca to be Philip's tutor. While he wrote Latin well and later composed religious treatises, his first interest was mathematics, in which he published several works. Not surprisingly, mathematics became Philip's strongest subject.

Assisting Silíceo in Philip's education were two well-known scholars, the humanist Honorato Juan, a disciple of the Renaissance educational theorist Luis Vives, and the Aristotelian Juan Ginés de Sepúlveda, who subsequently wrote Latin chronicles about the reigns of Charles

and Philip, and upheld against Fray Bartolomé de las Casas the rightness of conquering and enslaving non-Christian peoples.

Philip pursued his studies both privately and in small classes of five or
six children of courtiers, including young Requesens. For a while
Philip's cousin Maximilian (born in Vienna on 31 July 1527), son of
Charles's brother, Ferdinand, also shared these classes. Charles was particularly anxious that Philip master Latin and acquire some fluency in
French: he had himself learnt languages in the thick of events, as he
inherited realms with populations each speaking a different language or
dialect. Latin, the one tongue all educated Europeans knew, was vital;
French was important for the Low Countries, even in the Flemish-
speaking provinces, Castilian, on the othar hand, was understood outside Spain only in Portugal and Italy. We have no evidence that Charles
tried to have Philip learn German or any of the Netherlandish dialects.
Philip never became as good a linguist as his father – a fact for which
Charles blamed Siliceo, who, he claimed, did not work his pupil hard
enough.

Philip learned to read Latin easily and to speak it well enough to
sustain a conversation.[18] He understood Portuguese, his mother's
native tongue, and could use it. French, however, he was hesitant in
speaking and not able to follow well: he could read it, but ordinarily
had French correspondence translated into Castilian for his convenience.
Philip was fluent only in Castilian, but even in this no literary stylist.
His writings followed his thoughts at random, and his secretaries gave
them whatever polish they needed according to the bureaucratic
formulae of the times. Philip's biographer Luis Cabrera de Córdoba
(whose history of the Prudent King is still worth studying) grew up at
Philip's court and served his government as a secretary. He claimed
that the king, possessing a world empire, wanted to make Castilian
the world language, as Latin had been the language of the Roman
Empire and Greek of the Macedonian. Certainly Philip had before
him the example of Charles V who in 1536 chose to address the pope
and cardinals in Castilian rather than Latin.

Philip's childhood came to an abrupt and early end. Just before his
twelfth birthday, his mother died. Charles was present to console his
children, but not for long: affairs of state took him to the Netherlands
in late autumn, and he left Philip in Spain as a symbol of keeping
faith with his Iberian kingdoms. The young prince continued his
academic studies under Siliceo, but he also began to take part in the
affairs of state, by attending meetings of the royal councils and noting
their procedures. His instruction in statecraft lay in the hands of Zúñiga,

Archbishop Tavera of Toledo, Charles's lieutenant-general of Castile, and Francisco de los Cobos, Charles's secretary for finances. He took advice attentively, and observed closely the actions of those around him.

Charles returned to Spain in late 1541, but departed in May 1543 for Germany and the Low Countries to conduct a war against his many enemies, the king of France, the German Protestant league and the Ottoman Turks. This time he appointed Philip, not quite sixteen, his regent in Spain, and gave him the task of supporting his own efforts.

PHILIP'S APPRENTICESHIP FOR OFFICE: THE REGENCY OF SPAIN

Philip assumed regency powers in Spain in May 1543 and exercised them until October 1548, when Charles ordered him to join him in the Low Countries. During Philip's absence from Spain, Charles appointed his daughter Maria and her husband Archduke Maximilian as regents. Philip returned to Spain in July 1551 and replaced his sister.[19] He served as regent on this second occasion until June 1554, when business of state again took him north. This time he was replaced by his sister Princess Juana. When he next returned to Spain in 1559, he was king, and Juana already his regent, not Charles's.

Philip's exercise of regency powers in his father's absence was customary in Charles's dominions, which called for a member of the ruling house, preferably the heir to the throne, to stand in the stead of an absent sovereign. In practice Charles only employed members of his dynasty as regents in his most important dominions, Spain and the Low Countries; the rest had to be content with viceroys or governors of the high nobility.

Before leaving the sixteen-year-old Philip as his regent, Charles had two matters to settle: to obtain the recognition of Philip (already recognized in Castile in 1528) as heir to the crown of Aragon, and to provide Philip with a wife from Portugal in the interests of both the continuity of the dynasty and the maintenance of the long peace with Portugal. That a Portuguese marriage might lead to the union of Portugal with the other Iberian kingdoms could not have been far from Charles's mind. The death rate of King John III's children was extraordinarily high; in fact he outlived them all, to be succeeded by his sole and ill-fated grandson, Dom Sebastian.

Early in 1543 Charles summoned the General Cortes of the crown of Aragon* to Monzón to grant him a subsidy and to acknowledge Philip. Philip was duly recognized and Charles voted the traditional subsidy to succour his military operations.

A final piece of business concerned only the kingdom of Aragon proper. (Aragon means both the small kingdom with its capital at Zaragoza, and Aragon, Valencia and Catalonia taken together, which were ruled by the House of Aragon.) Charles intended to exalt the place of the crown and minimize the role of the *Justicia* of Aragon by symbolically altering the ceremony in which Philip, as heir, swore to uphold the famed 'liberties' of Aragon, largely vestiges of the feudal age, which favoured the nobility.[20] The *Justicia* had the power to over-rule the king in cases involving these 'liberties'. The office of *Justicia* had come to be hereditary in the Lanuza family; but the constitutional issue, whether the office was dependent on the royal pleasure, the Cortes, or both, had never been resolved.

When Charles himself had taken the oath in 1518, the ceremony, held in *La Seo*, the cathedral of Zaragoza, had been so arranged that he *knelt* on a dais, his back to the main altar, and faced the representatives of the Cortes and the *standing Justicia*, who administered the oath. An impression had thus been created that Charles had submitted to the sovereign authority of the magistracy and people of Aragon, or at least this was how many remembered it. Charles now saw to it that when Philip took the oath, he *faced* the main altar of *La Seo*, rather than the *Justicia* and the deputies of Aragon, thereby emphasizing that he submitted himself only to God, not to any temporal magistrates. Certainly in this Charles, and Philip his heir, showed their inclination towards divine right absolutism, and Philip, when king, resolved the issue of the *Justicia* in favour of the crown.

The marriage of Philip to the Portuguese infanta Maria Manuela took place at Salamanca in the autumn of 1543. We can see in Philip a touch of youthful ardour when he rode out to catch a glimpse of her prior to the wedding, as she approached the city in her cavalcade. According to contemporary sources, he fell quite in love with the pretty, buxom infanta, a girl of his own age. On 8 July 1545, she gave birth to a son, whom Philip named Don Carlos after his father. Four days later, the princess died of the complications of childbirth. Philip, who at twelve had buried his mother, at eighteen buried his first wife.

In the conduct of his regency government, Philip proved himself

* The General Cortes was an assembly of the Cortes of the kingdoms of Aragon and Valencia and the county of Catalonia in one place, though each Cortes sat independently.

diligent and grave. To guide him he had Charles's instructions, one of history's most remarkable political testaments, written on 4 and 6 May 1543,[21] as the Emperor embarked at Palamós to journey north to Germany and the Low Countries. These instructions deserve to be discussed in some detail, because of their impact on Philip's thinking.

Charles began by commenting on the gravity of the responsibilities being placed upon one so young, but he expressed confidence that Philip, with God's help, would give him 'reason to thank God for making me the father of such a son'. Claiming that he was a poor preceptor, Charles prayed that God would 'take me as His instrument' – an expression frequently invoked by Charles and later by Philip – so that the advice offered would be sound, since it was 'in His service'.

He urged Philip to uphold the Inquisition, and never to let heretics into his kingdoms. This advice of 1543 became more pronounced in subsequent years and made a particularly profound impression upon Philip. In Spain, the Inquisition authorized by Pope Sixtus IV and established in 1480 by Ferdinand and Isabella, was governed by a royal council, *de la suprema y general Inquisición*, staffed with royal appointees. Its purpose initially was to prevent backsliding by converted Jews (*conversos*) and Moors (*moriscos*), referred to as New Christians to differentiate them from the Old Christian majority of Spaniards. While royal control of the Inquisition made it a potential instrument of absolutism, it tended to have a life and momentum of its own, driven by the debates, jealousies and ambitions of the clergy, and the anxieties, prejudices and fears of the Old Christians, who doubted the loyalty of the New Christians to Church and crown. Staffed at the top by men well-versed in theology and canon law, it was served at the bottom by some 20,000 *familiares*, faceless informers fired by zeal or ambition, who permeated the life of Spain.

The more disillusioned Charles became by the failure of his policies, whether peaceful or warlike, to suppress heresy in the Empire, the more convinced he became that only a rigorous Inquisition could prevent Spain from going the way of Germany. In a later instruction of 1557 to the Princess Juana, Charles claimed that heretics disturbed the entire community and soon took up arms to overthrow the Church and established authority.[22] Heretics, he came to believe, should be considered rebels and treated as such. In Philip's reign, the expression 'rebel and heretic' became commonplace.

Along with defence of religion, Charles stressed the dispensing of justice. Philip should see that the magistrates administered it fairly. He reminded Philip to imitate Christ, tempering justice with mercy, but hastened to add, 'Too much mercy is a vice rather than a virtue.'

Charles implored the prince to be moderate in all things: 'Watch your temper and do nothing in anger. Avoid following the advice of the young, and ignore the calumnies of the elderly.' Surrounded as he now was in the government by mature men, Philip was to comport himself as a grown man, and not to tell jokes or behave foolishly.

Remembering his own past mistakes, Charles admonished his son 'to avoid bad people as you would the fire, because they are dangerous and have many ways of drawing near you. Be quick to find out about a man, so that if he is bad, you can dismiss him. Favour good men, so all know that you are served by them, not by the wicked.' This advice Philip heeded carefully – a hallmark of his own regime is the diligence with which he sought to find out, from whatever source, all he could about those who served him.

Charles had a good deal to say about the men he placed around Philip: Archbishop Tavera, Zúñiga, los Cobos and the duke of Alba. Only the instructions concerning Alba remained relevant since all but Alba were dead by 1547; he remained one of Philip's leading advisers until 1582. In general, Philip was advised by his father to let none of them exercise too much power, although several would surely try, whether from the best or worst of intentions. Drawing on Charles's remarks and what else we know about them, we can say that most of these associates of Philip during his apprenticeship in office were dedicated in principle and through interest to the monarchy, and were pious, intolerant and conservative.

In the case of Don Fernando Alvarez de Toledo, third duke of Alba, Philip's military chief, there were two problems. The first was personal: the duke, Charles warned Philip, would try to treat him as a child. Indeed, until the day he died Alba's manner towards Philip was avuncular; years later Philip's former page Requesens referred to Alba as *el tio* (the uncle).[23]

More serious was the threat of Alba's order, the grandees, to the sovereign authority of the crown. The forebears of the grandees had helped the royal bastard Henry, founder of the Trastámara dynasty, usurp the throne in 1369 from Pedro, whose policies they found objectionable. Indentured thus to the magnates, the Trastámaras alienated much of the royal domain to them, a process finally halted by Ferdinand and Isabella. To rebuild the power of the crown, the Catholic Monarchs obtained control of the Castilian military orders, and limited the participation by grandees in the administration of their realms. However, they left the grandees with most of their ill-gotten gains, broad if not absolute jurisdiction over their vassals, and exemption from direct taxation. Charles had no doubt that the grandees, given the chance, would resume control of the royal administration and start once more to plunder the royal domain. 'If they capture your will,' he cautioned Philip, 'it will cost you dearly.'

But the grandees could not be ignored, nor entirely kept from government. Their economic and social power was immense; the land could not be ruled without some sort of understanding between the crown and the magnates, who considered serving the crown their birthright, and plundering the crown a side-benefit of service. The solution was clear, even if its application did require eternal vigilance: speaking of Alba, Charles told Philip to consult him in matters of foreign policy and war (top items in the hierarchy of values of this warrior-nobility), render him honours and favours, but keep him from matters of ordinary administration – in other words from the routine business of handling lawsuits, estates and money.

The grandees were not the only order in the land likely to give the crown problems: there was another, the Church, the largest of early modern institutions, vital to effective government yet, in theory, responsible to an outside power, the pope. In the exercise of royal authority, and particularly in regard to justice, Charles warned Philip that the prince might have to contravene the pope, in which case he was to be respectful of the Holy Father, but uphold the laws of the land.

If Charles stressed one thing in the instructions, it was the problem of finance, 'upon which the success or failure of my policies depend. You must attend closely to finances, and learn to understand the problems involved.' Philip took this to heart, and indeed attended closely to his finances, if admittedly he never came to understand their intricacies.

Finances were closely tied to politics, since to raise revenues the crown had to deal with the Cortes, though (especially in Philip's own reign) the crown's rising income from the Indies gave it a powerful advantage. It could embark on some policy – usually a war – and then pressure the Cortes to contribute to its cost out of loyalty or fear.

Meeting with the Cortes to obtain revenues was not always a pleasant experience, as Philip discovered during his regency. Dependent on their vote for subsidies, the crown had to hear their grievances. The Cortes agreed that war and foreign policy were prerogatives of the crown but wanted a more significant share in making law and administering justice.

The presentation of grievances irritated the professional servants of the crown, a growing group of university men, trained in Roman Law and convinced of the efficacy of the government they administered. They conveyed their irritation to Philip who, as time went on, came to share it. Determined, as was his father, to uphold the constitutional arrangements of his God-given dominions, Philip throughout his reign convoked Cortes in Spain and representative bodies in all those of his dominions which possessed such bodies (which meant all save Milan). He did not, however, as he grew older, subject himself to the unpleasantness of hearing their grievances in person or dealing directly with their leaders; that he left to his ministers. Between his will and their abilities to manipulate representatives, and backed by the wealth of the crown he succeeded throughout his reign in getting supply before dealing with grievances, which were later accepted and at times acted upon or rejected, at the crown's convenience.

Again we encounter absolutism in its incipient phase under Charles and Philip, when representative bodies were convoked on the pattern of the Middle Ages to grant money and lay their grievances before the crown though their requests were not necessarily respected.

While crown and Cortes argued over grievances and taxes, the tax base in Castile was impaired by growing economic stagnation.[24] The clearest symptom was a steep rise in prices, not paralleled by a rise in productivity. The Cortes blamed the cost of Charles's wars, and indeed in 1545 Philip as regent complained to his father about the general misery caused by mounting taxes, which came on top of the many payments exacted from the population by the Church and the seigneurs.

The rise in war-related taxes was, however, but one factor in the economic woes of the Iberian peninsula, which, it must be stressed, seemed particularly distressing to contemporaries since the century had started out so full of promise with a rise in population, a continuing rich wool trade with the Low Countries and Italy, and above all the opening up of the New World. Yet certain lucrative export products, such as wool, wines and olive oil, drove grain production to marginal lands, chiefly in Old Castile. When the growth of population led to a rise in the price of bread, the government responded to public outcry and imposed a price ceiling on grains. This in its turn had the effect of depressing the economies of grain-producing districts, since the grain farmers could not pay the rising prices of other products. They often gave up and emigrated elsewhere, looking for new livelihoods, or became vagabonds, living on charity. Attempts to enforce harsh poor laws, which put vagabonds into workhouses, were half-

hearted and opposed by the mendicant orders which directed the organized charities. Vagrancy became an accepted lifestyle, celebrated in picaresque novels, and scarcely objected to by the Andalusian grandees, who employed seasonal labour, or by recruiting officers, who had little trouble filling their rolls.

What manufacturing there was in Spain suffered, since vagabondage or the military life seemed attractive. Willing workers were in short supply; they therefore demanded high wages, which cut profit margins. Moreover, the chief Castilian industries, textiles, hardware (in the Basque provinces) and shipbuilding, were less well developed than their Flemish and Italian competitors. Despite the Castilian monopoly in the Indies, they found it difficult to keep the pace set by others. Their problems were then compounded by the reaction of the Cortes and the crown to the rising cost of manufactures, which was, in the case of textiles, to restrict exports and allow increased imports. This resulted not in the reduction of prices, but in crippling the Castilian textile industry.

In fact, contemporary economic theory, still tied to theology, could offer no satisfactory explanation of what was happening, and statesmen were helpless to remedy matters. The learned men at the university of Salamanca held that the influx of specie from the New World was one cause among many of the general inflation; but their methodology was hardly adequate to develop the idea further, let alone suggest remedies to the problem.

The silver and gold arriving at Seville each year from the New World averaged by the 1550s some 2,000,000 ducats a year, of which the crown received roughly a quarter.[25] The money seldom stayed long in Castile because foreign bankers, often with crown licence, soon carried it from the country. As in other fields, the Castilians were behind their competitors in banking from Italy, Germany and the Low Countries. These were longer established, more efficient, had better connections, and could more easily deliver money when and where the crown wished.

The money from the Indies and the money raised through taxation in Spain was used to finance the crown's foreign wars. It was war, as the Cortes complained, that impaired the Spanish economy, not only because of the taxes it necessitated, but also because the money raised was spent abroad. The crown bought munitions in other lands, where they were more readily available, usually cheaper, and closer to the war zone; it hired foreign shipping, and spent hard Castilian cash for mercenaries from Lombardy and Germany.

Moreover, the wars had side effects equally harmful to the economic well-being of Spain. They gave purpose to an already swollen nobility who found honour in fighting, and stimulated the growth of a large non-productive bureaucracy. The most capable and ambitious men of Spain were attracted to the excitement of the wars or to prestigious posts in government and Church (itself partly a government institution), and left the management of Castilian commerce and crown finances increasingly to foreigners; while the too common disdain of noblemen and the lettered for manual labour found itself mimicked in the posturings of the idle *pícaros*.

The war crises that overtook Charles in 1552 (when he had to fight the German Protestants in alliance with the French king), just as Philip was beginning his second regency, caused the prince to borrow anew, to summon the Cortes for new grants and mortgage royal domains and rights. Despite contrary legislation, Philip granted allocations of Indian labour in the New World to Spaniards in return for hard cash (while to ease his own conscience, he reminded the grantees to treat the Indians well); and he yielded to necessity further by signing new contracts for the African slave trade, considered by many immoral, but none the less provided for by law.

Despite all steps to get more tax money, Philip, pressured by Charles, was forced to add more debts onto the already creaking edifice of Charles's credit. The monarchy's finances started their final dizzying descent towards the bankruptcy which confronted Philip when he succeeded his father to his thrones.

Affairs Abroad

Philip had far less experience with foreign affairs during his years of apprenticeship than he did with the domestic administration of Spain; and what experience he did enjoy was invariably under Charles's close supervision. Philip first left Spain in 1548, to see and be seen in those lands Charles wished to pass on to him, and to participate in determining the future of the imperial succession between the two branches of the House of Austria, Charles's and that of his younger brother Ferdinand. He returned to Spain in 1551. Three summers later, he sailed for England to marry Queen Mary Tudor and become titular king of England, all as part of a grand design by Charles to rescue his own situation and improve the strategic position of Philip's eventual inheritance.

By 1548, Charles had clearly in mind the manner in which he would dispose of his patrimony. Already in 1522 he had given his Austrian inheritance to Ferdinand, who acted as his lieutenant in the Empire during his absences, and who at the time needed lands of his own to be worthy of the hand of Anne of Bohemia and Hungary. Ferdinand's marriage to Anne in 1520 brought unexpected dividends to the Habsburgs (always fortunate in their marriages) when his brother-in-law Louis II, king of Hungary and Bohemia (married to his and Charles's sister Mary), fell fighting the Turks in 1526, and Ferdinand was subsequently elected king of both his realms. In combining Austria, Bohemia and those districts of Hungary along the Austrian frontier not occupied by the Turks, Ferdinand acquired the nucleus of a powerful territorial state of his own. Needing Charles's help in resisting the Turks and rivals for his Hungarian crown, he proved his brother's faithful ally. Charles confirmed Ferdinand's place in his system when in 1531 he arranged his election as king of the Romans and, as such, his probable election to the Imperial crown after Charles.

The rest of his patrimony Charles decided to give to Philip.[26] The Catholic Monarchy posed a fairly simple case: all of its components had been assembled by Ferdinand and Isabella through legitimate inheritances of several centuries' continuity, save for Naples and Spanish Navarre, which Ferdinand had seized with more might than right. Both were contested by the king of France, but Spanish Navarre was easily defended from Castile, upon which Ferdinand made it dependent, and the road to Naples was guarded by the duchy of Milan, which Charles had acquired in 1535 by escheat as Holy Roman Emperor upon the death of its last Sforza duke. In 1546 he quietly bestowed the duchy upon Philip.

The Netherlands and Franche-Comté were another matter. While sentiment inclined him towards giving them to Philip, Charles knew that strategically they were far removed from Philip's eventual Spanish and Italian inheritance, and would be difficult to defend against the king of France (who had claims upon them) if Philip did not control Germany.

In 1547 Charles had come as near to controlling that congeries of princely states and proud imperial towns known as the Holy Roman Empire of the German Nation as he ever would, when his armies crushed the German Protestant Schmalkaldic League. With a strong hand to arrange Imperial affairs as he wished, he decided to make a place for Philip in the Imperial succession, if not as his own successor instead of Ferdinand, then as Ferdinand's successor. To do this, he not only had to contend with Ferdinand, who became understandably concerned over his own place and the future of his son Maximilian, but with the Germans, Catholic and Protestant alike.

At this point, Charles ordered Philip north to visit the Empire and the Low Countries. Philip left Spain in the autumn of 1548, travelling via Genoa, since 1528 Charles's ally, and Milan. In the following spring he journeyed across the Alps through the Tyrol, Swabia and Lorraine to the Low Countries. He was received with festivities at every halt, but carried himself with such hauteur and reserve that not only the boisterous Germans, but even the Italians – accustomed to the digni-fied airs of Renaissance princes – found him cold and disagreeable. He performed poorly in tournaments and did not keep pace with his hosts at table or in drinking bouts, favoured pastimes of the German and Netherlands nobles. In the Low Countries men found little to like in Charles's heir, who seemed to conceal behind a mask of dignity no one could be sure what thoughts. In spite of his father's efforts to induce him to be more agreeable, Philip's only successes, if the Italian ambassa-dors are to be believed, were with the ladies.

To ensure that Philip's inheritance of the Netherlands and Franche-Comté should not be interfered with by the German Diet or some future emperor, Charles declared that the seventeen provinces of the Netherlands formed one indivisible patrimony and severed by edict many of the ties which bound them to the Empire.

This deed, coupled with the prospect of Philip's future election to the Imperial crown, raised fierce opposition in Germany. The elector of Trier said he would have no Spaniard ruling in Germany, and the bishop of Augsburg told the Venetian ambassador that there were many Germans 'who would rather come to terms with the Turk than elect Philip'.[27] And these were Catholics! The Lutherans were con-vinced that Charles meant to annihilate their creed, and Philip was his obvious heir to continue the work.

All Germans, Catholics and Protestants alike, feared that Charles and eventually Philip, with rich possessions outside the Empire, could mobilize resources the Germans could neither match nor control, and use them to dominate the Empire and overthrow its loose constitutional arrangements. Charles's victory over the Schmalkaldic League, in which he had used Spanish troops and money, and his subsequent maintenance of Spanish garrisons in Germany, proved their fears well founded.

Apart from these practical considerations, there was the matter of growing German patriotism to which Charles's repeated employment of Spanish mercenaries had given an anti-Spanish dimension. The

Germans wanted an emperor who was German. Ferdinand, though born in Spain, had spent his adult life in Germany, and his son Maximilian, keenly aware of German national sentiments, maintained a patriotic party to support his candidacy for the Imperial crown, after his father's, even while in Spain as regent.

Charles assembled the Habsburg family at Augsburg in the winter of 1550–51, and with his sister Mary, dowager-queen of Hungary, serving as mediatrix, hammered out an acceptable compromise agreement with Ferdinand for Philip's eventual election as head of the Empire. Ferdinand, as king of the Romans, was to be elected to succeed Charles as emperor; Philip came next, to be followed by Maximilian, thus establishing the principle that the Imperial crown should alternate between the two branches of the Habsburg family. As each in turn put on the crown, he was to seek the election of the next in line as king of the Romans. Ferdinand agreed moreover to give Philip the Imperial vicarate of Italy, which gave Philip a free hand in Milan, still technically a part of the Holy Roman Empire, along with most of the rest of northern Italy.

Philip want very much to be emperor, and before and during the family meeting pressed Charles to ensure a place for himself, and even his son Don Carlos. But when, in 1562, Ferdinand arranged with the connivance of Pope Pius IV Maximilian's election as king of the Romans, to Philip's exclusion, Philip made no serious protest. Why? Did he realize that the Germans would not accept him, or did the place in the Empire accorded the Lutherans by the Religious Peace of Augsburg (1555) make ruling the Empire contrary to his conscience as a Catholic king? We do not know; but he did reserve for himself the title 'Majesty', which then was supposedly the exclusive right of the Emperor, despite Ferdinand's and Maximilian's protests. Proper relations, however, were carefully maintained between the two branches of the family.

The Peace of Augsburg was the result of the utter collapse of Charles's position in Germany in early 1552, when he was simultaneously attacked by the revived Schmalkaldic League headed by Moritz, duke of Saxony, his one-time ally, and Henri II, king of France. From Spain Philip sent aid to Charles, who vainly tried to reconquer the three Imperial bishoprics (Metz, Verdun and Toul) from the French king, who had occupied them with the consent of the German Protestants. The Schmalkalders Charles left for Ferdinand to deal with. Ferdinand arrived at the 1555 settlement with them, and Charles acquiesced in it, though he considered it humiliating.

In Charles's eyes, his loss of power to the Protestants and to the princes of Germany in general isolated the Netherlands, beleaguered by the French, from the rest of his son's future inheritance. Yet he scarcely had time to consider his next move, when a solution to his problem appeared so suddenly that it seemed providential.

In the summer of 1553, Edward VI of England, aged fifteen, died. His legitimate successor was Charles's Catholic cousin the unmarried Mary Tudor, aged thirty-seven, daughter of Henry VIII and Catherine of Aragon. If Philip married her, then England would be linked to the Catholic Monarchy, and communications by sea from Spain to the Netherlands would be made safe.[28] On Charles's order Philip quickly broke off negotiations for his second marriage to another Portuguese infanta, while a painting of Philip by Titian was sent to England to sway Mary's heart.

English opinion was divided over Mary's marriage, though all agreed she had to take a husband if she meant to rule effectively. The majority wished to see her married to an Englishman, to keep England free of foreign entanglements. An influential minority, however, favoured a foreign prince to keep the crown above domestic faction. Mary's own preference was for a Catholic, foreign prince, who would best be able to help her in her life's mission to restore England to the Roman faith. Persuaded by Charles's diplomats, she chose Philip.

Mary's councillors, who loyally backed her wishes though they knew them to be unpopular, drew up a marriage treaty with Charles which strictly limited Philip's authority in England. Only grudgingly and at Mary's insistence did they concede Philip the title 'king'. Philip could not appoint foreigners to office in England, nor commit England to a foreign war. Any heir born to Philip and Mary would inherit not only England but also the Netherlands and – should Don Carlos die without issue – the rest of Philip's inheritance as well.

For Charles, almost any terms were acceptable to keep England from allying with France (as it had in 1551–53). He wished to restore the traditional alliance, forged in the 1490s, binding England, Spain and the Burgundian Netherlands to assist each other against the French.[29] The alliance, which had led to the marriage of Henry VIII and Catherine of Aragon, had experienced rough days at the time of the divorce, but in 1543 (seven years after Catherine's death) it had been formally renewed when Henry and Charles pledged themselves to support one another against 'the French and Turks' (in 1553, Charles was not only at war with France, but was also being attacked in the Mediterranean by the Turks).

Philip, who took no part in the negotiations for his marriage, did not like the prospect and resented the sacrifice of Don Carlos's rights in the Netherlands. Secretly he swore an oath that this concession had been made without his knowledge and that he regarded himself as not bound by it. Charles paid no heed to Philip's misgivings, but ordered him to sail for England, where he was to emulate the conduct of his great-grandfather Ferdinand in Isabella's Castile (an example of which the English were hardly ignorant when drawing up the marriage treaty).

Whatever his misgivings, the dutiful son obeyed the father. On Charles's order, he invested Princess Juana with the regency of Spain, arranged for the education of Don Carlos, and at the beginning of July 1554 embarked for England.

The marriage of Philip and Mary took place at Winchester at the end of July. Prior to the wedding a messenger announced that Charles had given Philip the crown of Naples, thus making him a king in his own right.

That autumn, Philip had his first encounter with the thorny politics of England, which chiefly concerned the restoration of the Church of Rome and the role England should play in Charles's wars. He sat in on sessions of the royal council, which for his sake were often conducted in Latin, and pored over state papers, translated for his convenience into Latin or Spanish.

But Philip was not a free agent. His father still considered him an apprentice in statecraft, and advised him from Brussels on what courses to follow so that England should best serve his Imperial purposes. Philip heeded his father's instructions and tried, by diplomacy in the council and, more persuasively, through Mary who adored him, to guide the direction of English policy. Keeping England out of war until the exchequer was refilled proved no difficult matter, especially since Mary's grand design, which Philip backed, was to arrange a 'summit conference' of Catholic rulers to make peace.

Philip had more trouble trying to temper the religious persecution, instigated by Mary and her hot Catholic advisers, which Charles feared might dangerously divide English society. We have no evidence of Philip's own attitude to persecution in England, a matter which would have been of interest in view of his own later persecution of heretics in Spain and the Netherlands.[30]

There seems no doubt that Philip was uncomfortable in English politics, did not love Mary and did not care for the English way of life. Early in 1555 he began to ask Charles to permit him to cross over to the Low Countries, perhaps to take command of an army fighting the French. His desire to leave England was heightened by Mary's false pregnancy; it seemed as if she would not be able to produce an heir.

At the beginning of summer, Charles ordered Philip to his side, not to command an army, but to prepare to succeed him. The death in April of Queen Joanna at Tordesillas had removed the last possible obstacle to Philip's succession in the Catholic Monarchy. The Emperor, broken in health if not in hope, had decided to abdicate.

SUCCEEDING CHARLES 1555–59

Philip arrived in the Netherlands in September 1555 and toured the country, while on Charles's summons the estates of each of the seventeen provinces met to acknowledge the abdication of the Emperor and the succession of his son. Charles's formal abdication took place on 25 October at Brussels in a grand ceremony before the States General (the assembly of all seventeen provincial estates) and noblemen from his many dominions. After an emotional farewell address the Emperor turned to Philip and urged him to keep inviolate the laws and privileges of his subjects. He thanked God that in Philip he had a son to whom with confidence he could hand the sceptre.

Speaking softly in French, Philip thanked his father for his confidence, and promised that with God's help he would govern justly. When he came to address the assembly, following the States' acknowledgment of his rule, Philip admitted that he could not express himself adequately in French, and had the bishop of Arras (Antoine Perrenot de Granvelle, a government minister and advocate of princely absolutism) speak for him. Altogether, it was an inauspicious beginning for Philip's government of the Netherlands.

On 16 January 1556 at Brussels, in the presence of Spanish and Italian nobles and jurists, Charles signed the instruments transferring the crown of Castile, the crowns of the Aragonese monarchy and the grand masterships of the Castilian military orders to Philip. In April he signed over to his son 'our fatherland', La Franche-Comté de Bourgogne.

Charles did not leave for Spain to go into retirement at the monastery of Yuste until September. Philip was able, therefore, during his first months of princely office, to draw upon the advice of the Emperor, and of Queen Mary of Hungary, who had since 1530 been Charles's governess of the Netherlands, but who now stepped down to travel to Spain with her brother.

At the same time, Philip was forming his own circle of advisers. Some had come in his household from Spain, such as Ruy Gómez de

Silva, prince of Eboli, a Portuguese who had been page first to the Empress and then to Philip, and now was Philip's confidant, a councillor of state, and keeper of treasury accounts; Don Gómez Suárez de Figueroa, count of Feria, councillor of state and Philip's representative in England; and Gonzalo Pérez, priest, Philip's private secretary and secretary of state. Others had long served Charles, such as Granvelle, bishop of Arras, and Don Juan Manrique de Lara, councillor of state. There were also those who had served both Charles and Philip, such as the duke of Alba, councillor of state, whom Philip at once appointed viceroy of Naples; and Alba's cousin, the prior Don Antonio de Toledo, councillor of state and grand equerry. All of these men began vying for Philip's favour, and two factions soon appeared: those who had served Charles, led by Alba, and those whose service had been strictly with Philip, led by Ruy Gómez. To be sure, a few, such as Manrique de Lara, steered clear of both.

Philip, aware of the formation of factions, did nothing to discourage it, since he believed that open debate would help him formulate the wisest policies. He also realized that he could play one faction off against another and hoped thus to safeguard his own power of decision.

The situation Philip and his advisers faced appeared relatively bleak. In the Mediterranean, the Turks had captured Tripoli (1551) and Bougie (1555) and, allied with the French, had overrun much of Corsica, which belonged to Philip's ally Genoa. The king of France still held Savoy, which his father Francis I had seized in 1536. Philip was committed, as Charles had been, to recovering it for its duke, Emmanuel Philibert, whom Philip appointed governor of the Netherlands and commander of his armies. The French also continued to occupy the three Imperial bishoprics, Metz, Toul and Verdun. These, however, Philip could leave to the care of his uncle, Ferdinand I, who in 1558 was elected Holy Roman Emperor to succeed Charles. Savoy and Corsica were Philip's business, vital to the monarchy's communications and position in Italy and the Mediterranean. But for the moment Philip had no money and was, moreover, anxious to attend to domestic government in the Netherlands and Spain, to implement reforms which everybody agreed were needed and overdue, but which Charles had neither had the time nor the energy to undertake.

In January 1556, Philip therefore accepted the Truce of Vaucelles with France, leaving Henri II with his gains for five years' duration. The truce lasted barely a year before it was broken by the French, honouring their mutual defence treaty with the pope, who had provoked Philip into war in Italy.

Pope Paul IV Caraffa, a Neapolitan opposed to Aragonese rule, who suspected that Charles and Philip meant to assassinate him, demanded extensive authority over the Church in Naples. Philip refused, fearing that Paul would employ the Neapolitan clergy and pro-French nobles to topple him from his first throne and pry Naples from the Catholic Monarchy.[31] Paul then raised an army and opened a campaign to divest Philip of Naples, which he claimed was a papal fief. Philip's viceroy, Alba, sent Paul an eight-day ultimatum to disband his army. On its expiry Alba marched on Rome.

At the French court, the faction headed by Francis, duke of Guise, and his brother Charles, cardinal of Lorraine, whose own interests clashed with Philip's in Italy and the British Isles, persuaded Henri II to send Guise with an army to aid the pope. In consequence, tension mounted along all the frontiers shared by France with Philip's dominions. A surprise French raid on Douai in January 1557 ended the truce and fighting was renewed everywhere.

In preparation for the certain renewal of war, on 1 January 1557 Philip took the drastic expedient of suspending all payments on past debts in order to free his income for the present emergency and entice lenders to make him new loans. Philip's declaration of what amounted to bankruptcy stunned the big banking houses of southern Germany, Antwerp and Genoa, and the money lenders of Castile, but all were too deeply involved in financing his monarchy to abandon him. They lent him money on stiffer terms but insisted that he come to a settlement for the old debts.

Philip had to comply. He could seldom lay his hands on enough ready cash in his own treasuries. To satisfy the financiers, Philip assigned them properties of the Castilian military orders to farm, and *juros*, annuities paying their holders from 5 to 7 per cent interest. This was considerably less than the 12–14 per cent Philip paid on short-term loans, but since *juros* were attached to specified income and customarily payable at the source, creditors found them secure investments and a means of steady income, since it was unlikely that the crown could pay back the principal. The crown thus saw more and more of its revenues taken at their source before they entered the royal treasury.

Worse still, during the mid-1550s, the activities of French corsairs on the sea lanes and a civil war in Peru combined to diminish the flow of treasure arriving at Seville, upon which the crown waited so desperately each year for the specie to pay its most pressing expenses and tempt its creditors into one more round of loans. The crown's share of the annual treasure fell from 4,354,208 ducats in the period 1551–55 to 1,882,195 in 1556–60, driving Philip to continue an expedient, begun by Charles in 1553, of virtually confiscating the treasure arriving for private persons, and also to have resort to forced loans, death duties and the sale of honorific offices. In 1557 Philip dispatched Ruy Gómez to Seville to oversee this process, through which many a merchant expecting silver had to settle for a parchment *juro* with its royal seal of lead.

In the vicinity of Rome, Alba in the meantime outmanoeuvred Guise, who that summer was ordered home to defend France's northern border against the huge army Philip had mobilized there. In Italy the pope stood alone, save for token help from the duke of Ferrara (Guise's father-in-law). Philip had won Cosimo I de' Medici, duke of Florence, to his side by granting him Siena (occupied in 1555 by Charles's army and stripped of its liberty for rebellion against his Imperial authority), and had gained the support of Ottavio Farnese, duke of Parma, by promising him Piacenza (not delivered till 1585). Venice remained neutral throughout the war.

Philip remained in the Low Countries and prepared his army, commanded by Savoy and Lamoral, Count Egmont, a Netherlands magnate. In March he went to England, where he had no luck in persuading the English council to declare war on France – he even offered Englishmen trading rights in the Indies, so desperate was he – until a band of English exiles, sailing from France, seized a castle in Yorkshire. When Philip sailed for the last time from England in July, he was accompanied by 6,000 English soldiers who joined the rest of his army in Flanders.

Crossing the French frontier under Savoy, the army invested St Quentin, and on 10 August 1557 annihilated a column sent to its relief, led by the constable of France, Anne de Montmorency (Guise's chief rival at the French court), who was captured.

Philip II was not present on the battlefield. He hastily drafted a letter to his father at Yuste expressing the wish that he had been there, then went in full armour to receive the acclamation of his soldiers. In fact, both Philip and Charles agreed that princes and senior commanders should not expose themselves to the hazards or confusion of battle, but rather remain somewhere secure, and from there keep track of overall developments, responding as necessary. Charles to be sure did not always abide by this principle, finding the smell of gunpowder irresistible; but Philip, on the other hand, found the carnage of battle disgusting. The conduct of each in regard to battle also fits their behaviour in office: Charles continuously travelled in person to the troublespots in

his dominions, whereas Philip remained aloof, trying to direct everything from his bureau by dispatch.

Philip's refusal to follow up his victory at St Quentin (and the fall,
two weeks later, of the town itself) with a march on Paris has been
much criticized, then and since. But he was short of funds, autumn was
coming on, and before him lay a formidable array of fortified towns
and Guise's army, back from Italy. Above all, Philip did not want war,
but peace; his ideals were religion and justice, for which he would fight
if he had to. At some point, he had ceased wanting to be a warrior
prince. He was no longer the youth who in 1552 had begged to be
permitted to fight at his father's side in Germany, and who in 1555
had wanted to lead an army. Was it the carnage of St Quentin, or
the embarrassing cost of war to his treasury and thus to the prosperity
of his subjects, that sapped his enthusiasm for war? Later in his reign, at
war on all fronts, he frequently complained in marginal notes about the
cost of war, but not about the human suffering it caused. But statesmen
seldom speak much of suffering, whatever they feel. What little Philip
did say suggests that it weighed on his soul, not because of his regard
for the judgment of mankind, but because of the judgment of God.

The victory at St Quentin did not end the war. Guise counter-attacked
in midwinter, after Philip had disbanded much of his army and sent
the rest into winter quarters to keep down costs. He surprised Calais,
taking it from Philip's English allies, then struck at Luxemburg in
April 1558, isolating Franche-Comté. In July, Philip gained a victory
when Count Egmont, aided by an English fleet, defeated the French at
Gravelines.

By autumn neither Philip nor Henri had gained a decisive advantage,
and both were sinking deeper into fiscal insolvency. They began to
put out peace feelers. On 21 September, Charles V had died at Yuste
and Philip was free to follow his own mind without concern for his
father's pride. Moreover, he and Henri shared a fear of Calvinism,
spreading with startling rapidity in French-speaking regions (and even
into the French court) in a climate of general unrest, aggravated by
the endless wars.

The death in November of Queen Mary of England brought the
first *pourparlers* between the two kings to a halt. Philip was faced with
an immediate dilemma. He had reason to believe that Elizabeth, the
daughter of Henry VIII and Anne Boleyn, would steer a Protestant
course; but the only alternative to Elizabeth was to see Mary Stuart,
queen of Scots and wife of the dauphin Francis of France, mount the
throne of England. Mary was soon proclaimed queen of England at the

court of France, and there was talk of a French invasion of England on her behalf. However much Philip wanted peace with Henri II, he did not quite trust him. He had no desire to see Mary and Francis bring England into Henri's orbit, permitting him to outflank the Netherlands. Philip therefore supported Elizabeth, though he meant to do what he could to keep England within the Roman fold.[32]

To maintain the English alliance and counter Henri, Philip and Feria, now his ambassador to London, took the time-honoured course of Habsburg diplomacy and sought for Elizabeth a suitable and reliable Catholic husband. The English rejected Philip's suggestion of the duke of Savoy, since they did not wish to help him recover his duchy. They were, however, willing to consider the Archduke Ferdinand, son of the Emperor.

Briefly and discreetly, Philip himself became a candidate for the hand of his late wife's half-sister. Feria had taken alarm at the rapid emergence of Protestants in London after Mary's death, their insolence and their confidence of Elizabeth's favour. The only way to keep England Roman Catholic, Feria wrote Philip, was for Philip himself to marry Elizabeth. The terms Philip proposed to Elizabeth were considerably less generous than those conceded by Charles for Philip's marriage to Mary. Any heir born to Philip and Elizabeth would inherit only England, not the Netherlands. Elizabeth proved evasive in her replies and Philip let his proposal lapse. He assured her of his friendship, however, as he wanted to maintain the English alliance against France, on which the security of his Netherlands depended.

Philip in the meantime, through the offices of his cousin, Christine of Denmark, duchess of Lorraine (whose son Duke Charles was betrothed to Henri II's daughter Claude), and the constable Montmorency, whom he paroled, was able to have negotiations with Henri II resumed. In February 1559, delegates representing Philip, Queen Elizabeth and Henri assembled at Câteau Cambrésis, Christine presiding over their sessions.

The obvious issues to be settled were territorial. Philip wanted Henri to restore Savoy-Piedmont to Emmanuel Philibert, Calais to Elizabeth and to withdraw from Corsica, to Genoa's benefit. For his part he would return to Henri the towns he had occupied in Picardy and acquiesce in Henri's occupation of the three bishoprics, Metz, Toul and Verdun.

Henri agreed to restore Savoy-Piedmont to Emmanuel Philibert, though he retained for himself the marquisate of Saluzzo and five fortresses in Piedmont, and insisted that Emmanuel Philibert marry his own sister, Margaret of France. Emmanuel Philibert agreed to these terms, but secretly signed a treaty with Philip to safeguard his position in the future, that is, to reconquer the French-occupied places. Henri also agreed to withdraw his soldiers from Corsica, and Philip II therefore gave him St Quentin and other occupied towns in northern France.

The matter of Calais proved more difficult. Philip's hope of marrying Elizabeth had gone, while Feria had become so concerned with her Protestant policies that he suggested an invasion of England by Philip to save the Church. Philip would not be deterred from making peace. He wished for a genuine rapprochement with Henri, although he still hoped not to alienate England. Calais gave him the lever he needed. Henri II wanted Mary Queen of Scots on the English throne, but did not want to surrender Calais. Elizabeth wanted Calais back, but feared Mary's claims to her throne. Philip therefore pressed only half-heartedly for the restoration of Calais to England, and obtained terms which saved Elizabeth's face: Henri would occupy Calais for eight years, at the end of which time he was either to restore the port to her or pay her an indemnity. Privately Philip assured Elizabeth that he would support her against Mary and any invasion from France, for which Elizabeth's Protestant government maintained, with no great enthusiasm, the Spanish alliance.[33]

Philip's rapprochement with Henri seemed to bear fruit. Their territorial differences settled, the two rulers arrived at an understanding of their need to cooperate in the suppression of Calvinism, while Henri agreed to break his alliance with the Turk. To seal their settlement and their new understanding, Philip accepted as his bride Henri's daughter, Elisabeth de Valois. The peace treaty was signed on 3 April 1559 at Câteau Cambrésis. England, seeing no hope of recovering Calais, had signed with Henri II the day before.

Henri did not live long enough to prove whether he meant to cooperate with Philip against heretics and infidels or to disturb the peace of Christendom, most likely in respect of the English succession. In early July he died of a wound received in a tournament. The crown of France passed to sixteen-year-old Francis II, and the one kingdom whose resources in many ways matched those of Philip's dominions fell victim to factious politics, which hindered its pursuit of any consistent domestic or foreign policy for a long time to come. The Peace of Câteau Cambrésis had in fact but acknowledged a certain balance of power in Europe between France and Philip's monarchy: it was Henri's death which made possible the 'Spanish Preponderance'.

II

Philip II: Character, Family, Interests

CHARACTER, VIEWS AND BEHAVIOUR

What sort of man was Philip II, this ruler who dominated the history of Europe in the second half of the sixteenth century? At his accession he was described as slightly below average in height, but well-proportioned, of fair complexion and handsome features, though his lips were thought too full. His blond beard concealed his Habsburg jaw, which, at any rate, was not so prominent as his father's. But the burdens of office took their toll: by 1575, when he sat for his portrait for Sánchez Coello, his hair was turning grey and his last portraits, painted after 1589 by Pantoja de la Cruz, show his hair to be white, his once ruddy cheeks pale, and the bright eyes sunken and red.

In talking to people, Philip gave the impression of listening intently, though he said little; and when he did speak, he spoke slowly as though he were weighing each word with care. His eyes fixed the person addressing him, and a small smile would often come to his lips, 'that shy, half smile' which has been called the protective device of rulers schooled to guard secrets.[1] From Philip's smile to his dagger, contemporaries remarked, was a very short distance.

In dress, Philip was neat and fashionable, though as he grew older he wore only black, with no ornament save for the emblem of the Golden Fleece suspended on a black ribbon around his neck. Looking at Pantoja's portrait of Philip in his early sixties, one is struck not only by the dignity of carriage, but also by the meticulous attention he still gave to his dress; it is a portrait to be sure, but it would make sense that the old man still persisted in the habit of dressing well.

Philip's health in his early years was relatively good.[2] He tried to avoid gout and other ailments of the sort that plagued his father by eating sparingly and travelling as little as possible, since physicians blamed Charles's gluttony and frequent journeys for his gout and poor health. Philip refrained from fish and fruit, which were thought to induce ill humours, and enjoyed a papal dispensation from the law of abstinence, so that even on fast days he could take meat. He drank little wine, and that watered. He was not, however, averse to a good table, and on one occasion asked the prince of Orange to make him a present of his renowned chef.

The medical historian, C. D. O'Malley, surveying Philip's married life and giving credence to reports of his many youthful affairs, decided that Philip had a normal and healthy sexual life. He was fifty when he sired the son Philip (1578–1621) who would succeed him; in all he had eight children who survived birth, of whom four reached maturity.[3]

Philip's chief form of exercise was the hunt, but after 1570 little is heard of royal hunting parties. In later life he became increasingly sedentary and avoided excitement, for he did not escape the curse of his forebears, the gout. It first struck Philip in 1563, and its attacks recurred with increasing frequency as he advanced in years. Towards the end of his life there were occasions when he could not sign his name; and when he could, the once neat flourish 'yo el Rey' (I the King), the characteristic signature of Castilian kings, was a blurred and ragged scrawl.

As Philip aged, he also became more susceptible to other ailments. His correspondence with his private secretary, Mateo Vázquez (from 1572–91), is full of mutual commiseration over fevers, migraines and gout.[4] In the summer of 1587, Philip, aged sixty, became so ill that his trusted ministers, Don Juan de Idiáquez and Don Cristóbal de Moura, virtually ran the government. From that time onwards, though he recovered to some extent and sometimes showed bursts of great energy, his health steadily deteriorated.

He continued none the less till the end to deal with the business of state, though a perusal of his papers for the 1590s reveals fewer of his customary marginal notes. In 1595, the Venetian ambassador to Philip's court reported that the royal physicians claimed Philip 'was so withered and feeble that it was almost impossible that a human being in such a state should live for long'.[5] O'Malley suggests that Philip in his last years suffered both from arteriosclerosis and nephritis;[6] but he survived till September 1598, seemingly carried by an indomitable will to see through undertakings he had launched, find a worthy husband for his favourite daughter, Isabel Clara Eugenia, and raise to manhood his only surviving son, Prince Philip. On his seventy-first birthday, bedridden, he found the strength to sit up and signal with his hands the steps for the dancing courtiers.[7]

To leave the matter of Philip's appearance and health for a discussion of his mind and character is to enter far riskier territory. Writing about Philip II in 1559, the Venetian ambassador Mula wisely said that it was bad business to try to come to firm conclusions about the minds of kings before there was time to observe their actions.[8] To come to grips with Philip II, one must study him throughout his life and reign, as he responds to situations, seeks advice, makes up his mind (and sometimes changes it), draws up plans, issues orders and attempts to justify what he does, to himself and his world. Yet coming to grips with Philip does not explain him. The historian has to deduce his motivation from his conduct with little evidence of the kind modern techniques demand. Philip was very reticent about himself. He left no memoirs, and neither said nor put on paper much of a personal nature. A slender bundle of letters to his daughters had survived, discovered by the Belgian historian L.-P. Gachard and published in *Lettres de Philippe II à ses filles Isabelle et Catherine*;[9] but for the rest the countless memoranda from his own hand to his secretaries and ministers and his marginal comments and postscripts to state papers only rarely reveal something private, and if they do, it is usually a complaint about gout or condolences on someone's death.

Evidence from the pens of others, though voluminous, seldom answers the questions we might most wish to explore, but which men of the sixteenth century did not ask. Most useful of all contemporary sources are the frank letters of men close to Philip to persons whom they could trust; but so far, only a limited amount of these has been discovered.[10] Best known is the correspondence of Granvelle to Margaret of Parma, Philip's half-sister, and to Don Juan de Idiáquez, whom Granvelle brought into the Madrid government in 1579; also significant is the correspondence of the brothers Don Luis de Requesens and Don Juan de Zúñiga, who served Philip as pages, ambassadors and governors, and the *epistolario* of the duke of Alba.

In describing Philip's character, his contemporaries used the terms 'phlegmatic' and 'melancholy', which imply coolness, sluggishness, apathy, self-possession and pensiveness. Certainly Philip seldom revealed emotion, was notoriously tardy in making decisions, and worried about their outcome; he was invariably in control of himself. The appearance of self-possession seems to be precisely the impression Philip wished to convey, combining the example of his mother, who raised him during the crucial years from two-and-a-half to four, and that proud Castilian composure called *sosiego*.

An air of dignity had been important to Philip since his childhood, but Philip and his mother did display warmth and affection within the intimate circle of the family. Philip once described to his daughters how he jumped from his carriage and ran to embrace his sister, the Empress Maria, before she could alight from hers; he had not seen her in twenty-six years. One indeed suspects that Philip needed affection very much, but given the nature of his office, he could enjoy it with few. At twelve he lost his mother, and throughout his childhood and youth, saw little of his revered father. He had two sisters and, at eighteen, an infant son. His need for affection might well explain the alleged amours of his life after the death of his first wife Maria of Portugal until the maturity of his third, Elisabeth de Valois. Later he seemed to cling to Elisabeth's oldest daughter, Isabel, considering suitors for her reluctantly – only when near death did he finally arrange for her marriage to Albert of Austria, his favourite nephew, when both were already past thirty. The marriage took place two months after his death.

In respect to Philip's procrastination, though all evidence shows that he was generally tardy in making decisions, not all sources are agreed why. Contemporaries who knew Philip best complained of the fact, but offered little in explanation. The captain of the Royal Guard referred to it as 'incurable',[11] as though it were a physical disease. Cardinal Granvelle, who repeatedly urged Philip to expedite matters, quoted Philip himself as responding only, 'I and time shall arrange matters as we can.'[12] This must have been Philip's standard reply, since it appeared in the book of his 'sayings and deeds' published in 1628 by Porreño.[13]

Contemporary observers not so close to Philip ascribed Philip's procrastination to prudence. The court secretary and historian Cabrera de Córdoba, though admitting that Philip often held important papers 'till they wilted', compared his prudence to that of his namesake, Philip II of Macedonia.[14]

But to the modern historian and physician, Dr Gregorio Marañón, 'prudence' in Philip's case should read 'timidity' or 'irresolution'.[15] Philip, he claims, was basically a weak and insecure person, over-awed by his father and the standards he set, and terrified of making decisions for fear that he might prove unworthy of the Emperor and of the awesome responsibilities he had inherited. Only Philip's iron self-discipline and assumed air of majesty permitted him to proceed with any success. Yet other twentieth-century historians stand with 'prudent', and hold that Philip's deliberate manner of proceeding, given the difficulties in communications and the complexity of unfolding events, made good sense: doing nothing, in fact, was often more efficacious than doing anything else.

I am inclined towards Marañón's analysis of Philip, but I must add that Philip's psychologically rooted irresolution fits nicely with his keen awareness of sixteenth-century realities; and given his determination, one might wonder how Philip would have behaved in different times.

A study of Philip's jottings and correspondence reveals that he had a prodigious memory and was full of bits of information about everything and everybody. He seems to have weighed all matters carefully in the light of this information, to which he continuously added more by requesting that all sorts of papers pertinent to whatever matter he was considering be brought to him. He reviewed all possible arguments, and encouraged disagreement among his advisers in order to obtain as many viewpoints as possible. But when he had the information and arguments assembled, he still hesitated to act. He admitted once to his trusted friend Don Luis de Requesens that arguments about what policy to pursue in the Netherlands had him thoroughly confused.[16]

Philip's dilatory ways, pessimistic pensiveness and frequent indecision may also have had physiological as well as psychological roots. From early in his reign, he worked such long hours poring over state papers, his eyes growing red from weariness, that his ministers and secretaries worried about his health. He admitted to his personal secretary Mateo Vázquez more than once that he felt burdened with heaps of paper, as though he were some pack animal.[17] As he grew older, his suffering from gout, his more frequent illnesses, and the ageing process itself certainly affected his thinking and therefore his ability to make decisions. Some deterioration in Philip's mental faculties for the last ten years of his reign must probably be admitted: the hardening of his policies in the 1590s would seem to parallel the hardening of his arteries.

The mental steps by which Philip II finally arrived at a decision remain mysterious, although if the pace of his speech provides a clue, they were taken slowly. His marginal notes on dispatches, reports and opinions sent him, and the memoranda he sent his secretaries, reveal chiefly random thoughts and little that resembles systematic thinking. At some point in the process, he closeted himself with trusted ministers or secretaries, no more than two or three others, and with them arranged for the issuance of orders.

None of these men, save for the secretary of state Antonio Pérez, left memoirs telling us about their close dealings with Philip. Pérez's purpose, however, was not to discuss Philip's statecraft, but rather to discredit Philip by accusing him of dissembling, sexual promiscuity and even assassinations, thus contributing to the debate about the king's moral character which began in his lifetime and still continues.

With his first publications in 1591–93,[18] Antonio Pérez joined a growing company of men who damned the Catholic king as Antichrist himself. Mostly Protestants, these men accused Philip of religious persecution and the martyrdom of true believers, and reviled his countrymen for the massacre of countless innocent Christians in Europe and Indians in the New World.[19] Specific charges against Philip II, contained in the works of Pérez, the *Apologia* (1580)[20] of William the Silent and similar writings, include incest, because he married his niece Ana of Austria, the murder of Elisabeth de Valois in order to marry Ana, the murder of Don Carlos and implication in the poisoning of the Emperor Maximilian II, both for being soft towards Protestants and for favouring the liberty of the Low Countries; sexual licentiousness and the siring of several bastards, whom he either ignored, found fathers for by forcing his courtiers to marry his mistresses, or placed in convents; and wanton disregard for the liberties and privileges of his subjects, which he had sworn to uphold, in order to tyrannize them.

Those contemporaries who lauded Philip, all Catholic, rejected out of hand the grosser accusations of murder and sexual promiscuity and found rational explanations for the rest. The Protestant 'martyrs' were, from the Catholic point of view, heretics, traitors and rebels. Philip's 'tyrannized' subjects were unruly children to whom he was giving good government; Philip issued good laws to protect the Indians, and his marriage to Ana was made under papal dispensation. These apologists in turn levelled sharp accusations at Philip's opponents: William the Silent was condemned for rebellion, duplicity, heresy and bigamy; Pérez for lies, pederasty, peculation, treachery and murder.

The praise or damnation of Philip II has continued from his own times to ours, but the arguments have become more sophisticated. On reviewing the evidence, men have dismissed most of the charges of a personal nature. However, valid accusations of religious persecution, arbitrary government, and the employment of illegitimate, questionable and often violent means to achieve otherwise acceptable or intelligible ends persist. Yet in the context of the sixteenth century, religious persecution was generally accepted, in order to protect the community from errors which insulted God's truth and might bring eternal damnation to those who accepted them: the duty to exterminate heretics was held by Catholics and Protestants alike (though for complex reasons, which include their smaller church establishments, the Protestants proved less thorough in carrying out this duty). As for arbitrary government, growing numbers of men in the sixteenth century were coming to favour what was called 'absolute monarchy', responsible to God and itself, which they understood to embody the principle of unity and function within the law, as the best and only means of achieving a just and harmonious society in a world where violence, strife and disorder were facts of life. The vehemence of the indictment against Philip II arises less from compassion with the real sufferings of those whom he persecuted or battled against than from the violent nature of the struggle between Catholic and Protestant, and between defenders of the old, decentralized order of society and the agents of the rising absolute monarchies. These issues of intolerance, arbitrary versus representative government, and the use of violence to achieve ends are, as we increasingly realize, hardly confined to the sixteenth century.

There was, then, both a moral and political aspect to the sixteenth-century debate on Philip II's conduct, and both aspects are reflected in Philip's own political testaments, which contain his thoughts on his kingly office and the behaviour proper to a Christian prince. Religion permeates his thinking, and his political maxims sound more like moral imperatives than guidelines for the practice of statecraft. To carry out these moral imperatives, Philip himself was prepared to use almost any means, although his scruples made him prefer to proceed through the ordinary channels of law before going outside them.

The most thorough of Philip's political testaments is that of 1597, drafted barely a year before his death, for the instruction of his son, the future Philip III.[21] Earlier he had drawn up others for the prince and for his own half-brother, Don John of Austria; and he had included similar moral injunctions in his instructions to his viceroys and governors.

Like his father, Philip stressed the need for God's grace in order to govern justly and well. 'To be a good prince,' he admonished his son, 'you must first be a good Christian, since the only way to rule is through virtue. Pray for help to God, Who has placed on your shoulders all the weight of governing His Christian people. Being a king . . . is none other than a form of slavery which carries with it a crown.'[22] That this was more than a weary sentiment expressed by a ruler close to death is shown by his instructions to the duke of Alcalá, dated forty years earlier, in which Philip asserted, 'The community was not created for the prince, but rather . . . the prince was created for the community.'[23]

For Philip, the chief concerns of the prince in the community were the maintenance of the Roman Catholic religion, the provision of justice and the keeping of peace.[24] From the beginning to the end of his reign these same imperatives guided his thinking; and to achieve these goals, Philip incessantly repeated in his instructions and correspondence that the treasury had to be kept solvent.

Of these imperatives, Philip placed the defence of religion first. He instructed his son, 'If you are forced to take a stand as champion or defender of our sacred religion, even should you lose all your kingdoms, God will receive you in glory, which is truly the one goal worth striving for.'[25] Philip had no doubt that God would one day sit in judgment on his soul, and was determined not to allow the slightest deviation from orthodoxy among those for whose temporal welfare and spiritual safety he was responsible.

Philip saw religious dissent not only as an insult to God and His Church, but also as a menace to the body politic. In Germany, from the moment he faced Luther in 1521, until he arrived at the humiliating settlement of Augsburg of 1555, Charles had fought a losing battle against the spread of heresy. Charles's ally, Charles III, duke of Savoy, had in 1536 lost Geneva to Protestant rebels; and in 1560, Mary Queen of Scots, the girlhood companion of Elisabeth de Valois, Philip's third wife, had been forced by her rebellious subjects to accept Protestantism in Scotland. It was therefore clear to Philip that heretics should not only be persecuted for their beliefs, but also, in his father's words, 'as creators of sedition, upheaval, riots and commotions in the state . . . Guilty of rebellion, they can expect no mercy.'[26] Prevention, Charles emphasized, was easier than the cure: at first sight or suspicion, heresy was to be uprooted, and rebellion thus averted. If not stopped early, it might not be stopped at all. Yet if one takes Philip's proscription[27] (1580) of William, prince of Orange, at face value, Philip did not learn his lesson well and trusted a man he had reason to suspect and was therefore remiss in stopping in time the growth of heresy in the Netherlands.

Philip's convictions in regard to heresy were in fact tempered by reality: he might have moved more quickly in the Netherlands had his Turkish wars not prevented him from doing so. Nor did he delude himself that he could forcibly change the European religious situation by warring against entrenched Protestant rulers, in spite of mounting pressures from militant Catholics to do so. Assessing with some accuracy the means at his disposal, he largely resisted their demands for more than token assistance, unless their purposes happened to coincide with his. But neither was Philip prepared to accept further Protestant gains at the expense of the Roman Catholic Church if he could prevent them, especially if such gains threatened the security of his own dominions.

He recognized that militant Protestants, primarily Calvinists, refused to acknowledge the right of Catholic rulers to uphold the old religion.

In regard to dispensing justice, the Castilian tradition of the king as *justiciero*[28] was of importance to Philip, as were the instructions of his father. The king must strive for perfection in justice, 'in such a manner that the wicked find him terrible and the good find him benign',[29] giving equal care to rich and poor alike. The ideal of perfection in justice meant the rule of law, to which crown and private person alike were subject. That Philip strove to realize this ideal is illustrated by the well-known anecdote concerning a difficult case between the crown and a subject. Philip instructed his legal councillor, Dr Martín de Velasco, 'Doctor, take note ... in case of doubt, the verdict must always go against me.'[30]

Writing to his half-brother Don John, Philip instructed him not to pass judgment while angry, an echo of what their father had once told Philip, and to take unusual care in cases involving friends or rivals. He was to remember that not Don John, but rather God and after him the king, were the offended parties; in the case of an enemy, he should remember that forgiving one's enemy is pleasing to God.[31]

Of course relatively few of the cases decided in Philip's many dominions ever came to his personal attention, although he believed ultimately that in the sight of God he was in some way responsible for all the judicial decisions of his reign. For this reason he took a deep and abiding concern in the appointment of men to high judicial posts. Charles had made Philip keenly aware of this responsibility when he scolded him for appointing men to such offices during his first regency without first thoroughly investigating their qualifications.[32]

In general Philip did not believe in interfering with the daily routine of the judicial system of which he was head. He was admittedly no expert in the laws of his many lands,[33] although he did order many of them to be properly codified for easy reference and uniform application. Judicial torture was legally accepted in the sixteenth century, and Philip did nothing to abolish it. He was, however, squeamish about bloodshed in his presence, and probably for this reason, though also from conviction, he disapproved of excessive torture designed to elicit confessions. He warned Prince Philip about a 'certain type and manner of men so savage and so inhumane, that they are not satisfied with any punishment unless it comes covered with blood. Such men ... look for new ways and means of punishment, causing those wretches who fall into their hands to confess through force of torture alone. Remove such judges from their posts: they are more fit to live among wild beasts than to serve a king and govern Catholic vassals.'[34]

About the death penalty, Philip wrote, 'Never condemn a man to death except unhappily and unwillingly, forced by the demands of justice and the necessity of law and order.'[35] Perhaps more terrible than torture or execution was condemnation to the galleys, which often brought slow death through exhaustion and exposure. When Philip first mounted the throne, he reminded his viceroys that men could be sent to the galleys only for certain crimes, and that it was 'a grave matter of conscience' to keep a man at the oars for a longer term than his sentence allowed.[36] Since there was a constant shortage of rowers for galleys, Philip ordered that his convicted subjects serve only in his own galleys, where the viceroys could ensure that their captains freed them when their sentence was up. As the need for rowers grew during the naval wars against the Turks in the early years of his reign, Philip was forced to extend the list of offences for which a man could be sent to the galleys, in order to keep his fleets at sea. But condemnation to the galleys, falling almost exclusively on the poor, was an unpopular penalty among Philip's subjects, and Philip was hesitant as much through fear of riots as qualms of conscience to press the matter too far.

Indeed, Philip's expressed views on justice seem to be contradicted by much of the conduct of his officers and armies and many of the events of his reign (including his own reaction to these events); but such discrepancies between precepts and practices are commonplace in history. Philip, like most men, had ways of not seeing contradictions, avoiding unpleasant facts, and attributing the disagreeable results of human actions to necessity or the will of God.

Philip recognized that justice should be tempered with mercy, but given his understanding of human nature, which, like most Europeans of his time, he considered sinful, he believed that clemency should only be used sparingly, 'lest men give themselves to vice in the certainty of royal pardon; it is preferable that all take heed from the public punishment of the few'.[37]

Waging war, which occupied so much of Philip's time, received little space in his political testaments or in his formal instructions to his governors. Philip perceived war not as an end, but as a means to defend – or sometimes to advance – the Catholic religion, his own rights and the security of his dominions.

While war in defence of religion was traditionally seen as the crusade against the infidel, it was Philip's fate that the costliest and bloodiest struggle of his reign grew from his efforts to suppress heresy and enlarge his authority in his own Netherlands. The political and religious revolt against Philip in the Netherlands, in which the rebels frequently employed guerrilla tactics, forced a dilemma on Philip that he was loathe to face: choosing between brutal repression of the rebels, thereby causing widespread suffering among the innocent, and the continued effort in dispensing justice and good government for the passive majority of Netherlanders, a hindrance to operations against the insurgents. The duke of Alba, commander of Philip's forces in the Netherlands in 1567–72, expressed the matter well when he said he could have crushed the revolt by laying waste to the countryside and forcing the population into a few fortified cities garrisoned by reliable Spanish soldiers; but while such means were acceptable in a conquered country,[38] they were unthinkable against the king's own subjects. Cabrera de Córdoba, commenting on Philip's ultimate failure to subdue the revolt, wrote, 'The affection the King bore them was a good part of the ruin of both.'[39]

Philip waged several naval and amphibious campaigns against the 'infidel' Turks and North Africans, actions more agreeable to his conscience. He had to end them through a truce in 1578, however, at an awkward moment, after the Turks had offset his victory of 1571 at Lepanto with their recapture of Tunis in 1574 and their subversion of Morocco in 1576. Yet the revolt of the Netherlands had reached such a point in 1576–77, that Philip had no choice but to leave the Turks with their gains and hope for a respite. He had to answer to God first for the faith of his own subjects, not for the devilish ways of others.

Philip could be uncompromising, at least verbally, when it came to his personal rights, which he certainly believed were God-given. To advance his claim to the crown of Portugal in 1580, he sent a warning to the duke of Bragança (whose wife claimed the crown) that if Bragança did not back down, the king of Castile was prepared to go to war though it meant the ruin of the Bragança estates and Portugal, and might involve the 'whole of Christendom'.[40]

Short of war, in carrying out his beliefs and in conserving his kingdoms, Philip when necessary violated the norms of legal procedure and ordinary decency. In 1578, for instance, he sanctioned the murder of Juan de Escobedo, a secretary who, he believed, was encouraging Don John of Austria to betray him. He gave his assent to several plots, the Ridolfi plot of 1571 being the most famous, to depose and if necessary to assassinate Queen Elizabeth, because he resented her interference in the Netherlands revolt, though he hesitated to declare war on her because his forces were committed elsewhere.[41] He succeeded in having William of Orange assassinated, although he first went through the legal procedure of proscribing him (in common law, outlawry), a then acceptable device in a case when a man under indictment could not be brought physically to trial. In the case of William, Philip did not violate the legal conventions of his time, but rather offended the codes of chivalry, which allowed the great vassal to rebel against his lord, when he felt wronged by him, and of course the sensibilities of William's Protestant partisans, who appealed to the higher judgment of God. Philip proceeded, without success, in similar fashion against Antonio Pérez, when he became a fugitive from justice.

At times, though doing what he thought right, Philip dissembled in matters of justice because of his fear of a public commotion. Due to the outcry raised by the execution of counts Egmont and Hoorn, who had been hastily, and many argued unfairly, tried and convicted, Philip decided to have Baron Montigny, convicted on the same charges, secretly garrotted in the castle of Simancas; he then ordered it said for public information that Montigny had died of natural causes.[42] Hasty and questionable trials, such as occurred during Alba's regime in the Netherlands, followed by dissimulation and official denials on Philip's part, have done no good for Philip's reputation, which, in general, deserves better. One must remember that the Netherlands after 1566 were gripped by rebellion, and that under such circumstances the execution of the laws tends to be heavy-handed, if not thoroughly martial.

Philip seems to have been able to justify all his deeds to himself, to his ministers and his allies, and even to many of his opponents, who understood his problems and shared his values. But it is not surprising, given such deeds, carried out in the name of God and dynastic right, that he once sighed, so Baltasar Porreño tells us, that had he his choice, he would prefer to be a private gentleman, with an income of 6,000 ducats a year, sufficient for comfort, but insufficient to support him in high office.[43]

Contemporaries took a lively interest in Philip's sexual morality, but the evidence, by its very nature second-hand, tends to be irresponsible gossip, often contrived in malice and of dubious quality. Between the ages of eighteen and forty, it can be assumed, Philip, a normal and relatively healthy young man, had several affairs.[44]

When Philip married Maria of Portugal he assured his father that he was still a virgin, but the rumour was certainly current that he was already married. Doña Isabel de Osorio (who died in 1589) claimed to be Philip's wife;[45] and William of Orange was later to accuse the king of bigamy – 'as Ruy Gómez could tell if he were still alive'. What can one believe? Whatever the case, Philip married Maria, and seems to have done nothing to silence Doña Isabel, with whom he certainly had an affair after he had become a widower. By her he allegedly had several bastards, but he never acknowledged any publicly. Nothing can be proven.

In 1548 Philip left Spain for the Netherlands, and the ambassadors claim that during his sojourn in Brussels (1549–50), he enjoyed great success with the ladies. This is hardly surprising for a prince of his era. In 1554, however, he was married again, this time to Mary Tudor, eleven years his senior. He seems to have been unfaithful to her, especially after he left England in August 1555 for the Netherlands. Though one might suspect that the reports of the French ambassador, the chief source, about Philip's infidelities were meant to sow discord, the behaviour of Mary when she saw him again in March 1557 appears that of a woman scorned. The doggerel that made the rounds, 'Better the milkmaid in her russet gown/Than Queen Mary without her crown', surely conveys some truth, though Philip probably committed his indiscretions among ladies of noble rank.

Mary died in 1558, and a year later Philip married, by proxy, Elisabeth de Valois, aged thirteen. She joined him in Spain in 1560, but not in the nuptial bed till 1564 when she was seventeen, the customary age then for consummation in high Spanish circles. Before 1564, Philip had several attachments, so the French ambassadors wrote Catherine de' Medici, Elisabeth's mother; but afterwards we hear little more of them.

Most notorious of the affairs of this period was the one with Doña Eufrasia de Guzmán. When she found herself pregnant, so the story goes, Philip arranged her marriage with Don Antonio de Leyva, prince of Ascoli, a member of his court. Naturally everybody concerned denied it, but Don Antonio's heir, Don Antonio Luis de Leyva, who sailed in the armada of 1588, was generally regarded as Philip's bastard. However, the investigations by Don Agustín González de Amezúa into Doña Eufrasia's later correspondence with Mateo Vázquez have convinced him that Don Antonio Luis was not Philip's son, although he believes that Philip had a brief affair with Doña Eufrasia.[46]

Philip was also alleged to have had another affair with Doña Ana de Mendoza, princess of Eboli and wife of Ruy Gómez de Silva. The source of this allegation, Antonio Pérez, hinted that he had an affair with her too, though after she had been widowed in 1573. Modern research has refuted Pérez's accusation.[47]

The matter of Philip's last marriage to his niece Ana of Austria also was raised by William. He accused Philip of murdering Elisabeth de Valois (she died in 1568 of natural causes after giving birth prematurely to a daughter who died immediately) and of incestuously marrying Ana in 1570. The real reasons for this marriage were otherwise. There were at the time available only two nubile princesses of childbearing age considered worthy of Philip: Ana, his niece,[48] and Marguerite de Valois, Elisabeth's younger sister. Marguerite was rejected for two reasons: first, that the daughters of Valois were considered relatively barren, and second that Marguerite had allegedly given her virginity to young Henri, duke of Guise. On the other hand, Ana's parents Maximilian II and Maria had given birth to six sons and three daughters who survived childhood, an important consideration for a king who wanted a male heir.

Another dimension of Philip's sexual life, apart from his attachments and marriages, is reflected ambiguously in his collection of paintings, chiefly from the brush of Titian, which he referred to as 'poetic subjects' and kept at the Pardo Palace, just outside Madrid. After meeting Titian in 1551 Philip commissioned several Venuses and a *Danaë and the Shower of Gold*, masterpieces whose eroticism few paintings can match. Philip, a great patron of Titian, later commissioned many more sober subjects, such as the splendid *Entombment of Christ*, delivered in 1574 to the Escorial, and the painting of Philip with his son Don Fernando (d. 1578) in his arms, thanking God for the victory at Lepanto.

Perhaps Philip's choice of paintings by Hieronymus Bosch to hang in his apartments at the Escorial after 1570 reveals best his change from a youth susceptible to sexual temptation to a man increasingly aware of death and the afterlife. The motifs of Bosch's paintings still puzzle art historians, but were possibly derived from an obscure Netherlands religious cult. In 1605 Fray José Sigüenza, a Hieronymite monk who wrote a history of his order and the Escorial, reported that many thought Bosch's work was tainted with heresy, though he himself defended Bosch's orthodoxy.[49] The most controversial works by Bosch in Philip's possession were the triptychs entitled *The Garden of Earthly Delights* and *The Haywain*, and a table on which were represented *The Seven Deadly Sins*. While all portrayed man's fall from grace and consequent punishment, they also vividly portrayed his vices. When set against the 'poetic' nudes ordered by Philip from Titian in the 1550s, Bosch's works suggest that Philip very much wanted to remind himself as he gazed at them of the eternal punishment awaiting those who surrendered to earthly pleasures. Marchers costumed like devils in a Portuguese procession once caused him to recall the frightening devils who punished the damned in Bosch's paintings.[50]

In dealing with Philip's sexual mores, however, one thing can be said for certain: none of the women with whom he had affairs influenced his conduct of office. Apart from that, his discretion in general suggests that he was more prudish and sensitive to the moral climate generated by the Reformation and Catholic Reformation than many if not most of the European ruling order. Philip openly admitted neither affairs nor illegitimate offspring, and kept his sexual life as best he could his own private business.

THE ROYAL FAMILY

The most agreeable aspect of Philip's character revealed itself within the circle of his family. The royal family lived in the world of the court, which in the sixteenth century meant both princely households, with their ceremonial and social activities and their function of giving expression to the kinship bonds between king and nobility, and the organs and agencies of the central government gathered around the person of the sovereign.

When Philip succeeded Charles in 1555–56, he was surrounded by a small entourage of Spaniards of his own household, and by his father's court, cosmopolitan in personnel and character. His wife Mary, queen of England, had her own court where Philip had another household, staffed by Englishmen as well as Iberians. The summer after Mary's death, Philip and his entourage returned to Spain, leaving the court of Brussels to Margaret, duchess of Parma, his illegitimate half-sister, whom he appointed regent. (In court parlance, she was known as *Madama* [de Parma]). Charles's Imperial court, of course, gravitated to Ferdinand, who in 1558 became Emperor.

In Spain, Philip established at his court five households: one for himself, one for his new queen, Elisabeth de Valois, one for his son Don Carlos, *el Principe*;[51] one for his sister Doña Juana (known as *La Princesa*, as widow of John of Portugal, prince of Brazil); and one for his illegitimate half-brother, Don John of Austria (called simply *Señor Don Juan*). His own household was allotted 250,000 ducats; the others received less in descending order; Don John's stood at 15,000.[52] From the money allotted to each household, expenses, salaries, endowments and alms to charities were disbursed.

The expenses for the royal households remained about the same throughout the reign, despite rising prices and varying numbers and changes in the royal family. After 1580, there was no queen, and Princess Juana and Don John were dead. There then remained the increasingly austere Philip himself, his two daughters by Elisabeth, the infantas Isabel and Catalina Micaëla, his heir Prince Philip, and the Empress Maria and her daughter, the Archduchess Margaret, who had come to Spain in 1582.

Court etiquette was rigid, and from the king down everyone enjoyed a distinct rank and title. When Philip dined in state, it was publicly in solitary grandeur, except when joined by someone of princely rank, for instance in 1591 by his son-in-law the duke of Savoy. Philip preferred, however, to avoid state occasions; at times he dined privately with his family, but most often he ate alone. His taste for simplicity prompted him to order the duke of Alba in 1579 to suggest ways for the court to replace some of the more costly and lavish ways of Burgundy with the less elaborate but dignified styles of the former court of Castile, and to end the recent proliferation of grandiloquent forms of address among the Castilian nobles.[53] For himself, he ordered that he be addressed simply as 'Señor', and no longer as 'Sacred Catholic Royal Majesty'.

His refusal to accord the form 'Your Highness', applied then to royal children, reigning dukes and even some monarchs, to Don John of Austria, has then and since caused many to deduce that he was jealous and suspicious of his natural half-brother. Yet the respect and affection shown Don John by Philip clearly contradicts this idea. It was only briefly in 1577–78, just prior to Don John's death and years after he had first complained to Philip about not being recognized as 'Highness', that Philip mistakenly entertained suspicions of Don John's loyalty. Apart from the immediate circumstances of the case, two episodes in Castilian history may have influenced the king: one was the forcible displacement from the succession by Sancho el Bravo (1284–95) of his eldest brother's sons (the *infantes* de la Cerda); the other, the murder of King Pedro the Cruel in 1369 by his bastard half-brother, Henry of Trastámara.

Philip learnt from Charles of the existence of Don John,[54] who was born in 1545 at Regensburg and raised in Spain by Charles's confidant, Don Luis de Quijada. The Emperor asked Philip to favour the boy and find him a place in the Church. On meeting Don John, then a twelve-year-old lad called Gerónimo, Philip decided that he was too lively for the Church and would better serve at court. When Don John reached the age of twenty-one, Philip gave him command of the galleys of

Spain and, from then on, raised him to ever higher and more important posts in the monarchy, culminating in 1576 with the governor-generalship of the Netherlands. Philip was even willing to consider Don John's wild ambition to invade England and liberate Mary Queen of Scots, but only after he had succeeded in his mission to restore order in the Low Countries. Philip saw Don John as he saw himself, first and foremost a servant of the monarchy and its mission.

Philip may have been subconsciously a little jealous of Don John, who had a flamboyant and martial personality, was better looking, and reminded everybody of Charles. He was adored by women and most men; but Philip had the comfort of knowing that he was the only legitimate son of Charles and Isabel, and was the king.

The happiest days in Philip's generally sober court came during the years of his marriage to Elisabeth de Valois. Married to her by proxy in the summer of 1559, Philip met her in January 1560 at Guadalajara, where they wed in person at the palace of the duke of Infantado. On 15 August 1566 she bore him a daughter, Isabel Clara Eugenia, and in October 1567 another, Catalina Micaëla.

During Elisabeth's first springtime in Spain, her lady-in-waiting Mme de Clermont kept a diary, which presents a charming picture of court life.[55] The young queen wore sumptuous gowns and robes of satins and velvets, and dressed her hair in the Spanish fashion, adorning it with strings of pearls and jewels. Accompanied by Don Carlos and Don John, she went with Philip and the Princess Juana to the bullfights. The diary tells of lovely days in Aranjuez, where the queen dined in the afternoon under poplars with Philip and the rest of the royal family. On formal occasions she received ambassadors and attended court functions. She often danced with her ladies after dinner; and when she suffered from migraines, she stayed in bed and received comforting visits from Princess Juana.

Elisabeth died in October 1568, having given birth after five months' pregnancy to an infant girl, who died immediately. Philip's grief was great. As they grew to maturity, he became increasingly attached to his two daughters by Elisabeth, and it was to them that he wrote in 1581–82 the letters which provide our best account of Philip in his unguarded moments, as a man who loved his family.[56]

In the letters he expresses his concern for their education, and urges them to learn the language of his new kingdom of Portugal. He is sorry that a basket of fruit they sent has rotted; he wishes that he were with them in Aranjuez among the roses, listening to the song of nightingales; he keeps the children informed about the court women who had been their nurses and the jesters who were with him, and describes for them churches and castles he visited. In a general way he also tells the children of the progress of his affairs: he mentions the comings and goings of officials at court, and recounts court ceremonies, his attendance at religious festivals and *autos de fé*, and describes the ships in the Tagus.

In July of the year Elisabeth died, Philip suffered the loss of his son Don Carlos in perhaps the most tragic personal episode of his reign, which grew into one of the more celebrated myths of history.[57] For some years before 1568, evidence had been accumulating that Don Carlos, born in 1545, was mentally retarded and probably unfit to rule. Charles V had his doubts about the boy's stability in 1556, and the next year Ruy Gómez de Silva informed Philip that not only should Don Carlos be rejected as a possible regent of the Netherlands, but indeed he should not even be seen there. He had been pledged for the hand of Elisabeth de Valois, but his condition was such that in 1559 all held it better that Philip himself marry the young princess for the sake of peace between the houses of Valois and Habsburg.

Philip, however, proved an indulgent father, and kept up hope that Don Carlos would improve, in spite of reports that the prince was morbidly cruel to animals and molested young women in the streets of Madrid. He sent him off to the university of Alcalá in the company of Don John and Alexander Farnese, Margaret of Parma's son (who was being brought up at Philip's court), expecting that the university might help him. There Don Carlos fell downstairs, apparently while chasing a porter's daughter, and received serious head injuries. Philip's own physicians, including Andreas Vesalius, attended the prince, while the local clergy brought to his bed the relics of a long-dead saintly Franciscan, the Blessed Diego. After several weeks on the threshold of death, the prince recovered. The physicians of course took credit for the recovery, but Philip seems to have believed that it was at least partly miraculous, for in 1588 he arranged for the canonization of Fray Diego.

The recovered prince became yet more erratic and scandalous in his conduct. Yet Philip still persisted in his hope that his son would outgrow his perverse ways, and assigned him to preside over meetings of the council of state. Don Carlos abused the councillors and showed interest in only two matters: his own marriage, preferably to Ana of Austria, and his becoming regent of the Netherlands. After 1564 the affairs of the Netherlands grew daily more tense as the local magnates defied Philip's orders (which entailed increased religious persecution), sending to Madrid various delegates, including Count Egmont, Baron Montigny and the marquis of Bergen, to explain their reasons and gain Philip's assent to their position. Don Carlos took to meeting with them and came to favour their position, which it seems unlikely he understood. He saw in the regency of the Netherlands a chance to escape court and a father towards whom he became openly contemptuous for neither sending him to the Netherlands nor going there himself.

When Alba received orders in 1567 to go to the Netherlands as captain-general of Philip's army, Don Carlos in a rage attacked him with a dagger and had to be forcibly restrained. He then wrote secretly to the Castilian grandees that he needed help for a special mission he was undertaking; Ruy Gómez told Philip about it. He confided to his secretary Martín de Gaztelu his vainglorious ambitions to follow in the footsteps of his grandfather, the Emperor, and derided his sedentary father; Gaztelu told all to Philip. Finally Don Carlos began to sell his jewels for money, and asked Don John to join him in an escape to Italy or the Netherlands. Don John went to Philip and told him that Don Carlos was on the verge of fleeing Madrid.

This report convinced Philip at last that his son had to be put under restraint. He intended to travel in 1568 to the Netherlands, and leave Spain under a regency government. He therefore could not take the chance of leaving Don Carlos free. In the middle of the night of 18 January 1568, Philip, wearing a helmet and carrying a sword, accompanied by Ruy Gómez, Feria, the prior Don Antonio, Quijada and a few guards, entered the prince's chamber and placed him under arrest. The stunned young man at first joked: 'Are we having a meeting of the council of state?' Then seeing his father, he screamed, 'I am not crazy, I am desperate! Does Your Majesty want to kill me?'

Philip told the prince to compose himself, then left. Don Carlos was confined to his chambers. Philip convoked the council of state for their opinions, and sent letters to the pope, the Emperor, the Empress Maria and other rulers, explaining the arrest of the prince: 'There seemed to be no other remedy for complying with the obligations I have to the service of God and the public welfare of my kingdoms and estates.'[58]

He was most concerned with the reactions of the pope to whom he confided that the deed had been done 'with the sorrow and grief Your Holiness would expect, since he is my only son and first born'.[59] He instructed his ambassador, Don Juan de Zúñiga, to speak freely with the pope about what he had seen of Don Carlos's conduct at court, but to insist on his orthodoxy in religion. Rome was rife with rumours, attributed to French Huguenot sources, that Philip arrested Don Carlos for heresy.[60]

Don Carlos behaved erratically and fatally impaired his fragile health with hunger strikes alternating with bouts of gluttony, indifference to cold and putting ice in his bed during hot spells. Tertian fevers, a form of malaria from which he had suffered before, gripped him. On 24 July 1568, a few days after his twenty-third birthday, Don Carlos died with the last rites of the Church. C. D. O'Malley, evaluating the reported symptoms, 'his anxiety and mental confusion, his dyspepsia, vomiting and diarrhoea', believes that Don Carlos succumbed to 'some intestinal infection, such as ambiasis or bacillary dysentery that represented simply one too many complications for survival'.[61]

Among Philip's enemies, the deaths of Don Carlos (July) and Elisabeth de Valois (October) coming so close together soon gave rise to an untrue story that they had been lovers, for which Philip had them both murdered. Elisabeth had indeed been kind to Don Carlos, but no more; and he, when not searching for nocturnal adventures in the streets of Madrid, thought only of Ana of Austria, the unseen bride of his dreams. The story of their love joined the idea that Don Carlos had become the champion of liberty and religious freedom for the Netherlands against his tyrannical father and the Inquisition. From this material, Schiller wrought his great drama *Don Carlos*, to which Verdi later gave splendid music.

Modern scholars have absolved Philip from the old charges that he had Don Carlos murdered, although R. B. Merriman's argument on Philip's behalf, that there was nothing he had to do because he foresaw that the prince would not live long in confinement, leaves open the possibility that Philip might have ordered the prince's death. But this seems out of the question: Philip could count on the commitment of Spaniards to stable government, proved by their acceptance of Queen Joanna's long confinement, an issue the *comuneros* had tried vainly to exploit in 1520. This tragic episode reveals Philip as an affectionate and indulgent father, but far more importantly, and in the last analysis, as a king who placed the obligations of his office above all other considerations.

Lost in the drama around Don Carlos, Elisabeth and Don John is Philip's sister Juana, who played an important role at court until her death in 1573. She had left Portugal in the spring of 1554, having that January successively lost her husband, Prince John, and given birth to a son, Dom Sebastian, and had taken over the regency of Spain from her brother, who on Charles's order was departing for England and his marriage to Mary Tudor. When Philip was planning to journey to the Netherlands in 1568, he intended to leave the regency of Spain to the experienced Juana rather than to the queen, who was too young and was French and, moreover, that spring became pregnant.

After the death of Elisabeth and Don Carlos, Philip was without wife or male heir. His two daughters, Isabel and Catalina Micaëla, were aged two and one respectively.[62] At his court were, besides Don John, Philip's two nephews, the teenage archdukes Rudolf and Ernst, sons of Maximilian II and Maria, whom the Habsburg family, despite some protests from Maximilian, had decided should be educated in Spain for the sake of their religious orthodoxy.

For Philip, aged forty-one, another marriage became an immediate order of business. As explained, he selected his niece Ana of Austria. When she came to Spain in 1570, she brought with her two more brothers, the archdukes Albert and Wenceslas. Rudolf and Ernst returned the following year to Vienna.

Wenceslas died in 1578. Albert survived and became like a son to Philip. Inclined towards a clerical career, he entered the Church; and though never ordained, he became a cardinal in 1583 through the offices of Philip, who ultimately had in mind for him the see of Toledo held by Cardinal Quiroga, who lived longer than anyone expected. However, the needs of the monarchy and dynasty required that Albert fill political offices. His career became entwined with the history of the last twenty years of Philip's reign, culminating in 1598 in his marriage to the Infanta Isabel and receiving jointly with her the sovereignty of the Low Countries.

Philip's last queen, Ana of Austria, bore Philip four sons, Fernando (1571–78), Carlos (1573–75), Diego (1575–82) and Philip (1578–1621), and a daughter, Maria (1580–84). Cabrera de Córdoba stated that Philip loved Ana best of his wives.[63] In October 1580, both Philip and Ana were stricken with *catarro* (influenza) during an epidemic. The king recovered, but Ana, still weak after the birth of her daughter earlier in that year, died.

On Ana's death, her mother the dowager Empress Maria took leave of the Imperial court and hurried to her widowed brother's side to take charge of bringing up the royal children. With her came her daughter, the Archduchess Margaret, who some thought would become Philip's fifth wife, but in 1585 she entered a Carmelite convent in Madrid. Philip never remarried.

Of Philip's daughters, the younger, Catalina Michaëla, married

Charles Emmanuel, duke of Savoy, in 1585 at Zaragoza. The marriage, which underscored the continuation of the alliance between the Habsburgs and the House of Savoy, was the last great service of Cardinal Granvelle (formerly bishop of Arras) to Philip. Catalina died in 1597.

Isabel Clara Eugenia remained at the side of her father, whose plans for her marriage to Rudolf II foundered on the mutual suspicions of the rulers for each other. She took to sitting with Philip in his bureau, silently passing him papers of state. Not until 1598, shortly before Philip's death, was she betrothed at the age of thirty-three to her cousin Archduke Albert.

Philip ceded to the 'Archdukes', as the couple were called, the sovereignty of the Netherlands (in effect the provinces not lost in the Dutch revolt), but with the provision that should they have no children, the sovereignty would revert upon the death of either to his son Philip and his descent, as in fact happened in 1621 upon Albert's death, when Philip IV became sovereign ruler of the 'Spanish' Netherlands. The Archdukes' sovereignty, however, had always been limited, since Philip II had made Spain responsible for their territory's defence.

Isabel lived most of her life in the shadow of important men – her father till 1598, Albert till 1621, and the brilliant commander (1604-28) of the army of Flanders, Ambrogio Spinola – and her talents have therefore been obscured. After Albert died, she remained in the 'Spanish' Netherlands as Philip IV's regent till her death in 1633. Competent and widely loved, she sometimes annoyed Madrid by her independence.[64]

Philip II's heir to all but what he gave Albert and Isabel, Prince Philip, grew up to be an agreeable but indolent young man, with the sort of bland character that might be expected of one who supposedly never committed more than a venial sin. The king had appointed as governor for him in 1585 Don Juan de Zúñiga, the son of his own governor, but as Zúñiga died the next year, the prince continued under the control of women until the end of 1589 when Philip set up a separate household for him.[65] Philip himself supervised the prince's education and from the mid-1590s gave him increasing responsibilities in government. Many state papers from Philip II's last years bear the signature *yo el principe*. While the prince proved docile, Philip could see that he had no mind for hard work and reportedly confided to his intimate adviser Don Cristóbal de Moura his fear that young Philip would be ruled by others.[66]

PHILIP II AND THE ARTS AND SCIENCES[67]

Philip II, if for nothing else, would have to be remembered for his great construction, the monastery palace of San Lorenzo de Escorial,[68] an enduring monument to the man and his reign, and the counterpoint of the Catholic Reformation played against the classical and rational thrust of the High Renaissance. Philip conceived the Escorial as a monastery and royal residence, where masses and prayers would incessantly be offered for the souls of his parents, his family, himself and his descendants, whose final resting place would be the mausoleum beneath the main altar. He dedicated it to St Lawrence, on whose feast in 1557 his army had defeated the French at St Quentin.

Philip frequently visited the construction site and pored over the plans with his architects, chief of whom was Juan de Herrera. The central feature of the edifice is the royal chapel, whose dome dominates the great rectangular building – laid out in a gridiron pattern to commemorate St Lawrence's martyrdom on a gridiron – and containing within its confines eight small and three large courtyards. The royal apartments lie beside the chapel's sanctuary, and from the window of his bedchamber, Philip could follow the Mass being said at the high altar. When at the Escorial, Philip worked, worshipped, ate and slept in a few small rooms, near which was an austere throne room where, sitting in a simple chair, he received important visitors.

At the Escorial Philip established a library for which he ordered manuscripts and books relating to all the sciences known to man, collected all over Europe. The secretary Gracián, who was involved in cataloguing the acquisitions, frequently mentioned Philip's interest in the library and occasionally his requests that books, usually theological, be brought to him.[69] Philip seems to have done much of his reading while travelling and often read while riding in his litter. Apart from pious works, he preferred histories, above all the works of Tacitus.

Philip employed various painters and sculptors, chiefly Italians, to embellish the walls and ceilings of the Escorial's chapel with religious motifs, its library with the story of learning, and, in one grand corridor, with scenes commemorating victories, including St Quentin (1557), Gravelines (1558) and Terceira (1582–83) in the Azores against a Franco–Portuguese fleet.

For his private apartments, Philip favoured the panels of the Flemish painter Hieronymus Bosch, as has already been mentioned. He also kept in the Escorial, the Pardo Palace and the *Alcázar* of Madrid portraits of his parents and relatives, painted chiefly by Titian and Anthonis Mor. In general he favoured the Italian and Flemish schools, although he did give several commissions to El Greco, whose work strongly influenced the direction of Spanish painting at this time. El Greco's first work for Philip was *The Adoration of the Name of Jesus* (often called *The Dream of Philip II* and even *The Allegory of the Holy League*), painted in commemoration of the death of Don John, the victor of Lepanto, and modelled after Titian's *Gloria*, painted for Charles V. A second commission, *The Martyrdom of St Maurice and the Theban Legion*, was not well received by the king and proved to be Greco's last from him.

In addition to books and works of art, Philip collected maps and scientific instruments. At the palace at Aranjuez he kept wild animals in a small zoo and exotic plants from the New World and Africa in a botanical garden, tended by the noted botanist Andrés Laguna.

Musically, Philip wanted his royal chapel to match in splendour the Burgundian chapel of his father and ancestors. He appointed to it several fine musicians, the most famous being Tomás Luis de Victoria, whom many rank with Palestrina as the greatest composers of the High Renaissance.[70]

Philip believed in promoting scholarship, so long as it lay within the bounds of orthodoxy, and gave gifts of money to the leading universities of his dominions. For the most famous – Salamanca, Valladolid, Coimbra, Louvain and Douai – his reign proved the golden autumn of their medieval splendour. In 1593 Philip appointed the great Jesuit political theorist Francisco Suárez to a chair of theology at Coimbra, and at the same time provided a pension to Justus Lipsius, the renowned editor of Tacitus and Seneca, to enable him to continue his historical work at Louvain.

A scholarly enterprise in which Philip II took particular interest was the publication in 1568–72 of the *Poliglota Regia*, the Bible in eight volumes, with the sacred texts in Hebrew, Aramaic, Greek and two Latin versions (the Latin were St Jerome's Vulgate, upon which Philip insisted, and a modern translation), and supporting notes and glossaries. To Philip, the success of the enterprise would culminate the work launched in the reign of his great-grandparents by Cardinal Cisneros, which resulted in the trilingual Complutensian Bible of 1514–22, and give Christian scholars a definitive edition of Scripture.

Proposed by the Antwerp printer Christopher Plantin, who organized the undertaking, the Royal Polyglot was published under the supervision of the sympathetic Spanish biblicist Benito Arias Montano,[71] sent by Philip to Antwerp, and with the guidance of the theological faculties of

Louvain and Paris. To Philip's embarrassment, the publication came under heavy criticism from conservative Spanish theologians and the papal curia. Indeed, Plantin, and through him Arias Montano, and several others associated with the Royal Polyglot were members of a secret, quasi-heretical sect called 'the Family of Love'. Philip apparently knew nothing of this and stood by Montano, who fended off his Spanish critics and obtained the approval of Rome for the Polyglot. But in that era, to be controversial was as good as being condemned: Catholic scholars shunned the *Poliglota Regia*, which for Plantin turned out a financial disaster.

Arias Montano continued, however, to serve Philip as librarian of the Escorial until his retirement in 1590, and led there a small, secret band of Familialists, from the Hieronymite community. Since their doctrine allowed outward conformity, it probably did not come to the attention of Philip.

Philip, on the urging of his architect Juan de Herrera, established an academy of science in 1588 at Madrid, for the study of mathematics, astronomy, navigation and military and civil engineering. Prompted by the cosmographer Juan López de Velasco, he issued instructions for the coordinated study of the solar eclipse of 1577 in his dominions. Unlike many of his contemporaries, Philip paid no heed to astrology, and took no action on petitions from the Cortes to establish chairs of astrology at universities where medicine was taught, that physicians might learn 'to relate the movements of planets with the critical days of the illness'.[72]

The provision of astrologers could probably have done little to help or hinder the study of medicine in Spain, where it was associated with Jewish and Muslim traditions, and clung strictly to the work of Galen. Spanish clinical medicine was not well regarded elsewhere in Europe: a Tuscan ambassador commented, 'Who hasn't seen it can't believe it.'[73] Andreas Vesalius,[74] whom Philip brought with him from Brussels as his personal physician, found his Spanish colleagues nearly impossible to work with, and to get away from Spain and them, he undertook a pilgrimage to the Holy Land, to which Philip could hardly refuse his permission. He had no intention of returning to Spain, where the Galenists maintained their dominance and provided physicians for the court.

In the long run, Philip's wish to promote scholarship foundered on the rock of his determination that it stay within the bounds of an orthodoxy imposed largely by Thomism and enforced by the Inquisition. He feared that outside Spain the old orthodoxy was neither so steadfast nor so vigorously enforced, and therefore in 1559 issued an edict forbidding Spanish students to attend universities outside the Iberian peninsula, save for Rome, Naples and Bologna. Publicly he claimed that his reasons were economic, but privately he admitted to his sister Juana that he feared they would be contaminated by heresy and acquire bad habits.[75]

The effect of Philip's ban on foreign study on intellectual developments in Spain, especially in the field of science, had been a topic of debate among scholars since at least the time of Marcelino Menéndez y Pelayo (1856–1912), who defended Spain's Catholic traditions.[76] More recent scholarship, however, without denying that the edict was significant, treats it as a symptom of a general reaction against the freedom of Renaissance thought. It was no accident that the edict came at about the same time as the great *autos de fé* of 1559 in Valladolid and Seville. Moreover, universities in general during the sixteenth century and for some time later were not the main promoters of modern science but rather proved in the main resistant to any innovation. And, as a recent article explains, Spanish students in Philip II's era were far more interested in training for careers in government and the Church than in engaging in speculative thought, whether theological or scientific.[77]

Since Philip II was chiefly interested in pious, historical and scientific literature, he had little direct impact on the writing of poetry, pieces for theatre and novellas, which provide, along with the novel *Don Quixote*, the chief glories of what is called the *Siglo de Oro* (Golden Century – roughly 1450–1680) of Spanish letters. However, the residence of the court at Madrid made that city a centre for entertainment, and by the mid-1580s both Lope de Vega and Cervantes were contributing their early works for the stage. The great age of Spanish theatre, however, had to await the fun-loving court of Philip III; it received no particular encouragement from the austere one of Philip II.

III

The Catholic Monarchy
of Philip II

MADRID: THE CHOICE OF A CAPITAL

Philip II's court settled in Madrid in 1561 and, except for a shortlived effort by Philip III to move the court to Valladolid, Madrid, *villa con corte* as it was known in Philip II's time, has since been the capital of Spain. A recent study by Manuel Fernández Alvarez on Philip's selection of Madrid[1] for the residence of his court rejects the traditional view that the choice was a brilliant stroke of Renaissance statecraft, putting the court in the geographic centre of Spain and in a town with few historic traditions. Philip, upon his return to Spain, had first settled in Toledo. He rejected Valladolid, the seat of his regency governments, because, according to Cabrera de Córdoba, the discovery of a nest of heretics flourishing there had made the city 'odious' to him. Toledo, the 'Imperial City', he knew well from his childhood days, and perhaps entertained happy memories of it.

But soon after Philip took up residence in Toledo, his new queen, Elisabeth de Valois, became ill with pneumonia, which was made worse by the dampness of the city on the Tagus. He therefore decided to move his court to a healthier place which could be easily supplied, particularly with firewood. For some months the courtiers did not know if Philip meant to take them to Madrid or to Segovia, since both places fitted the king's requirements. Philip finally selected Madrid, which at the time had some 20,000 inhabitants. Beneath the city and its environs were underground reservoirs supplying fresh water, and the mountains with their forests were close by.

Courtiers and ambassadors complained about the inconveniences of the raw town, about high rents and the cost of labour. Philip, however, went ahead with his plan to settle the court at Madrid, and had the *alcázar* (royal citadel), which stood on the site of the present Palacio Real,[2] refurbished. It was after he was established in Madrid, not before, that he chose the site for the monastery palace of the Escorial, that combination of monastery, mausoleum and palace, built to the glory of God and his family on the slopes of the Sierra de Guadarrama, some nine leagues to the north-west.

While the government took its seat, grew and became immobilized in Madrid, Philip regularly made a circuit with a few councillors and secretaries to nearby royal residences. At Easter he left Madrid, where he customarily spent the winter, and went via the small Pardo Palace, just outside Madrid, to the Escorial (under construction 1563–83). Thence he would wend his way to Toledo, and next to Aranjuez, where he spent late April and May among his rose gardens and orangeries. Passing through Madrid in June, he would journey into the mountains to his palace at Valsaín, referred to in dispatches as 'in the woods of Segovia'. From Valsaín, the road to the Escorial was short. Once the royal apartments of the Escorial became habitable, around 1570, Philip spent the hot summer months there rather than at Valsaín. None the less, he usually went to Valsaín in the autumn to hunt, until he gave up that exercise and began to stay more often at the Pardo Palace in late autumn, before taking up residence in the capital once more for the winter.

Philip's settling the court permanently in Madrid, and almost always remaining in the neighbourhood himself, is in some ways another sign of his phlegmatic temperament. He was a creature of habit and mindful of his own convenience and health as well as others'. In 1563 he began to suffer from gout, and Charles had claimed that no climate was better than Madrid's for the gouty.[3]

THE IMPERIAL INHERITANCE

Between 1546, when he invested Philip with the duchy of Milan, and April 1556, when he transferred the Franche-Comté to Philip, Charles V endowed his son with a grand inheritance quite as impressive as his own had been, but rather different in character. Charles's Austrian inheritance had been given in 1522 to Ferdinand, who early in 1558 succeeded Charles as Emperor. The rest, which had grown considerably during his reign with the conquests in the New World of Mexico and Peru, he passed on to Philip. Thus in Europe Philip ruled over the Netherlands (which Charles intended should be buttressed by England, ruled by Philip's wife, so that together they could resist the French) in the north, and Milan and the Catholic Monarchy in the south; beyond Europe lay Castile's New World empire, the North African fortresses of Melilla, Oran and La Goleta, and the Canary Islands.

1 The Spanish monarchy: Their Catholic Majesties Ferdinand and Isabella

3 Portrait believed to be of Philip as a youth

2 Isabel of Portugal, mother of Philip II

4 Charles V, father of Philip II and the man against whom he measured himself. Philip sits on the right

5, 6 Later influences on Philip: the duke of Alba (left) and Cardinal Granvelle (right)

7 The riches on which Charles V and Philip II depended: the silver mines of Potosí

8 An entertainment provided for Charles and Philip during their visit to the Netherlands in 1548

9 Philip's army defeats the French: the battle of St Quentin (1557) as depicted in the Sala de las Batallas, the Escorial

10 Titian's portrait of Philip sent to England to be shown to Mary Tudor

11 Philip in the sober dress of his later (c.1575) years

12 Philip with the courtesy title 'king of England' during his marriage to Mary Tudor (1554–58)

13 A musician (traditionally held to be Philip) admiring Venus in a painting by Titian

14 The palace at Valsaín, a favourite retreat in the woods of Segovia

15, 16, 17 Philip's first, third and fourth wives: Maria Manuela of Portugal,
Elisabeth de Valois and Ana of Austria

18 Don Carlos (1545–68), whose tragic life inspired legends

19 Philip III, son of Philip's fourth marriage and his successor

20 Isabel Clara Eugenia and Catalina Micaëla, Philip's two daughters by Elisabeth de Valois, to whom he wrote fatherly letters and who provided comfort in his old age

21 The Escorial under construction

22 The princess of Eboli–'the
Eboli'–a political intriguer with
a romantic reputation

23 Antonio Pérez, a secretary
and minister who was disgraced

Le Prince Gauere, Conte d'Aiguemont.

24 The struggle for the Netherlands: the execution of Egmont and Hoorn

25 Pius V who at times worked with Philip and at other times opposed him

26 The battle of Lepanto, 1571

27 (Opposite) Don John of Austria, hero-victor of Lepanto, Philip's half-brother

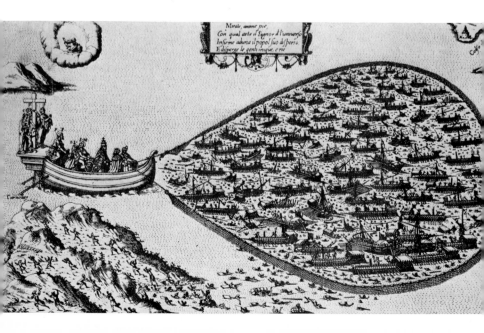

28 Philip II of the Catholic Reformation: El Greco's allegory *The Adoration of the Name of Jesus*

The assassination
(1584) of William of
Orange, outlawed by
Philip

30 An English
celebration of the
defeat of Philip's
Armada, 1588

31 A commemoration of the Peace of Câteau Cambrésis

32 Four members
of the *Cortes* of
Valencia

33 Three servants of the crown:
Gian Andrea Doria,
Don Álvaro de Bazán,
marquis of Santa Cruz,
and Don Luis de
Requesens y Zúñiga

34 Philip in his last years, painted by Pantoja de la Cruz. Note his only jewel, the Golden Fleece

During his reign, Castilian *conquistadores* consolidated Spanish rule in Chile (1558) and, pushing southward from Paraguay, established Buenos Aires (1580) on the Rio de la Plata. In the South Seas an expedition led by Miguel de Legazpi raised Castile's banner in 1565 over the Philippines, which he named after Philip II. In 1580, Philip joined Portugal and its empire in dynastic union with his monarchy, thus reconstituting in his eyes Roman and Visigothic *Hispania*: from this time, Cabrera de Córdoba remarked, Philip called himself king of Spain.[4]

Philip's titles, listed in full after 1580, read: king of Castile and León, Aragon, Portugal, Sicily, Naples, Sardinia, Navarre, Valencia, Majorca, Granada, Toledo, Seville, Córdoba, Jaén, Murcia, Gibraltar and Algeciras, the Algarve and Jerusalem, of the Islands of the Indies, East and West, and the mainland of the Ocean-Sea; archduke of Austria, duke of Burgundy, Lorraine, Brabant, Limburg, Luxemburg, Gelderland, Athens and Milan; count of Habsburg, Flanders, Tyrol, Artois, Burgundy, Hainault, Holland, Zeeland, Namur, Zutphen, Barcelona, Roussillon and Cerdagne; prince of Swabia and marquis of the Holy Roman Empire; lord of Friesland, Mechelen, Overijssel, Groningen, the (Basque) Provinces and Molina de Aragon, lord in Africa and Asia.

Philip, notably, kept the titles for the Austrian dominions given by his father to the cadet branch of the house, and the name *de Austria* for the children of Spain. The name Habsburg, which today we use for the dynasty to separate it from the Austrian state, heads the list of Philip's manifold countships. Some of Philip's titles pertained to extant kingdoms, duchies, counties and lordships, others to former ones which had been subsumed under some greater realm but still existed as provinces, referred to by their historic titles in official correspondence. Titles such as king of Jerusalem or duke of Athens carried only historic significance, and implied neither possession of territory nor dynastic rights.

Philip was also grand master of the Burgundian Order of the Golden Fleece, the Castilian Orders of Alcántara, Calatrava and Santiago, and assumed during his reign the grand masterships of the Order of Montesa in Aragon and of Christ in Portugal.

In Europe, after 1580, Philip ruled over some 16,000,000 subjects, about as many as did the king of France.[5] Of these some 9,000,000 lived in the Iberian peninsula: 6,500,000 were Castilians, 300,000 Aragonese, 400,000 Catalans, 600,000 Valencians, 150,000 Navarrese, and about 1,000,000 Portuguese. The population of the Burgundian lands was around 3,000,000, with all but roughly 200,000 living in the seventeen provinces of the Netherlands. In Italy, Philip's subjects included some 2,500,000 Neapolitans, 1,000,000 Sicilians, 1,000,000 Milanese and 100,000 Sardinians.

It is almost impossible to attempt to estimate the population of Philip's dominions in the New World or the Philippines, but the total Spanish population of the New World in 1570 was probably about 120,000, with an estimated 230,000 *mestizos* and blacks. Some figures can be given for the Indian population of Mexico, which reveal a drastic demographic decline: at the time of Cortés's conquest in 1519, the Indian population may have been 25,000,000; but by 1568, the ravages of disease had reduced it to 3,000,000. Later epidemics caused a further drop, so that around 1595 there survived some 1,375,000 Indians.[6]

⌐ In its organization, Philip's monarchy followed the pattern developed by the Aragonese monarchy in the late Middle Ages. Each dominion was seen as independent of the others, and maintained its own institutions and customs. Only the person of a common ruler linked them together. Philip was recognized by the appropriate title, king, duke, count, etc., so that to Castilians he was king of Castile, to the Milanese, duke of Milan, to Flemings, count of Flanders, and so forth.

Since Philip could be resident in only one of his dominions at a time, he appointed persons to represent him to each of the others. Philip began his reign in the Netherlands, but in 1559 returned to Castile where he remained for the rest of his life, save for three short visits to Aragon (1563, 1585, 1592), two to Catalonia (1564, 1585), one to Valencia (1586), and a twenty-seven month sojourn in Portugal (1580–83). During his absences from Castile after 1559, he in effect continued to rule that kingdom directly, being never very far away. The rest he governed through representatives, known as viceroys in the kingdoms of Aragon, Valencia, Navarre, Naples, Sicily, Sardinia, New Spain (Mexico) and Peru, as governors-general in Catalonia, Milan and the Netherlands (considered as a whole), and as governors in the Canaries, the Philippines, the Antilles, Chile, Rio de la Plata and the African fortresses. In the Netherlands, in addition to appointing a governor-general for the whole, Philip appointed a governor, called stadholder,[7] for each of the seventeen provinces. These stadholders reported to the governor-general, as did the governor of the Franche-Comté.

CASTILE

Much has already been said about Castile, since it was there that Philip served his apprenticeship for his royal office. It is a mountainous land, not rich, and still rather thinly populated. Yet during the first years of the sixteenth century, both population and prosperity grew, and Castile provided its rulers with men and money, which the rulers in turn employed chiefly abroad. By mid-century, both population and economy began to stagnate, in large part the result of providing for Habsburg wars.

Castilian society, and that elsewhere in the Iberian peninsula, was dominated by the Church and the nobility, who between them controlled the better lands and enjoyed immediate jurisdiction over much of the rural population. One Spaniard in ten claimed to be an *hidalgo* of gentle blood, and enjoyed exemption from direct taxation. The *hidalgos* were most numerous in the northern provinces; few were wealthy. They provided fine soldiers, and were willing to serve in the infantry as privates; and as the government swelled in size, many went to the university to earn a law degree and find suitable careers.

At the pinnacle of society were the titled nobles, numbering no more than 200 heads of families. Some thirty grandees, so designated by royal patent, stood well above the others in wealth and far higher in prestige. The king called them his cousins; a few, such as the dukes of Medina Sidonia, Infantado, Béjar, Frías and Alba, were probably richer than any other non-reigning noblemen in Europe. Medina Sidonia enjoyed an income of 200,000 ducats a year and could raise 10,000 militiamen on his estates.[8]

Government in Castile or any other of Philip's dominions could not function without the cooperation of the nobles and churchmen enjoying jurisdiction over vassals. Power in the sixteenth century did not extend straight from the crown to subjects, but rather descended through broadening strata of secondary powers until it touched everybody in the realm.

The most efficient way from king to every corner of the kingdom lay through the Church, which explains why control of the Church was of such vital concern to the old European monarchies. In Spain, Ferdinand and Isabella had obtained from the papacy, in the name of Church reform, the right to provide bishops and control the Inquisition. Since devotion to the monarch's person was chiefly limited to the politically articulate minority and patriotism remained an uncertain force, often too narrowly local for the purposes of the greater monarchies, monarchs depended on the pulpit to inculcate in their subjects the sentiments of fidelity and obedience.

Local justice and keeping the peace were therefore in the hands of traditional authorities, whom Philip accepted. He did, however, want to supervise them in their work. In the case of the royal municipalities, he enjoyed the right to appoint *corregidores*, who looked after his interests. These officers were most often lawyers, except in the case of fortress towns, where the *corregidor* was a soldier, assisted by a lawyer. In the case of seigneurial estates, Philip worked through the hereditary lords, but he gleaned information from the *corregidores* of neighbouring towns and, interestingly enough, from inquisitors. If his personal appeals to wayward seigneurs or the efforts of *corregidores* did not bring compliance with the royal will, Philip then employed the great royal tribunals, above all the chancelleries of Valladolid and Granada and the *audiencias* of Seville and Galicia, before which recalcitrant municipal officials or unresponsive nobles could be brought. Titled nobles generally balked, and insisted that their cases be taken up at court.

As for civil jurisdictions discharged by clerics, the king with his powers of nomination saw to it that men he trusted were provided. If they proved recalcitrant, he found ways to remove them or, at least, render them ineffective.

To oversee home defence Philip appointed captains-general to the frontier regions. In this he was largely dependent, as in other matters, on local power structures, and the captains-general were in fact the leading grandees of their provinces: the marquis of los Vélez in Murcia, the marquis of Mondéjar in Granada, the duke of Medina Sidonia in western Andalusia, the marquis of Cerralbo in Galicia, and the constable of Castile on the Cantabrian coast. Philip often turned to his soldier-*corregidores* to review the work of the regional captains-general, which naturally generated friction between the professional officers and the generally amateurish grandees.

Castilian society, heavy at the top, was in its middle reaches inflated but unproductive. Practising law, playing local politics and investing in lands, government bonds and personal loans appealed to the Castilian middling sorts more than the risky, time-consuming world of industrial or commercial enterprise.

Most Castilians, like most other Spaniards, were poor and worked the soil. The average income *per capita* was eleven ducats. Some owned small plots, others rented lands from lords, while others, especially in Andalusia, worked vast seigneurial estates. The Mesta, the medieval guild of sheep-herders, was still active, but less influential than in previous times. Still, the privileged sheep made cultivation next to impossible in many areas, especially in Extremadura. The hard life of the 'have-nots', as Sancho Panza called them, was somewhat disguised in Castile by the colourful vagrants, the *pícaros*, whose mischievous antics Cervantes and Alemán relate in their *novelas*.

CASTILE'S INDIES

For those who broke the spell of home and Europe, and had enough money or luck to secure a passage overseas, there was the lure of the Indies. 'Here you will earn more on your job in one month than there in one year,' wrote one emigrant to his brother in Spain. 'God has given us more here than there,' wrote another from the New World, 'and we shall be better off.'⁹

The mines of Potosí, discovered in 1545, were already a legend, drawing men across the oceans in search of other eldorados, and bankers to Madrid to lend Philip II money on the security of wealth arriving from the Indies (i.e. the West Indies, Mexico [New Spain] and Peru).

Philip II spent much thought on the problems of the Indies, not only because he needed their riches, but also because they were his to govern and defend in God's name. Through the council of the Indies he pursued matters of religion and justice, worrying about the rights of Indian and settler alike, and about the righteousness of importing black slaves, and having laws codified and published. Yet driven by those necessities that know no laws, he pawned justice for cash, sold Indian labour, made deals with slavers and confiscated the treasure of private persons.

Whatever he thought, the Indies were for him in fact little more than sources of revenues for his European policies. In the first five years of his reign, Philip received a little less than 2,000,000 ducats from the Indies; after 1580 he averaged that much or more per year. While the 'Royal Fifth' from the mines was the chief source of revenue, there were other imposts, such as customs duties, and in 1558, Philip opened the way to extending the *alcabala* (a sales tax) to the New World by eliminating the exemption hitherto enjoyed by the colonists. He first ordered its collection in Mexico in the 1570s, and in 1591 extended it to Peru in spite of local protests and riots. In the same years he improved the viceregal fiscal agencies in the New World.

His revenues from the New World permitted Philip, who was no absolutist in theory, to practice in effect royal absolutism. He was freed from too much dependence on representative assemblies in his dominions, and could push ahead when he wished with unpopular policies, intimidating or buying off those who opposed him. He was moreover able to wage war on a scale which his increasingly exhausted European dominions could not support.

Philip's dependence on the routes to the Indies along which his treasure travelled to Spain was clear to Philip and his enemies, and their protection was a major problem of his reign.

Defence for the Indies, which depended much on efforts made in Spain, Philip could adequately supervise; but good and vigorous government in lands thousands of miles across the ocean from Madrid was another matter. To begin with, few Spaniards with talent and enjoying high social status wanted to serve in the Indies when there were so many posts available in Philip's European dominions. No Spanish grandee held office in the Indies during Philip's reign.

Viceroys, governors, captains, judges and clerics, once posted to the Indies, encountered a situation in which the Spanish colonists, especially the sons of the *conquistadores*, lorded over Indians on vast estates and were as entrenched in their stations, or more so, as any lord of vassals in Spain, despite all efforts of the crown to prevent this state of affairs. Quarrels between those sent from Spain to govern and colonials were frequent, and Philip was under steady pressure from one faction or another to replace his officers almost as soon as they took up their posts. Philip, who had so many doubts about who was right, wavered in supporting his officers, and thus made vigorous government doubly difficult. Yet Philip sometimes entertained his doubts for a long time, and as communications were slow, his decisions were not soon known. Therefore his officers often enjoyed tenure long enough to be relatively effective, as was the case with the controversial and dynamic Don Francisco Álvarez de Toledo, who served as viceroy of Peru from 1569 until 1581, when at last Philip ordered him home.

Over the Church, which must always be seen in part as an instrument of government, Philip enjoyed in the New World full powers of clerical provision, conferred upon him by the *Patronato Real de Indias*, granted by the papacy to Ferdinand and Isabella. In 1571 Philip extended the Inquisition into the New World when he set up a tribunal at Santo Domingo. His decision may have been influenced by attempts a few years earlier by French Huguenots to colonize Florida, but its source certainly lies in his determination to suppress heresy before it became dangerous anywhere in his realms. There was in fact during his reign little for it to do in the Indies, save harass a few *converso* families and try the occasional Protestant smuggler or pirate who fell into its grasp.

Dependent always upon crown officers and clerics far away to realize

Philip's wishes, the council of the Indies' successes frequently remained on paper. In 1570–72 ordinances for the functioning of the council and defining its authority were promulgated, and a *recopilación* of laws pertaining to the New World was started (finally published in 1681). But the rules laid down did affect the structures concerned and their procedures, and despite distance and other difficulties, Philip's reign in the Indies, as J. H. Parry has stressed, saw the establishment of an administrative system which survived in its essentials for a century and a half after his death.[10]

Yet the system was wedded to a form of imperialism which, as Pierre Vilar tellingly points out, remained feudal in its mentalities and vital substructures:[11] Castilian imperialism aimed to conquer, keep and exploit land. The result in Spain ('reconquered' from the Moors) and in the conquests overseas was a congeries of personal domains upon which was superimposed a bureaucracy which tried to enforce law, organize defence and collect taxes. The land holders and those dependent upon them, while asserting their loyalty to the crown, had little real sympathy for the tasks of the crown's agents.

Moreover, few individual Spaniards, and hardly the government, seemed interested in developing new, more rational organizations for the exploitation of capital acquired in the New World, or for the promotion of industry. The prevailing feudal spirit tended to stifle capitalist tendencies, which were beginning to infect many Englishmen, Netherlanders and Italians. Thus the system built by Philip II, however impressive, consumed wealth without promoting the production of new wealth, save for what could be taken from the earth, and his administrative system came in time to symbolize governmental inefficiency.

These same remarks can also be applied to the Philippines, which were colonized from New Spain. In 1565 the *conquistador* Miguel de Legazpi landed at Cebu and set up a base. A few years later he founded Manila, which became the capital of the new conquest. He and his successors alternated persuasion with force to subdue the natives in a generally pacific conquest, during which the chief battles were fought against the Portuguese, who tried to defend their monopoly in the western Pacific, and Chinese pirates.

Philip, with his concern for justice, soon replaced the regime of the *conquistadores* with government by *audiencia*, the supreme local court of law. But the needs of defence in the East Indian world of rajahs and pirates required that governors be soldiers. In 1590, Philip ordered the armada veteran Gómez Pérez Dasmariñas to Manila with orders to suppress the *audiencia*. Dasmariñas was murdered by Chinese pirates, and the *audiencia* revived, but his son assumed his office, thus maintaining the military nature of the governorship. The result was that the Manila government, like governments elsewhere in Philip's dominions, was constantly caught up in the rivalries and value conflicts between soldiers and legists, government officers and clerics, with none able to prevail.

THE CROWN OF ARAGON: ARAGON, VALENCIA AND CATALONIA

Philip's subjects of the crown of Aragon had few privileges in regard to the Indies, and needed special licence to do business or emigrate there. They were, however, in a weak position, economically and geographically, to exploit the opportunities offered in the New World, and, moreover, were far more interested in Italy, where their kings, soldiers and merchants had been active since the thirteenth century.

Aragon proper, with its capital at Zaragoza, was largely a barren land, dominated by an unruly nobility who hid behind a hedge of privileges. The Cortes was jealous of the famed 'liberties' of Aragon, which chiefly benefited the nobles (who, among other things, could execute their vassals on their own judgment), and made the redress of grievances precede supply. Since the kingdom could supply little, Philip II did not concern himself much with it until a revolt broke out in 1591 at Zaragoza.

Neighbouring Catalonia gave him much more anxiety, because of its vulnerable frontier with France and proximity to the Huguenot strongholds of Languedoc. The Cortes of Catalonia were as stubborn as those of Aragon, and represented a region in the throes of a long depression. Barcelona had little left but the shell of its medieval greatness. In the countryside, banditry was rife and provided Philip's governors-general with one of their chief problems – the others being defence and protection against the infiltration of heresy, which, with little justification, they linked with banditry. Pursuing the bandits was no easy matter, and not always popular, since many were from, or sheltered by, prominent but impoverished families.

The life of the kingdom of Valencia was somewhat different from that of the other Aragonese realms. The capital city, Valencia, was relatively prosperous, while the great Valencian nobles, who lorded over vast estates, were the only Aragonese subjects who approached the Castilian grandees in wealth. The great menace to the ease and security of Valencia was the large *morisco* minority, of nearly 150,000 persons, or about one-fourth of the population. In some regions, especially in the hills above the Valencian *vega*, *moriscos* formed an absolute majority. Most of them worked noble estates and therefore enjoyed the protection of the nobility in the face of the hostility of the 'Old Christian' commons who, not always mistakenly, believed that *moriscos* collaborated with the North African corsairs in their raids on the Valencian coast, and awaited liberation by the Turks.

ITALY

Of his dominions in Italy Philip only visited the duchy of Milan, and that during the reign of his father, when he travelled to the Netherlands and back in 1548–51. There was occasional talk during his reign of his visiting Italy, but nothing ever came of it.

Of all Philip's dominions, Milan alone had no general representative assembly for the whole, but the municipal corporations, often working together, served as a limiting influence on Philip's governors. The most powerful Milanese institution was the Senate, a supreme court of law modelled by Louis XII of France, who occupied the duchy in 1500, on the Parlement of Paris. The twelve members of the Senate were appointed by the sovereign for life; nine of the twelve, including the president, had to be native Milanese. All government edicts and appointments had to be ratified by the Senate; Philip II advised his governors always to heed the Senate before taking action.

But during much of Philip's reign, the legal power of the Senate to limit his will was eclipsed by the moral power of the archbishop Carlo Borromeo, who recognized few restraints to the Church's right to intervene in the affairs of society. Philip once casually noted on a letter from Borromeo, who claimed to be working for the people, 'I am not sure that he is not doing perhaps more than he ought to.'[12] Don Luis de Requesens, governor-general in 1571–73, put it more dramatically: Borromeo was more dangerous to Philip's rule of Milan than 'an army of one hundred thousand Frenchmen at the gates'.[13]

Control of Milan was vital for the security of the Catholic Monarchy in Italy and the maintenance of communications northward to the Netherlands and Austria. Moreover, the Milanese arsenals were prime suppliers for Philip's soldiers marching north or boarding the Mediterranean galleys, and surrounding Lombardy was a chief recruiting ground for troops. Philip was therefore extremely jealous of his authority and conceded nothing. Through his governors he resisted Borromeo's designs, which ultimately aimed at the establishment of an archiepiscopal theocracy.

The kingdom of Naples was the richest and most populous of Philip's Italian dominions. Much of what has been said about life in Spain can be applied to Naples, and also to Sicily and Sardinia. Philip's viceroy held court in the city of Naples, where a strong squadron of galleys, paid for by Naples but invariably commanded by a Spaniard, had its station. Philip and his ministers were always gravely concerned about the loyalty of Naples to his dynasty. The kingdom had been conquered after the death (in 1435) of Queen Joanna II of Anjou by Alfonso the Magnanimous of Aragon, who insisted that she had willed it to him. She once had, but had since changed her mind. On his death Alfonso willed his conquest, Naples, to his bastard Ferrante I, while the traditional possessions of the crown of Aragon passed to his brother Juan II. The rule of Ferrante was brutal, and the land was rent by faction as supporters of the House of Aragon clashed with the supporters of the Angevin pretenders. Ferrante's death brought in 1494 Charles VIII of France, who had acquired the Angevin claim, to occupy the kingdom. Ferrante's sons sought the help of their cousin Ferdinand the Catholic (Juan II's successor in Aragon), whose armies drove the French from Naples by 1504. Ferdinand then proceeded to set aside his Neapolitan cousins and take Naples for himself. Charles V was able through strong viceroys to keep control of Naples, and made a triumphal entrance into the capital in 1535, on his return from the conquest of Tunis. In 1547, however, he backed down from an attempt to establish in Naples a royal Inquisition on the Spanish model because of riots.

The nobles and burghers of Naples remained factious, and the Aragonese and Angevin parties continued to exist; however, a certain indifference to anything but local issues pitted the factions more against one another than against the policies of the crown, which, to buy their loyalty, was inclined to treat everybody generously. The Neapolitan *parlamento*[14] met almost every two years during Philip's reign, but in general did little but vote the *donativo* the government asked; in effect a conquered nation, they could not make redress precede supply. The one tactic employed with some success to make the viceroy responsive to their petitions was threatening to send a delegation to Madrid to complain to the council of Italy and so reach the king's ear.

Higher policy, decided in Madrid, was chiefly concerned with defending Naples against the Turks, and enjoyed general support. The viceroy contented himself with collecting taxes, recruiting Neapolitan soldiers, who were held in high repute, and overseeing the dispensation of justice, aided by Neapolitan lawyers who supported the royal prerogative; and for the rest, let the kingdom follow its own logic. The countryside was dominated by the barons, who were plentiful if only in rare instances wealthy, and plagued by bandits. The need to defend the coasts against corsairs permitted the barons to maintain militia companies to augment royal garrisons of Spanish and German mercenaries.

As tensions mounted in Philip's Netherlands in the 1560s and rioting escalated into rebellion, Philip and his ministers feared that the same might happen in Naples and Milan, which were considered latecomers to the monarchy and uncertain in their loyalty. As feared, the peace of Naples was shattered when riots broke out in the capital in May 1585, initially over a steep jump in the price of bread.[15] The duke of Osuna, then viceroy, feigned sympathy with the rioters until the royal galleys arrived in the harbour in July, giving him overwhelming military advantage. He then began a systematic suppression of suspected dissidents and their sympathizers. Eight hundred and twenty persons were brought to trial, of whom thirty-one were tortured and executed, seventy-one sent to the galleys and 300 sent into exile. During the repression, perhaps 12,000 persons fled the city in fear.

The result of the riots and the subsequent punishment of rioters was a heightened awareness of the Neapolitan population of the nature of the 'Spanish' viceroyalty, with its foreign officers, which had effectively emasculated the politically articulate elements in Neapolitan society. A regime once accepted with relative indifference now became increasingly unpopular.

The chief difference between the governments of Sicily[16] and Naples lay in the greater effectiveness of the Sicilian *parlamento*. Its recalcitrance in the face of viceregal requests for grants, in Philip's reign as in his father's, gave rise to the *bon mot*, 'In Sicily the Spaniards nibbled, in Naples they ate and in Milan they devoured.' In general the viceroys of Sicily found their tours unpleasant and their tenure short. Like the Neapolitans, the Sicilians accepted direction from Spain because of the need for a common defence against the Turks. In addition, Sicily's ties with the House of Aragon were old, dating back to the Sicilian Vespers (1282), when the Aragonese came not as conquerors, but as liberators, to help the Sicilians in their rising against Charles of Anjou's oppressive rule. The *parlamento* elected Pedro III of Aragon as king of Sicily in place of Charles. Unlike the Neapolitans, the Sicilians were considered reliable subjects of the monarchy.

With their ancient feuds, Sicilians came to believe that in distant Spain more even-handed justice might be obtained than in Messina or Palermo, though the king and council of Italy in Madrid preferred that verdicts given in Sicily not be ordinarily appealed to the king himself. Upon his accession Philip therefore undertook to improve the administration of justice in Sicily, and remove from it the element of personal rivalries, by reforming the Great Court of Sicily on which several feuding barons held seats by right of inheritance. He did not, however, move directly against these baronial seats, which might have provoked an outcry, but rather proceeded in an oblique fashion by modestly proposing to the Sicilian *parlamento* that Spanish jurists be eligible for legal offices in Sicily. This raised a storm of opposition. Soon afterwards, Philip promulgated his judicial reforms, adding several seats to the Great Court for professional legists, leaving the barons their seats but stripping them of all judicial powers. Since Philip reserved all legal offices in Sicily for natives, the *parlamento* thought it had won a victory over the king. In their elation, they did not realize till later that in fact the crown had gained in power, since the new members of the Great Court were its creatures, Sicilian or not. And since the ideal of royal justice, whether Philip's or the legist's trained in Roman Imperial Law, was the equality of all under the laws, the complaints of the privileged barons, who lost out, were overshadowed by general acceptance of Philip's reform.

There is another dimension to the place of Sicily, and also of Naples, in Philip's eyes, apart from the fact that they were God-given dominions to govern and defend. They formed the forward echelon of a general system of defence, viewed perforce from Spain where the king was resident and found his chief military advisers. The enemy was the Ottoman Empire, expanding aggressively along the coast of North Africa. Blocking the Turkish advance stood Naples, Sicily, Malta and allied Tunis. Algiers, controlled by the Turks, lay isolated to the west, cut off from Constantinople, and exposed to the attack constantly talked about in Spain. The conquest of Algiers would round out the Catholic Monarchy's dominance over the western Mediterranean. Without the expectation of Turkish help, France could do nothing about it.

The Sicilians were well aware of their crucial role in the defence of Mediterranean Christendom, and despite their defence of privilege in their *parlamento*, they proved, in their contributions for defence, surprisingly generous, as one viceroy put it, for so poor a kingdom.[17] Sicily ordinarily maintained a squadron of a dozen to twenty galleys.

Between Milan, the northern bastion of the Catholic Monarchy in Italy, and Naples, lay several independent Italian states. Savoy, Parma and Genoa were firm allies, the first bound to Spain by gratitude, the second by blood and the third by money. The papacy was a special case, but by its nature it could not easily become a military threat to the monarchy without powerful allies, as Alba's rout in 1557 of Paul IV's army proved. What most concerned Philip II was Tuscany, which had been Charles VIII's high road to Naples in 1494. For different reasons, the people of Pisa, Florence and Siena were pro-French, and had a history of revolting with French help against the Medici regime, which depended upon the support of the Catholic Monarchy. Cosimo I (ruled 1537–74) married Eleonora de Toledo, a cousin of Alba, and in 1557 received Siena from Philip, who wanted to hold Cosimo as an ally. But both to support Cosimo against dissidents in his own dominions, and to assure his honesty, Philip retained of the Sienese lands a series of fortresses along the Tuscan coast (which moreover provided havens for his galleys coasting from Naples to Genoa). These fortresses and the lands around them formed the so-called states of the Presidios: Orbetello, Porto Ercole, Porto San Stefano, Talamone and l'Ansedonia on the mainland, and Porto Longone on the island of Elba. All were made dependent upon Naples, except Elba, which was divided between Cosimo and the Appiani family, who in addition received Piombino as a fief from Philip (who, however, maintained a permanent Spanish garrison there).

Sardinia seemed almost a world apart from the life of the Catholic Monarchy and the rest of Italy. Militarily, it gave Philip few advantages other than that his possession of it kept it from the hands of a potential foe. On the other hand, its coasts, like those of his other Mediterranean dominions, were subject to raids by corsairs and needed protection. The island was sparsely inhabited, by perhaps 100,000 persons, governed by the historic combination of Church and barons. Philip's authority was exercised though a viceroy, who dealt with a Cortes on the Catalan model, and on a lesser scale confronted the same sort of problems faced by his counterpart in Sicily. In Madrid Sardinia was administered though the council of Aragon rather than that of Italy, and its chief petition, that its Cortes meet triennially, was rejected at the outset of Philip's reign.[18] By custom they met once every ten years to vote a *donativo* for the next decade, a custom Philip could see no advantage in changing.

With his powerful position resting on his hereditary possessions, Philip II gave Italy a generation of peace after 1559, something Cabrera de Córdoba found no mean feat, since 'for nine hundred years some one or another has ravaged this loveliest province of Europe'.

Spain and Italy

A Catholic Monarchy based on Spain and Italy made much sense in the sixteenth century. The peoples of the two peninsulas spoke Romance tongues, and could understand one another. Their appearances were not dissimilar – to northern Europeans their soldiers were the 'blackbeards' – and they shared the climate and unity given by the Mediterranean and lifestyles which in many ways seem alike. Their foods had much in common and were cooked or moistened with olive oil, flavoured with garlic and taken with wine. The resources of both peninsulas and the different talents of their various peoples complemented each other in dealing with the three great challenges that confronted them: defence against Ottoman aggression, revitalizing the Reformation-torn Church which nourished their civilizations and exploiting the opportunities offered by the opening of a New World.

The Italo–Spanish Catholic Monarchy's response to these challenges was largely conditioned by existing social realities, the prevailing values of its societies and certain compelling physical considerations. The belligerent confrontation with the Turks and the revitalization of the Church not only appealed immediately to the two dominant orders of society, the nobility and clergy, and provided them with more than enough occupation, but also justified in the eyes of the commons the existence of these essentially unproductive orders. To them the vast majority of commoners rendered obedience and paid taxes, dues and tithes.

By their very size and prestige, as well as their overwhelming concern with war and the Counter Reformation, the nobility and clergy tended to stifle the development of productive activities beyond those needed for subsistence and the maintenance of a minimal military technology. The low levels of production had difficulty keeping pace with the growth of population and the improvements in weaponry. But those middling elements of society in the Catholic Monarchy, whose opposites were beginning to develop new productive techniques, preferred to ape the nobility and clergy, and did not respond sufficiently to new developments to maintain the pace set in northern Italy (especially Milan) and north-western Europe. Braudel and others call this the 'treason of the bourgeoisie' of the Catholic Monarchy, but this of course implies certain value judgments which favour modern industrial society; although to be sure the monarchy was not lacking in critics among its own subjects, who challenged its prevailing values and ways of doing things.[19] They could clearly see that the monarchy was becoming increasingly dependent on Milan and northern Europe for manufactured goods, and the Netherlands for shipping to carry needed foodstuffs from the North Sea and Baltic regions to Spain and southern Italy.

The monarchy's own shipbuilding industry in the meantime was responding to the problems of war and piracy, and yards that might have provided more merchantmen produced war galleys, which were good for little but combating piracy and quick amphibious operations. The gentlemen who might have improved the productivity of their estates, preferred to ride these galleys when not engaged in gallantry in some provincial capital.

Nature was no longer so generous in the south in yielding her bounty: the soils were eroded and depleted, and the better forests were long ago cut down. As agricultural productivity fell off, and necessary commodities had to be brought from farther away, costs went up and the economic life of the southern monarchy deteriorated.

The third challenge faced by the monarchy and its peoples was the exploitation of the opportunities offered by the opening of the New World, but the challenge was not met. To the most vital elements in Spanish and south Italian society, the other two proved more compelling and were certainly more immediate. The challenge of the New World drew comparatively minimal response, and its chief beneficiaries in the Mediterranean world were the Genoese bankers. The gold and silver mined in the Indies ultimately worked its way northward to pay for munitions and foodstuffs or eastward to pay for the spices and luxury products of the Orient, unless by chance it was used to embellish a church or a palace.

In the final analysis, the Catholic Monarchy rested on a society which was fundamentally feudal and agrarian in outlook and structures. Though in matters of finance and military organization Philip II's government showed some ability to build rationally as well as merely expand, its guiding principles remained the medieval ideals of justice, religion and the crusade, all of which worked in one way or another against the systematic development and exploitation of its natural and human resources for the production of wealth and power, whether by government, corporations or individuals. The result in retrospect reminds one of a grand edifice of the time, in which the dynamic elements are powerfully contained within an imposing and massive structure of traditional and classical forms.

THE NETHERLANDS AND THE FRANCHE-COMTÉ

If Philip's southern possessions persisted in their traditional structures, the rich, populous and crowded Netherlands were beginning to break from them, not without a good deal of social tension and unrest. Exploiting the products of the land and sea, manufacturing textiles on a large scale and developing a large carrying trade by sea, Netherlands merchants and entrepreneurs competed fiercely to win an ever-growing share of European and even world markets.[20] Their bottoms carried grains and timber from the Baltic and fish from the North Sea to Seville, Naples, Palermo and Lisbon, returning with spices from the Indies, wines, salt, citrus fruits and Castilian wool. Thus, economically, the developing Netherlands provided useful and necessary services for the stagnating Catholic Monarchy. Their growing share of its markets did not fail to attract attention and raise some jealousies, but the South, like a man who fears he is drowning, clung tightly to its buoyant northern partner.

Strategically, however, the Netherlands seemed an embarrassment to some after the death of Mary Tudor in 1558, since England was no longer a dependable ally, and they were exposed to attack from France and the Lutheran parts of Germany. On the other hand, many of Philip II's advisers, from Granvelle onwards, saw the Netherlands as the monarchy's forward bastion, absorbing the blows of the monarchy's northern European enemies, who dared not move against Spain and Italy until they had been reduced.[21] Therefore, the Netherlands had to be powerfully fortified and garrisoned. However they were viewed, Philip intended to conserve them.

For Philip, the government of the Netherlands posed many problems; and the divisions among his advisers over how to respond did not help. He wanted his regime in Brussels to repair its finances and provide for the common defence, while at the same time dispensing justice and safeguarding the Catholic religion. This would be no easy matter, since the Netherlands had borne so much of the cost of Charles's wars that their prosperity seemed – for a moment – jeopardized. They scarcely defrayed the costs of their own administration, and from the beginning of his reign, Philip had to send money from Castile to support his rule in the Low Countries.

The most fundamental problem facing Philip, from his point of view, was that the Netherlands, despite the work of the Burgundian dukes and Charles V, had never been unified. Each of the seventeen provinces maintained its separate identity, its own estates, and looked upon Philip, in a strict legal sense, only as its particular ruler. Thus in Flanders, as in Holland, Philip was count, in Brabant, duke, etc. This provincialism was compounded by language divisions: in the northern provinces, Netherlandish was spoken, itself broken into many dialects such as Flemish, Dutch and Frisian; in the regions south of Brussels, Walloon French.

None the less, a sense of a unified Netherlands, nurtured by the Brussels government, did exist, represented in such institutions as the Great Council (High Court) at Mechelen, the States General, to which each of the provincial estates sent delegations, and the Order of the Golden Fleece.

The Order of the Golden Fleece, founded by Duke Philip the Good in 1430, enjoyed a special place among Netherlands institutions. The knights, of the greatest families in the Low Countries, were free in chapter meetings to speak directly to the sovereign of government matters without fear of giving offence. To protect this right, knights could only be tried by the chapter. Charles had found it easy and natural to work with the chapter, but Philip, uncomfortable in so free a situation, did not. Increasingly he used the Order as an honour to be bestowed on the high nobility in any one of his dominions. He effectively ended its political role when in 1568 he had several of its members tried for treason by a special tribunal, arguing that they had forfeited their right to trial by the chapter. They were convicted and executed as traitors.

In Philip's defence, it must be stressed that the Order had become a centre of opposition to those of his policies which displeased the magnates, for whatever reason. In its meetings they concerted the line to be taken by its members who sat on the Netherlands council of state, the chief advisory body to the governor-general and one of the three collateral councils. The other two, the privy council, which supervised justice, and the council of finance, which supervised the fiscal business of the government, were less of a problem to Philip: their members were chiefly 'new men' with law degrees, while on the council of state the old nobility predominated. The knights of the Fleece moreover provided most of the provincial governors, and the stadholders, who captained the militia, supervised the royal garrisons and looked after the sovereign's business in general.

Like the nobility in Philip's other dominions, the Netherlands nobility were powerful and lorded over the countryside. Government could not function without them. Yet following an older feudal geography,

they married their scions into the noble houses of France and the
Empire, as well as into other Netherlands houses; and their interests, in
consequence, frequently stretching beyond the confines of the seventeen
provinces, often did not coincide with Philip's. The greatest of them,
William of Nassau, prince of Orange, ruled the sovereign principality
of Orange and possessed estates in France and the Empire as well as in
Philip's Netherlands and Franche-Comté. Count Hoorn and Baron
Montigny were Montmorencys, kinsmen of the constable of France.
Then there was another problem, according to Granvelle: these
nobles lived lavishly and amassed debts, which they owed to rich
merchants, to whom they therefore became in effect politically indentured.[22]

In the Netherlands, above all in Brabant and Flanders, the merchants
and entrepreneurs of the towns carried more political weight than in
any other of Philip's dominions, save perhaps for Milan. Town governments were oligarchic and jealous of their control over the ordinary life
of their municipalities, and favoured the sort of monarchy which
guaranteed the hierarchical social order without interfering with the
power of local authorities or overburdening them with taxes. Within
each town oligarchy existed fierce tensions, caused not only by family
rivalries, which were common in all Philip's realms, but also by rivalries
between *rentiers*, who lived off government bonds, rural holdings and
rental properties, and engaged in law and government, and entrepreneurs, who engaged in manufacturing and trade, and therefore
thought pragmatically rather than in terms of legal precedents. Among
the entrepreneurs themselves there were also divisions, between those
in commerce, who wanted a free market, and those in manufacturing,
who wanted protection; between those in the old guilds, who wanted
to control production and keep wages high, and those who employed day
labourers and cottagers, and wanted to expand production and screw
wages down; between large shopkeepers, who wanted competitive
prices, and small shopkeepers, who wanted prices fixed by government
decree. All of these men put pressure on the Brussels regime, which
tried to find policies pleasing to at least the most influential, if not to all.
It enacted protectionist legislation favouring Netherlands manufacturing and shipping and, at the same time, negotiated trade treaties,
especially with neighbouring England.

Needless to say, the condition of the poor in this fluid economic
situation was not always agreeable. In the countryside, a certain traditional stability mitigated the effects of fluctuations in the non-agrarian
economy, but the spectre of famine remained as terrifying as ever. But

for urban workers, conditions were uncertain and often desperate; and confronted by the establishment of Church, nobles and oligarchs, they frequently found release in the fervour of Calvinist preaching, and were always ready to vent their despair through riot. There was nothing new in this; for three hundred years the history of Flanders had been punctuated by bloody rebellions of 'low people', often with strong chiliastic overtones.

Philip II seems not to have grasped the economic and social problems of the Netherlands, which were more intense than the same problems in his more traditionally structured southern possessions. He expected more revenues, more control of local institutions and more submissiveness in matters of religion than most of his officers in Brussels and certainly his stadholders in the provinces thought they could obtain without provoking popular uprisings. Because of his aloofness, his dependence on too few advisers and his language limitations, Philip failed during his sojourns in the Netherlands, as heir apparent (1549–50 and 1555) and as sovereign (1555–59), to learn as much as he might have about his Netherlands subjects and, in consequence, they remained foreign to him and he to them. He was, however, Charles's son, and they meant to prove themselves his loyal subjects.

Philip was likewise regarded as foreign in the last remnant of Burgundy proper, the Franche-Comté. The *Franc-comtois*, however, were devoted to the House of Burgundy, which he represented, and wanted no more than the Netherlanders to be ruled by the French monarchy. Charles V had been well served by many *Franc-comtois*; Philip only employed three in important posts: Antoine Perrenot de Granvelle, bishop of Arras (after 1561, Cardinal Granvelle), his brother, Thomas Perrenot de Chantonnay, ambassador successively to France (1559–63) and the Empire (1563–70), and Simon Renard, who negotiated his marriage with Mary Tudor and the Truce of Vaucelles, and advised him on the Burgundian lands. All had been employed first by Charles V. The Perrenots and Renards had lands and connections in the county, and had been friends before the truce, which Granvelle opposed. The development of a rift between Granvelle and the prince of Orange (who possessed large domains in the Franche-Comté) over control of the Netherlands government after Philip left Brussels in 1559, deepened their emnity because Renard supported Orange's ambition to become governor of the Franche-Comté.[23] Through their friends, Renard and Granvelle troubled the county until 1564 when Philip ordered Renard to Madrid (where he died in disgrace in 1573). Granvelle, on Philip's orders, proceeded in 1566 to Rome and in 1579 to Spain, always in the royal service. He became Philip's principal adviser on the government of Franche-Comté, and in effect was the chief architect of the extension of Philip's control over the county's traditional institutions.

While the county was to be sure a God-given dominion for Philip, it was also a vital link in the military road from Milan to the Nethernds. Though treaties between himself and the king of France pledged that there would be no war between the two halves of Burgundy, the French duchy and the Franche-Comté, Philip feared French subversion or invasion of the county, if not by the French royal army, then by French Huguenots aided by Swiss Protestants. For this reason, Philip and Granvelle proceeded through appointments to office and the provision of clergy, through patronage, intimidation and bribery, to dominate the provincial estates and the magistracies, through which opposition to Philip's policies could be vented.

In 1586 the cardinal died in Madrid, but the regime he had built for his native Franche-Comté persisted, despite some dozen years of troubles caused by the last wars of religion in France, and Philip's intervention in them. In 1598, the county was included in the dowry of the Infanta Isabel when she married Albert, and then passed under the benign reign of the 'Archdukes'.

The Franche-Comté, like the other components of Philip's monarchy, was looked upon by Philip above all as a part of the entire dynastic patrimony; for the sake of the whole, the ancient 'liberties' of a province, or an old and proven minister, would be sacrificed.

THE RELATIONSHIP OF CASTILE TO THE MONARCHY'S OTHER DOMINIONS

The settlement of Philip and his court in Castile in 1559 had profound consequences for his monarchy, as has already been suggested, in an age of nascent nationalism. Philip had been born in Castile, raised in Castile, spoke easily only in Castilian, learned to govern in Castile, and as soon as he had arranged his affairs in the Netherlands (1555–59) hurried back to Castile. To be sure, he hoped to have better luck in getting money in Castile than in the Netherlands, but he had been hankering to return 'home' before bankruptcy became inevitable. There were in fact good reasons why he should have based his monarchy on Castile: it was his most populous realm, his prime source of revenues, his chief recruiting ground for soldiers and the kingdom where, as a native son, he inspired the highest loyalty. Resident in Castile, Philip perforce saw the world from a Castilian viewpoint.

Despite his preference for Castile as the seat of his government, Philip insisted that he had the same concern for his subjects and for good government in each and every one of his realms. This was sincerely meant, and proved at least within the peninsula by Philip's journeys, even at times that were inconvenient, or even threatening to his health. In 1592, for example, he insisted on travelling to Tarazona to meet with the Cortes of Aragon; he brushed aside his physicians' objections to the trip, saying, 'If I die, it will be in the office in which God put me, to minister to His people for the sake of peace and justice, in Aragon as in Castile.'[24]

Non-Castilians, however, believed that Philip favoured Castile and Castilians. They saw his chief councils dominated by Castilians and the great posts of the monarchy a virtual monopoly of the high Castilian nobility. The secretaries who handled Philip's correspondence, the commanders who led his armies and armadas and the diplomats who represented him at foreign courts were predominately subjects of the crown of Castile. Vespasiano Gonzaga, an Italian prince who had the rare fortune to be viceroy of Valencia, told Philip's secretary Mateo Vázquez in 1578 that Philip ought to keep in mind that he ruled Italians and Flemings as well as Spaniards.[25] When saying Spaniards, Gonzaga, like most non-Iberians, did not differentiate among the nations of the Iberian peninsula: its natives did. Aragonese, Valencians, Catalans, Portuguese, even Andalusians, who were subjects of the crown of Castile, complained about the prevalence in government of men from the provinces of Old and New Castile.

Though Castilians indeed predominated at Philip's court and therefore in the government of the monarchy, many of his leading ministers and councillors were not Castilians. The ordinances governing the regional councils of the monarchy prescribed that at least some, if not all, of their members be natives of the region concerned. And two of the men most influential in shaping policy during his reign were Portuguese: Ruy Gómez de Silva, until his death in 1573 Philip's closest adviser, and Don Cristóbal de Moura, the most trusted councillor of Philip's declining years, elevated in 1585 to the council of state. One might add to this list of non-Castilian confidants Don Juan de Idiáquez, who began to serve at court in 1579 and, like so many of Philip's ministers and secretaries, was a Basque, and thus ethnically not Castilian, though a subject of the Castilian crown. All three, however, were from the Iberian peninsula. The only man from outside the peninsula to

enjoy a major role in the shaping of the higher policies of the monarchy
was Cardinal Granvelle, the *Franc-comtois* whom Philip in 1579 put in
charge of foreign relations (save for relations with Portugal which
Philip conducted directly with Moura, his ambassador in Lisbon), and
in 1580, in charge of the administrative offices of government in Madrid,
when Philip himself went to Portugal. Yet despite his Burgundian
origin Granvelle, when he served in the government of the Netherlands
(1559–64), was called the 'Spanish' cardinal and shared the Castilians'
unpopularity.

Overseas conquests, military successes in Europe and a belief that
they alone maintained unsullied the old Catholic faith caused Castilians
to treat with condescension Philip's other subjects, as well as his allies
and enemies. When a Spanish official in Milan, in a letter to Madrid,
stressed that the Italians abhorred the Spanish nation and regime, the
recipient wrote on the back, 'These Italians, although they are not
Indians, have to be treated as such, so that they understand that we are
in charge of them, and not they in charge of us.'[26] Cabrera de Córdoba,
who served as a secretary to Philip's government in Brussels in the 1580s,
wrote that Spaniards were looked upon as 'enemies of the Germanic
peoples', and with the myopic vision of those sure they are in the right,
found it hard to understand how Spanish soldiers, who were laying
waste the Netherlands in their attempt to crush the Calvinist insurgents,
could be so hated by a population whose ancestral religion they had come
to save.

Philip's non-Castilian subjects did indeed fear Castilians as the
instruments for carrying out a policy imputed to Philip and his ministers
imposing a Castilian-style regime on the other states of his monarchy.
A Castilian regime, to those not familiar with the realities of Castile,
implied a supine Cortes, a dependent nobility and clergy, a crown-
directed Inquisition unhindered by ordinary legal procedures, a compliant
judiciary and towns governed by royally appointed *corregidores* –
in other words, absolute monarchy, run by Castilians appointed from
Madrid to the chief offices in each of Philip's dominions without regard
for local privileges. *Non curamus vestros privilegios* ('We regard not your
privileges'), William the Silent in his *Apologia* has the Castilian jurist
Vargas say in bad Latin.[27] Philip II's non-Castilian subjects meant to
resist the imposition of the feared Castilian regime. Their fears and
consequent resistance run like a *leitmotif* through his reign, which
appears in such diverse forms and places as Borromeo's anti-govern-
ment activities in Milan, in the hostility to the 'Spanish' viceroyalty in
Naples that grew in the wake of the repression of the riots of 1585, in

the resistance of the Portuguese to Philip's strong claim to their throne (and his generosity in respecting their privileges after he made good his claim), in the riots inspired by the appointment of a Castilian viceroy for Aragon and, above all, in the revolt of the Netherlands, those provinces where the ideals and forms of Castile were most entirely foreign and most deeply mistrusted.

IV

Philip II, the Court of Madrid and the Government of the Monarchy

Through this discussion of the man, his attitudes and his dominions, we begin to come to grips with Philip II, the king in office. Regardless of the theories of the King's Two Bodies (the fallible, mortal man; the infallible, immortal monarch), one cannot separate the private Philip from Philip the king; nor can his dominions be studied without reference to Philip, whose will affected all of them. We cannot proceed linearly in our investigation, but rather must work our way across the mosaic of his reign, finding each piece and trying to relate it to the others, studying what we see develop, and observing how events affected Philip and how he responded to them.

Philip, in regard to his office, believed simultaneously in his sovereign prerogatives and in the inviolability of the fundamental laws and institutions of each of his dominions, which he had sworn to uphold. The monarch was responsible to God for all of his subjects; the subject was responsible only for himself. The subject therefore generally stood for selfish interests and often had to be overruled for the good of the community by the prince, whose duty was to serve the community. Both scripture and history supported monarchy as the best means of assuring the well-being of the community.[1]

But principles supporting monarchy are one thing, the conduct of kingly office another; and in office, if one thing is certain about Philip II, it is that he was determined to have his way and loath to brook opposition. To have his way, however, Philip needed willing agents, bound to him either through personal loyalty, the royal purse or both. He required reliable judges, ministers, lieutenants, secretaries, fiscal officers, churchmen, soldiers and sailors to execute the law, collect taxes, deal with private subjects and their institutions and defend his dominions against his enemies.

To assist him in directing the activities of all those needed to carry out his intentions, there was the court, the royal government that had grown up around the crown to deal with its widening range of concerns. For in the sixteenth century, royal government was becoming ever more involved in the increasingly complex affairs of society. The expansion of business and commerce, religious differences and the rising costs of bigger wars required more government action and arbitration. To put it simply, Philip II's government had to cope with steadily changing circumstances and situations which often developed with surprising rapidity. And, arguably, his regime was not well suited to cope with these new developments, since it grew from the traditional *curia regis* and household offices characteristic of medieval monarchies, which had presided over seigneurial, feudal and agrarian societies. Effective response above all demanded a shift in values, which would have permitted a more sympathetic approach to the 'novelties' and changes of early modern European society: it was chiefly here, in my view, that Philip's court fell short.

By Philip's time, the various tasks of state, such as the administration of justice, farming the royal domain, collecting taxes and providing for defence, had been divided among several councils directed and co-ordinated by the king and his closest ministers. Each council had its own sphere of competence, action and concern, either functional, territorial or both. From councils were often formed committees called *juntas*, which included members of one or more councils, and addressed themselves to special issues.[2] Similar patterns of governmental organization had developed in Philip's other dominions as well as in Castile, so that Philip's viceroys and governors found themselves at courts similar to Philip's.

THE KING'S MINISTERS

Fundamental to the study of the court of Philip II is an examination of his ministers and their administrative procedures. 'The king can govern well,' Philip II claimed in his 1597 instructions to his son,[3] 'only through good ministers. If you cut yourself off (God forbid!) from the advice of your best ministers, and disregard it and run matters alone ... you would want to be more a god among men rather than a king: or at least, and this seems more likely, you would appear a very foolhardy king. But then you would not be worthy of the crown, but, instead, an enemy of the public well-being of your vassals. If after important matters are discussed, with care and mature deliberation, by the wisest and most prudent ministers, they can make mistakes and draw wrong conclusions, what can be expected of a king, who is no more than one man,

subject to passion, error and equivocation, who takes counsel with none
and asks about nothing?'

Philip II always intended to be served by good ministers. The words
he used repeatedly to describe the kind of ministers he had in mind were
prudent, wise, well-informed, experienced, mature, just, righteous and
honourable. He wanted these qualities in all his officers, whether they
be ecclesiastical, judicial, civil or military. When he commissioned Don
John of Austria to take charge of the galleys of Spain, he admonished
him to be pious, just, diligent in their administration and prudent in
battle, stressing that he would be 'more content to see you victorious
through prudence than through rashness or some desperate gamble'.[4]
Philip said nothing about the qualities of decisiveness or bravery, but
at the time these were thought to be attributes of good blood, rather
than consciously or environmentally developed personality traits.
Philip did leave his commanders and governors some leeway to take
independent action in his instructions to them, usually by the phrase,
'or whatever occurs to you'.

Few of Philip II's ministers, secretaries, governors and commanders
have been adequately studied; and such studies are necessary before
Philip's share in the making of the policies of his reign can be assessed
with any certainty. Many of the documents needed to study the evolu-
tion of policy during Philip's reign are in print, but the bulk of the
material for the study of his reign lies in archives, both public and
private, throughout Europe and even in the Americas. The largest
collection of papers engendered by his regime is certainly in Spain, in
the Archivo General de Simancas, where many papers remain yet to be
adequately catalogued. From some of the documents in Simancas the
sand used to dry the ink still falls when they are unfolded.

Recently, some English scholars have found that the British Museum,
the Bibliothèque Publique et Universitaire, Geneva, and two private
libraries in Madrid hold in their manuscript collections some of the
most important working papers of Philip II, his chief ministers and
secretaries.[5] These papers, which cover most of his reign, were apparently
lost from the Palacio Real in Madrid and somehow acquired by the
count of Altamira in the nineteenth century. When his estate was
sold, the papers were unfortunately acquired by several different
collectors, whence they arrived at their present locations. These papers
may shed new light on Philip's regime, but first they must be
correlated and catalogued, which promises to be a hard and lengthy
task.

Apart from the state papers themselves, certain contemporary histories, most importantly that of Luis Cabrera de Córdoba, who served in Philip's government as a secretary, reveal something about policy-making and mention the names of Philip's collaborators. The reports of the Venetian ambassadors about Philip's court, though they have been repeatedly used, can still offer new insights.

Philip II's collaborators were men of all stations of life, from grandees to commoners, but their stations affected and delimited what they might achieve in a rank-conscious society.

Philip naturally employed members of his own family and dynasty when he could, but these filled only the highest offices, and generally represented him where he was not present himself, rather than served him at court. The privileges of certain of his possessions, most notably the Netherlands, Aragon proper and, after 1580, Portugal, required that when Philip was not present in the possession himself, he appoint either a member of his dynasty or a native-born subject to serve as his governor (called 'regent' if a member of the dynasty). Those dominions which did not enjoy such privileges usually got Castilian grandees as Philip's representatives. Philip's own convictions, which he expressed on the occasion of a revolt in Aragon in 1591, were that he should be able to appoint whomever he wished to represent his person, without restriction. None the less, since on his accession he had taken an oath to uphold the privileges of each of his dominions, he neither could nor would abrogate them lightly.

Local privilege was only one factor limiting Philip's freedom to choose whom he wished to advise and serve him. The social hierarchy was an obvious consideration, which Philip accepted along with the other traditions of his age. He had to cope with the assumption by great nobles that seats on royal councils, governorships of provinces and high military commands were part of their birthright. He also had to accept the men appointed by his father in the government he had inherited, unless he wanted to cause confusion.

Philip had little choice, even had he desired it, in the matter of giving governorships and high command to great nobles: the social and political realities of his age (as noted in the survey of his dominions) demanded that he do so. But because great nobles would not study for years to obtain law degrees and disdained the necessary work of secretaries, clerks and book-keepers, Philip had to employ the services of men of the petty nobility or common birth for essential tasks of government. Philip certainly did not mind employing such men, since he knew very well that they were dependent upon him alone for their positions. Great noblemen, on the other hand, had their ancestral estates to fall back on,

and large clienteles of their own who might join them in making trouble
for the crown, if the nobleman were so minded.

Aided by the many posts available in his vast monarchy, Philip had
little difficulty in finding positions of honour for the high nobility. He
therefore allowed into his inner circle only those grandees he wanted,
usually to advise him on foreign policy and military affairs, assuming
they had some knowledge of these fields. But for matters of administration, law and finance, though occasionally a titled noble might preside
over a department, the work was done by experts, usually of gentle
birth, but not infrequently commoners. Many holding important posts
in the government had taken holy orders and thus had become members
of the clerical estate.

Ill feeling between great noblemen and those of lesser station at court
was often intense. The duke of Alba once ranted to the Venetian ambassador about the impudence of the secretary Francisco de Eraso, who
kept him waiting in the king's antechambers;[6] the duke of Medinaceli
had a violent quarrel in 1572 with Cardinal Espinosa, whose meteoric
rise had dazzled the court[7] – the Cardinal, who had even become
imperious in his dealings with Philip, was soon after disgraced.

Men of lesser rank, who served the government well, long and
loyally, did not always hide their resentment of great nobles who
received higher posts, regardless of their qualifications. Cabrera de
Córdoba critically commented that the Turks had the better system,
selecting officials for their proven worth rather than on the promise of
blood.[8] Philip seems to have shown little disposition to change the practices of the prevailing system, and certainly not in the field which was
the specific target of Cabrera's criticism, high military command. On
the other hand, several commoners rose through talent to powerful
positions not in the public eye as Philip's private secretaries, and were
treated with deference, even by grandees. But as shown by the case
of the fall of Antonio Pérez, secretaries who wanted to keep their influence had to be somewhat self-effacing and avoid public display.

The notorious slowness of Philip's court in dispatching business
reflected Philip's own slowness: 'The original sin of our Court', Don
Luis de Requesens once complained to his brother, 'is neither starting nor
finishing anything on time.'[9] Yet it must be remembered that no
European court of this era had much experience in conducting government or waging war on so grand a scale. There were few tried and
proven routines, and it should not appear surprising that matters
frequently proceeded in a disorderly fashion. The very nature of
bureaucracy tends to generate excessive and often unnecessary work.

One of Philip's secretaries described the processing of a petition thus: 'The man presenting the petition gives it to Juan Ruiz; Juan Ruiz gives it to his Majesty; and the King refers it to Juan Ruiz: Juan Ruiz to Gasol, Gasol to Vilella; Vilella makes a report; Vilella gives this to Gasol, Gasol gives it to a committee, the committee gives it to his Majesty; the King refers it to Juan Ruiz, Juan Ruiz gives it to Gasol, Gasol to Vilella, back to Gasol. Gasol gives it to the concerned party. It takes long enough to draft a petition, much longer to get an answer. This much is certain: the poor petitioner waited two months for one small settlement.'[10]

Yet perhaps more crucial than either confusion in the matter of routines or diffidence in the matter of decisions was the vast extent of Philip's monarchy and the slowness of the then available means of communication. 'Space', as Fernand Braudel puts it, was 'enemy number one'[11] in the conduct of government or commerce. A fast courier from Lisbon or Seville might reach Madrid in four days, from Brussels in ten days, from Milan in a fortnight. The ordinary mails to Rome took just under a month. The record run across the Atlantic, from Sanlúcar de Barrameda to Cartagena (de Indias) was twenty-seven days; the return voyage took longer. Drake captured Santo Domingo on New Year's Day 1586; Philip did not get the news until late March.

In sum, Philip's regime, based on councils and *ad hoc juntas*, was from the start encumbered by red tape and rivalries; at the centre of a world-wide congeries of dominions, it was faced by the insuperable problems of distance, and ultimately dependent on direction from a wilful yet diffident and dilatory sovereign.

It needs to be stressed, however, that diffidence was not uniquely a characteristic of Philip, but rather was common to his court and era. Philip's empire was largely built through conquest and inheritance in Charles V's generation. Philip and his generation found it their task to consolidate and conserve what their forebears had put together so quickly that, when Philip came to the throne, all seemed on the verge of collapse. They were therefore conservative by temperament and, aware of the dangers that threatened the monarchy from within and without, understandably cautious.

Most prestigious of the monarchy's councils was the council of state, which advised the king on the conduct of foreign affairs, matters common to the monarchy as a whole (usually strategic defence) and important issues the king chose to put before it.

The members of the council of state were generally of the high nobility and had prior experience in important governmental, military or diplomatic posts. When Philip succeeded to the throne, he inherited a council from his father which included Italians, Netherlanders and Burgundians, as well as Spaniards. On his return to Spain, however, he took with him only the Spaniards and the Portuguese Ruy Gómez. The rest continued to be councillors of state, but were no longer attendant upon his person, and therefore had little influence in policy decisions that affected the whole monarchy, even when such decisions involved their native lands. Of the non-Iberian councillors, the Netherlanders and Burgundians (Granvelle, still bishop of Arras, the prince of Orange and Count Egmont) remained in Brussels with the Netherlands council of state on which they had seats already; the duke of Savoy returned in 1559 to his duchy; and the Genoese admiral Andrea Doria (d. 1560) and his nephew the successor Gian Andrea Doria were fully occupied in the government of Genoa and their galleys. The younger Doria visited Spain in 1585, 1594 and 1596, though he seems not to have sat with the council, but rather conducted his business directly with Philip and his chief ministers. Thus after 1559, the foreign policies of Philip's monarchy appeared to be Spanish foreign policies, despite tensions between Spanish and Habsburg dynastic interests.

Philip as king was president of the council of state, but seldom, some claim never, attended its meetings. Cabrera de Córdoba wrote that Philip was present at some of the most important meetings of the early part of his reign, but these meetings mentioned by Cabrera took place at Valsaín, in the woods of Segovia. Surrounded by only the most trusted members of the council who were attending him, Philip may well have sat in on their sessions.

Until his death in 1566, Gonzalo Pérez, Philip's personal secretary, served as secretary of (the council of) state; afterwards, Philip divided the post between two men, Antonio Pérez, Gonzalo's son, and Gabriel de Zayas. The former became secretary of state for Italy, and handled the correspondence concerning the Italian states, including the papacy, and the war with the Ottoman Empire. The latter became secretary of state for the North, and handled correspondence dealing with the states north of the Pyrenees and Alps, and also Portugal and Morocco.

What most impressed contemporaries about the council of state was the open rivalry between Ruy Gómez de Silva and the duke of Alba. The Venetian ambassador, Michele Suriano, whether in real awe or just turning a good phrase, called them the 'twin columns that uphold the great machine of state, and upon their counsels depends the fate of half the world'.[12]

The roots of their rivalry were many, and often crossed. Alba was the leader of those who served Charles V, men like himself and Don Juan Manrique de Lara; Ruy Gómez, of those who had been in Philip's entourage, such as the count (after 1567 duke) of Feria. Generally it can be said that Alba's outlook was Castilian and imperialistic, Ruy Gómez's Iberian and cosmopolitan. Ruy Gómez's experience had been in diplomacy and finance, Alba's in war.

Alba headed a noble faction in Spain, which included his own House of Toledo, and the houses of Enríquez (the admiral of Castile), Enríquez de Guzmán (count of Alba de Liste) and Pacheco (marquis of Cerralbo). His close relatives in high office included the prior Don Antonio de Toledo, councillor of state, and Don García de Toledo, marquis of Villafranca, who served as governor of Catalonia, commander-in-chief of the Mediterranean armada and viceroy of Sicily before joining the council of state.

Ruy Gómez de Silva, when he came to Spain, had no such connections. He was dependent upon Philip, who made him prince of Eboli in Naples, duke of Pastrana in Castile and grandee of Spain, and arranged for his marriage to Doña Ana de Mendoza, the heiress of the duke of Francavilla, Don Diego Hurtado de Mendoza, an important councillor. Through his marriage, Gómez was linked to the powerful Mendoza family (the duke of Infantado, the marquis of Mondejar, and others) and their allies, the Zúñiga (the duke of Béjar and the count of Miranda), the Velasco (the constable of Castile) and the Guzmán (the duke of Medina Sidonia and the count of Olivares).

Ruy Gómez and Alba, representing two great blocs of Castilian families (and these were, of course, not the only such blocs), were thus engaged in a continuous struggle to secure positions, patronage and preferment for them, in which each achieved considerable success. Their clienteles extended to the lesser nobles and commoners at court (for example, Antonio Pérez was a protégé of Ruy Gómez, Zayas was Alba's). Consequently the court seethed with intrigue, nowhere better shown than in Gregorio Marañón's *Antonio Pérez*. Though Philip had a stronger hold over the middling sort of men, they none the less aspired to acceptance in aristocratic society as well as to government promotion.

The membership of the council of state naturally changed as the reign wore on and the king outlived his original councillors, who had mostly been men older than himself. We might list their names, for they are important men of whom we know little: Don Luis de Quijada (d. 1569), Don Juan Manrique de Lara (d. 1570), the duke of Feria (d.

1572), Cardinal Espinosa (d. 1572), Ruy Gómez de Silva (d. 1573), the second count of Chinchón (d. 1575), the fourth duke of Medinaceli (d. 1575), Don Luis de Requesens (d. 1576), the prior Don Antonio de Toledo (d. *c.* 1577), the third duke of Sessa, the third marquis of los Vélez, Don García de Toledo and Don John of Austria (all d. 1578), the duke of Alba (d. 1582) and, finally, Cardinal Granvelle and Don Juan de Zúñiga (d. 1586).

Granvelle, the old imperialist who in 1579 came to Madrid after so many councillors had already died, provided, as Leopold von Ranke correctly stressed, the chief link between Philip II's 'first' and 'second' ministries.[13] Less influential in this transition was Don Juan de Zúñiga, who served Philip in Italy as ambassador to Rome (1568–83) and viceroy of Naples (1579–83) before coming to court in 1583, where he headed the Spanish opposition to the Burgundian Granvelle.

The 'first' ministry had been balanced between Ruy Gómez and Alba, and continued after Ruy Gómez's death (1573) because his followers were successfully held together by Antonio Pérez. In 1579, both Alba and Pérez were disgraced, and Granvelle took over direction of the administration and became Philip's chief foreign policy adviser. His opponents, Spaniards who resented his administration of the court during Philip's absence in Portugal (1580–83) and his Burgundian foreign policy, lacked a capable leader until Zúñiga arrived at court from Italy. Zúñiga and Granvelle, who had served together in Rome, did not differ greatly on foreign policy – both favoured the Enterprise (i.e., the conquest) of England, for instance, although Zúñiga gave higher priority to Mediterranean undertakings, such as the conquest of Algiers, than did Granvelle, who wanted the monarchy to concentrate almost exclusively on Netherlands and Atlantic matters and strictly assume the defensive in the Mediterranean. But Zúñiga's balance of Habsburg and Spanish interests was more to the liking of Spaniards than Granvelle's Burgundian dynastic views, and thus Zúñiga became the centre of the nearly universal opposition at court to Granvelle.

Zúñiga was, moreover, closer to the king than was the cardinal. Zúñiga's father had been Philip's governor, and he himself was appointed governor to Prince Philip. Soon after the king's return to Madrid, in early 1583, and Zúñiga's arrival at court, the personal influence of Granvelle began to wane steadily until his death in 1586. It was noted that the king did less for the cardinal's funeral than for Zúñiga's a few months later.

Granvelle's success in forming Philip's 'second' ministry lay not in his own influence with Philip, but in his friendship with Don Juan de Idiáquez, whom he had brought with him from Italy. Their fathers had both served Charles V. Idiáquez had served successively as ambassador to Genoa (1571–78) and Venice (1578–79), and had been posted to France when Granvelle persuaded him to change his plans. Granvelle, on his arrival in Spain, was made president of the council of Italy, although his duties were far greater in scope. He in turn arranged for Idiáquez's appointment as secretary (to the council) of state for Italy, the office lost by Pérez when he was disgraced. The office of secretary to the council of Italy, recently made vacant by the death of Diego de Vargas, went to Gabriel de Zayas (who continued to be secretary of state for the North) as the result of bureaucratic politics, but Idiáquez's nephew, Don Francisco de Idiáquez, was appointed Zayas's assistant for Italy. During their seven years of friendship in Madrid, Granvelle seems to have schooled Idiáquez carefully in the Burgundian and Imperial traditions of the monarchy's diplomacy.

Around 1585, when Don Juan de Idiáquez took a seat on the council of state, the 'second' ministry began to appear, with Idiáquez the spokesman and heir of Granvelle's thinking. But, as in all Philip's ministries, there was another major minister who seems not to have been a protégé of Zúñiga or anyone else: Don Cristóbal de Moura. His views on foreign policy seemed to rest more on moral positions than on experience, which in his case was chiefly of his native Portugal. His diplomatic activities there (1578–81), however, had been so instrumental in winning for Philip the Portuguese crown, that when Philip was given the keys to Lisbon he turned them over to Moura. Of Philip's ministers only Ruy Gómez ever enjoyed as much confidence with Philip as did Moura, who gave the king moral support in times of trial.

Both Moura and Idiáquez were of the middle nobility, and therefore were not the natural leaders of vast family blocs. Rather than become rivals, they formed a team to guard the king's favour. They chose not to work through the council of state, where men in the tradition of Alba still sat, led by the late duke's natural son Don Hernando de Toledo (d. 1592), the true heir of his father's talents, and survivors of Antonio Pérez's faction such as the ageing relic Cardinal Gaspar de Quiroga. Instead, Moura and Idiáquez preferred to work through the *junta de noche*, a small, informal committee that met at night with Mateo Vázquez, Philip's private secretary (who died in 1591 and was succeeded by Don Martín de Idiáquez), and the king's confessor. Zúñiga (d. 1586) sat with them, and frequently they were joined by the third count of Chinchón, who was appointed to the council of state in 1585. They went through the important business of the monarchy, and determined how it was to be presented to the king. In this they presaged the seventeenth-century institution, the *despacho universal*.

In the summer of 1587, when Philip was seriously ill, Idiáquez consolidated his position and, in doing so, that also of the new ministry at court by turning his office of secretary of state for Italy over to his cousin Don Martín de Idiáquez (Don Juan was by now councillor), and in effect giving his nephew Don Francisco the business of the council of Italy, leaving Zayas with only the bare title of secretary. Zayas complained to Vázquez about these moves of 'the Basque', but Vázquez hushed him, saying it was for the good of the royal service.[14]

And so the 'second ministry' took its final form. Idiáquez directed foreign policy, advised Philip on the Netherlands, and oversaw military and naval affairs. Moura worked closely with him in these matters, and in addition oversaw the monarchy's finances and advised Philip on the affairs of Portugal and matters of great delicacy in Castile. Chinchón shared with Moura the task of advising Philip on Castilian affairs, but his chief provinces were Aragon and Italy. Mateo Vázquez was the 'arch-secretary'; Martín de Idiáquez, who replaced him in 1591, never achieved his influence with Philip. This 'second ministry' continued until Philip II's death in 1598, when it was broken up by the duke of Lerma, Philip III's favourite.

What opposition there was to the 'second ministry' was led by Don Hernando de Toledo, a veteran of his father's wars, with experience in the Low Countries and Italy as well as in the Iberian peninsula. In 1570–79 he had served as governor-general of Catalonia, and in 1580 led the cavalry in the Portuguese campaign. In addition to taking a seat on the council of state in 1585, he also joined the council of war. He particularly resented the control of foreign and military affairs by Moura and Idiáquez, and blamed them for the defeat in 1588 of the Enterprise of England, for which they had coordinated the planning. 'Things must go ill,' he told the Venetian ambassador Contarini in 1589, 'when all decisions are taken by the inexperienced.' Moura, he added, had never been outside the peninsula, while Idiáquez had never seen war.[15]

In the aftermath of the Armada's defeat, Toledo and his fellows from the council of war, Don Juan de Cardona, a Lepanto veteran, and the soldier Alonso de Vargas, gained in influence. But by the mid-1590s, all had left the scene; on the council of war sat Idiáquez, Moura, Pedro de Velasco, captain of the Royal Guard, who had soldiered with Alba and served in 1580 as *corregidor* of Badajoz, and Don Juan de Acuña Vela, scion of a family of professional soldiers and diplomats, who was captain-general of the artillery. The presence of Idiáquez and Moura on the council of war, of whom only Moura had seen any combat at all, only underlines their dominance of Philip's last ministry.

THE COUNCIL OF WAR AND PHILIP'S ARMED FORCES

The council of war, to be sure, was closely associated with the council of state. The presidency pertained to the king himself, and on it customarily sat those members of the council of state who had military or viceregal experience, and a number of veteran officers, each of whom was expert in some aspect of warfare, such as land or naval operations, ordnance and military engineering. While the council of state was purely an advisory body, the council of war presided over a growing department which administered armies, armadas and fortresses, reviewed the decisions of courts martial, dealt with the petitions of veterans or their widows for pensions and issued rules for the conduct of the local militias. Until 1586 one secretary, Juan Delgado, handled both land and naval matters. Upon his death in that year, Philip appointed two secretaries to the council, Andrés de Prada for land and Andrés de Alva[16] for sea.

Sixteenth-century wars were largely fought by mercenaries, who expected pay and booty. Some of them had a sense of patriotism; more, strong religious convictions which provided them some motivation above money. Officers, generally noblemen, often had a sense of personal loyalty to their natural sovereign.

When the money ran out, or was in arrears, however, discipline in the army broke down and men began to desert when they could. Among one's own people, desertion was easy. There were no uniforms, no serial numbers; men merely vanished into the population. Among foreign peoples, it was different. Soldiers were generally despised, and a foreigner could usually be identified as a soldier if he were such, and ran the risk of being mobbed. Therefore soldiers in the midst of foreign populations remained banded together for the sake of security, and when disaffected, mutinied.[17] They sent off their officers, elected leaders (in Spanish *electos*, Italian *elettos*), and demanded their pay from their generals and the governments in their neighbourhood. If not satisfied, they sacked towns and villages, and held cities up for ransom.

A mutiny of his troops was the nightmare of every commander in the sixteenth century, but so long as governments did not adequately organize their resources (and they did not till the late seventeenth century) to pay and supply their armies regularly, mutiny was likely.

Soldiers were recruited by force and persuasion in all parts of Europe. In Philip II's Spain, captains received commissions at court to raise companies, and orders were sent to seigneurs and municipal officials in designated districts to give each captain all possible assistance in filling his quota of men. The commissions were often granted to those with the right connections at court. The problems that ensued are well illustrated in a letter by the duke of Medina Sidonia, concerning captains freshly sent from court to recruit companies in Andalusia.[18] The duke explained that to recruit men, one had to exploit a network of local connections, of relatives and *compadres*. If the king would not commission worthy Andalusians, then the new captains would do best to wait until the duke and his agents had collected the men and got them aboard ships, from which they could not desert, before the new captains took charge of them.

Philip II and his council of war developed a system in the late sixteenth century whereby in general the raw recruits (*bisoños*) could be drilled and disciplined before being committed to combat. The recruits were shipped *presidios*, chiefly in quiet Italy, to receive their basic training, while the soldiers who had been garrisoning the *presidios* would be sent to a war theatre. After the *bisoños* had been drilled for a year or so, they would be ready to march, while a new contingent of recruits arrived at the *presidios* to take their place.

Manning armadas was far more difficult than manning armies. Sailors were highly skilled, and mercantile voyages were far more rewarding than naval expeditions. From beginning to end, the commanders of the 'Invincible Armada' complained of the shortage of sailors and navigators. Country boys and urchins from the Lisbon streets were pressed into service, and the ships with fewest sailors were assigned soldiers who had served in the Indies fleets and had their sea legs.

Getting ships was not simple. At the beginning of the sixteenth century, only the English monarchy and the Venetian republic had fleets of government-owned warships. Other rulers had only a royal galley or two; for the rest, they hired ships from private subjects. Leasing ships to warring rulers became a big business from which the Genoese Doria family and the Spanish families of Bazán, Mendoza and Toledo grew rich.

Philip II took advantage of the loss of Juan de Mendoza and twenty-five of his galleys in a storm off Málaga (1562) to rebuild the Spanish squadron with state money and bring it under his control. At the same time, he had constructed the armada of the Indies route (*armada de la guarda de la carrera de las Indias*) with crown funds. By the mid-1590s the Spanish galleys and more than thirty galleons in the Atlantic were owned by the crown.

A constant problem for Philip in building armadas was his need to maintain galleys in the Mediterranean to combat swift-moving corsairs, and big sailing warships, chiefly galleons, in the Atlantic, to weather the ocean. The vessels were not easily interchangeable. A galleon might be becalmed in the Mediterranean and watch helplessly while corsairs sacked a fishing village two leagues away; a fifty-yard long fragile galley might founder or break up on the long, high Atlantic swells. When Spanish commanders did consider using galleys in the Atlantic they had in mind coastal operations, involving carrying troops and supplies, not fleet actions.

For Atlantic combat, the galleon, carrying from twenty to forty cannon and dozens of smaller pieces, formed the backbone of Philip II's armadas. The first galleons were built to serve as flagships for the Indies fleets, to ward off pirates, but in the 1560s, Pedro Menéndez de Avilés built the armada of the Indies, a squadron of a dozen galleons which sailed together. When Philip acquired the crown of Portugal in 1580, he also acquired the Portuguese armada of a dozen galleons, built or in the yards. The Portuguese squadron and the Indies armada (rebuilt in 1580–84), called the *armada de Castilla*, provided the main fighting strength of the 'Invincible Armada' of 1588.

Mounting the campaign of 1588 (although it ended in defeat) caused Philip II and his naval secretaries to improve the administration of the armadas; and in the 1590s, they maintained in the Atlantic two and sometimes three powerful armadas, varying in size from twenty to more than a hundred ships (for example the ocean armadas of 1596–97), which operated from Cadiz, Lisbon and La Coruña-El Ferrol across the Atlantic to the Indies, and northward into the Irish Sea and the English Channel. At the same time Spain, Naples, Sicily and Genoa continued to deploy strong galley squadrons in the Mediterranean each summer, although by the 1590s these had been somewhat reduced in size because of the diversion of available money to the armadas in the Atlantic.

Expenditures for armies and armadas easily formed the largest item in Philip II's budgets. What the total figures for all his dominions were awaits further research, but we do know something of the cost of war to the Castilian *Hacienda*, which bore the brunt of it. In 1572, for instance, when Philip deployed some one hundred fully manned galleys in the Mediterranean (his contribution to the Holy League) and 60,000 men in the Netherlands, sending in addition an armada of some fifty ships carrying 1,200 soldiers to the Netherlands,[19] it cost the Castilian treasury move than 6,000,000 ducats. The budget for the last year of his reign projected expenditures of more than 3,000,000 ducats for the army of Flanders, 1,500,000 for the Castilian guards and frontier defences, 500,000 for Mediterranean galleys and 500,000 for the ocean armada, though a comment in the margin about this last claimed that it would in fact cost more than 1,700,000.[20]

Since his expenditures were always more than his revenues, Philip borrowed constantly, and his annual interest payments must be considered part of his war expenses. It is thus hardly surprising that recommendations made to Philip by his councillors of state and war often concluded with the proviso that the finance officers of the crown be consulted about the availability of money to carry them out. Repeatedly in his marginings and correspondence Philip made the point clear: 'Without money, nothing can be done.'[21]

CROWN FINANCES AND THE CORTES OF CASTILE

Charles and Philip had an overriding concern about finances. What were the monarchy's revenues? All of Philip's dominions owed dues and paid taxes voted him by representative assemblies. In regard to taxation, Philip accepted the Roman Law adage, used in support of the medieval custom of his dominions, 'quod omnes tangit ab omnibus approbetur' (what touches all must be approved by all): to ignore it in an age when most men went armed was likely to provoke sedition, riot and even rebellion.

In principle Philip was supposed to spend the money raised in each dominion only for that dominion's needs and interests, which in essence meant close by and for reasons acceptable to that dominion's subjects, or at least those who had voice in the various Cortes, *parlamenti* or estates. Philip II and his father before him had found, however, various ways to circumvent this principle by pleading special necessity, and the need to defend Christendom and their 'reputation'. Philip, answering an objection by the council of Italy to his levy of taxes in Sicily for the Enterprise of England (1588), answered, 'Except in the most urgent cases, it is not the custom to transfer the burdens of one kingdom to another ... [but] since God has entrusted me with so many, since all are in my charge and since in the defence of one all are preserved, it is just that all should help me.'[22]

'Urgent cases' kept arising, but the hard fact was that Philip could not find more than token support anywhere but in Castile and from Castile's Indies; and even that was not always a simple or certain matter.

The problems of finance, *lo de hacienda*, was the reason he repeatedly gave for always remaining in or near Castile.[23]

Charles's finances had rested as much on the Netherlands as on Castile, but his wars against France, fought so often in or near the Netherlands, had exhausted their will to pay more, and Philip II from the beginning of his reign had to augment what he raised in the Netherlands with money from Spain. During his reign the Netherlands were divided by rebellion, and the revenues derived from them therefore dwindled to a fraction of what they had been in Charles's day. The rebellion, at first chiefly of religious 'malcontents', was able after 1572 to spread rapidly in large part because of the attempts of the duke of Alba, Philip's governor-general (1567–73), to increase taxes, put them on a permanent basis, and take their collection from the hands of the States General. On a plan of 1592 for raising more revenues from the Netherlands, Philip tersely noted, 'The author of this relation is one of those who think there is a lot of money there.'[24]

Naples, Sicily and Milan mainly supplied just enough for their own needs, though occasionally a bit more for the general defence of the Mediterranean.

So the burden of paying for Philip II's wars fell chiefly on Castile, which, becoming economically stagnant, was therefore not able to bear substantial increases in taxation without suffering. (It must be remembered that in pre-modern Europe most men lived on the subsistence level, and there was seldom much surplus.)

Philip began his reign bankrupt, and knew that he had to increase his revenues and make more efficient and reliable those departments of government concerned with their collection and disbursement. Philip's Castilian revenues can be placed into three categories: those he collected in his own right, those conceded him by the Church and those for which he needed a vote of Cortes.[25]

The first included revenues from the royal domains, the lands of the Castilian military orders – and the sale of knighthoods in them – and the customary royal dues (vestigial feudal dues, pasturage and mineral rights, customs duties, salt taxes and the playing card monopoly).

What interested contemporaries most was the crown's share of the Indies treasure, the 'Royal Fifth' (derived from its mineral rights). At the beginning of Philip's reign, his income from the 'Royal Fifth' fluctuated between 400,000 and 900,000 ducats a year; after 1575, it rose sharply to more than 1,600,000 ducats a year; and after 1590, averaged close to 2,000,000, giving his government a *largueza* (abundance) which permitted him to pursue policies he might not otherwise have dared, and tempted bankers, thrice burnt by his bankruptcies (1557, 1575, 1596), to risk loaning him money once more.

The estates of the military orders earned more than 300,000 ducats per year, but much of this was mortgaged to financiers for past debts. The rest of the crown due came to about the same amount.

The revenues conceded to Philip by the Church included the 'Royal Third' (a third of all Spanish tithes), granted the Spanish crowns in perpetuity by Alexander VI Borgia in 1494, and the 'Three Graces', the *subsidio* of the clergy, the sale of the *cruzada* (an indulgence) and the *excusado*, which had to be renewed periodically and therefore were crucial issues in Philip's relations with the papacy. When all three were in force, Philip derived from them about 1,200,000 ducats annually. Since Philip's income from the 'Royal Third' rose because of inflation during his reign, and the amount moreover was calculated together with the *encabezamiento*, a precise figure for it cannot be given. It would seem reasonable to say that it rose from about 400,000 ducats annually at the time of his accession to perhaps double that at the time of his death.

The *encabezamiento* was related to a tax which legally was the royal due, the *alcabala*, an impost on sales and other business transactions ranging from 2 to 10 per cent. The Cortes, representing the Castilian municipalities, considered the *alcabala*, which dated from Moorish times, detrimental to business, and in 1525 persuaded Charles V to accept, in return for their granting him a larger subsidy, a poll tax, the *encabezamiento*, in place of the *alcabala*. Collected by the municipalities, the *encabezamiento* was fixed at a sum supposedly yielded at the time by the *alcabala*, and could not be increased without the consent of the Cortes. At the beginning of Philip's reign, the *encabezamiento* and 'Royal Third', calculated together, came to about 1,200,000 ducats per year.

But since prices were rising steadily throughout the sixteenth century, Philip, as regent and as king, saw the actual worth of the sum paid by the *encabezamiento* decrease. The crown thus became increasingly dependent upon subsidies voted by the Cortes, the third category of revenues, an 'ordinary' subsidy of 800,000 ducats, payable over a three-year period, and an 'extraordinary' subsidy of 400,000, payable at once.

Soon after his return to Spain in 1559 Philip therefore succeeded in persuading the Cortes to increase the *encabezamiento* by threatening to reinstate the *alcabala*. At the same time, to get yet more revenues, he raised old customs duties, established new ones, recovered control of customs houses alienated by his Trastámara forebears to seigneurs (for example, in 1562 from the constable of Castile, and *c.* 1583 from the duke of Medina Sidonia), and increased rates on salt and the price of playing cards.

He also reformed the fiscal departments of his government for the sake of increased efficiency. He extended the jurisdiction of the *Consejo de Hacienda*, the governing board of the treasury, to include the *Casa de Contratación* (House of Trade) in Seville, which regulated the Indies trade and received the incoming treasure. Philip's treasury officers could now lay hands on the king's share of the treasure at once and, through various devices, obtain money from merchants. Philip also gave the *Consejo de Hacienda* authority to review tax cases for his final judgment, with few exceptions. The Cortes protested at this, since it preferred to have the legists of the council of Castile review such cases, as in the past, rather than let those responsible for collecting taxes also recommend judgment in tax matters. Because of such protest, Philip initially had tax cases reviewed by a panel of six, of whom three were legists, who sat on the council of Castile as well as on the *Consejo de Hacienda*. One by one, however, he added *contadores* (keepers of the accounts) of the *Hacienda* to the panel, until it had eight members, of whom five were treasury officials. The importance Philip gave the *Hacienda* is underscored by the fact that he made his trusted confidants Ruy Gómez and Don Cristóbal de Moura *contadores*. Since, however, the task of undertaking the reforms was in general assigned to lawyers and not to financiers, the *Consejo de Hacienda* never became an efficient instrument for the management of the crown's finances, which according to a modern scholar 'partially explains the bleak financial history of the reign'.[26]

While reorganizing the fiscal institutions of government, Philip had to be constantly on guard against the venality characteristic of his age, when public office was seen as much a source of private profit as a locus of public trust. He was willing to put up with a modicum of peculation, for it would have been impossible to fill important offices, which usually carried low salaries, with competent men unless there were some opportunity for them to line their own pockets.

There were, of course, limits. Complaints about gross mishandling of funds were promptly investigated, and at the end of each man's tour of office, an official *visita* was made to audit his accounts. Miguel de Cervantes was hardly unique among Spanish treasury agents in being sent to jail (in 1597 and again in 1602) on charges of peculation. In 1584, Juan Fernández de Espinosa, one of the two treasurers-general (who chiefly arranged terms of loans taken by the crown), was briefly incarcerated, and not until 1593, when he agreed to pay the king 614,000 ducats were his goods released. His colleague, the marquis of Auñón, escaped imprisonment, but his accounts were frequently under investigation by government auditors. Francisco Duarte, factor of the *Casa de Contratación*, was arrested several times for peculating, but was always released as his services in getting the Indies fleets under way were recognized to be indispensable. Litigation over the accounts of Francisco de Lixalde, paymaster of Alba's army in the Low Countries, was opened by the crown against his heirs in 1577, and was only settled in 1614, when the defendants were ordered to pay 13,000 ducats to the royal treasury.[27] And one of the principal charges that induced Philip II to relieve Alexander Farnese of the governor-generalship of the Netherlands was that his aides, and perhaps even he himself, were misusing government money.

Philip's increase of rates on customs and other items due the crown, and certain of his reforms in the fiscal departments of government, annoyed the Castilian municipalities, and when he summoned them in late 1566 to grant him an ordinary and extraordinary subsidy, they were in a mood to challenge his authority to make such increases or reforms without their consent.[28] They well knew that Philip desperately needed money for the war raging in the Mediterranean against the Turks and for an army to suppress unrest in the Netherlands.

The Cortes, by 1566, was not in a strong position to so challenge the crown. In 1520, at the beginning of Charles's reign, the Castilian municipalities had rebelled – the revolt of the *comuneros* – against Charles and his policies. The nobility, fearing social revolution, had rallied to Charles and defeated the *comuneros*. In 1538, Charles acknowledged the nobles' privilege not to pay direct taxes and, in consequence, the 'military' estate ceased sitting in Cortes, and dealt directly with their sovereign at court. Since in theory the Church could not be taxed, but rather 'gratuitously' donated money to the crown through arrangements made in Rome, the clerical estate, like the noble, had no reason to sit in Cortes. As a result the Cortes of Castile in fact meant the assembly of thirty-six *procuradores* (delegates), two each from eighteen privileged royal municipalities, who, unaided by the nobility or clergy, faced the might of the crown.

Philip ordered the *corregidores* to ensure that no delegate was bound by any oath to his constituency which limited his powers. This was a touchy issue, since all knew what pressures the crown could bring to bear on delegates. Municipalities sending delegates to the Cortes wanted important matters referred back to them before the delegates voted.

When the Cortes assembled in January 1567, Cardinal Espinosa, president of the council of Castile, and thus *ex officio* president of the Cortes, made the delegates swear that their powers were unrestricted. This only served to irritate them, and they at once raised the challenge: redress of grievances must precede supply. Espinosa pleaded with them to vote supplies first, since the king was in such necessity, fighting to defend his patrimony and Christendom against infidels and rebellious heretics. Philip in the meantime allowed that in the future he would seek their consent before adding or increasing taxes.

The Cortes was not satisfied, but demanded that the need for consent be stated clearly as the law of the land. Appealing to their sense of loyalty, however, Espinosa and his assistants succeeded in convincing the Cortes that the king would be more agreeable to their demand *after* he had been voted the money he so desperately needed. On 18 March 1567 the Cortes voted Philip an extraordinary grant of 400,000 ducats and an ordinary three-year subsidy of 800,000.[29] They continued their deliberations until June, and presented Philip with a resolution embodying their demand that he obtain their consent in all matters of taxation, which Philip published in July. His reply which followed in effect rejected their resolution; and in enforcing the law, the royal courts, staffed by royal appointees, followed the royal will. Philip, banking on the delegates' loyalty to his person and their commitment to his wars, had won a major battle in making the Cortes of Castile the subservient tool of monarchical government.

Three years later, Philip told the Cortes summoned to Córdoba that matters everywhere were going well: the Mediterranean war had subsided, and Alba in the Netherlands had suppressed all dissent and was arranging for those provinces to meet all their own expenses, including that of his 'occupation' army, so that Castile would no longer need to support it. Within weeks after making this claim, Philip was caught up in a new war with the Turks, and in 1572 faced a renewed outbreak of revolt in the Netherlands and the threat of war with France and England. In the period 1571–73, Philip's military expenditures charged to the Castilian treasury came to more than half his total income from Castile, some 5,500,000 ducats per year, of which a third was committed in advance to funding his debts, while another third went to the upkeep of the court and routine administration and defence of Castile.

He therefore resorted to borrowing on a grand scale. It soon became apparent, however, that he was sliding once more towards bankruptcy. In Genoa, whose bankers had advanced him several million ducats, opponents of the pro-Spanish regime threatened to seize the government, while on the battlefields of the Netherlands, the discipline of Alba's army, whose pay had fallen far in arrears, was collapsing.

In November 1574, he convoked the Cortes of Castile for the third time since the spring of 1570 to inform them of his straits: in defence of the Faith and his patrimony he had gone deeply into debt. He asked them for this reason to vote to triple the rate of the *encabezamiento* to aid him. If they did not, he warned them as he had before, he would resume his right to collect the unpopular *alcabala*, which arguably would have yielded more. In the bargaining between crown and Cortes that followed, the Cortes agreed to the tripling of the *encabezamiento*, on the condition that Philip would cease paying 'usurious' rates of interest, consolidate his debts at more favourable rates, and break his dependence on foreign, especially Genoese, bankers. In the formulation of the Cortes' demands, Philip's officers seem quietly to have taken part, in order to make his creditors believe that he had no choice but to cut interest payments if he wanted more money.

With the increased revenues voted, Philip on 1 September 1575 declared the suspension of payments on his debts, and thus opened the way for their renegotiation and, in general, to getting his fiscal house in order. It took him nearly two years to settle matters with his creditors, during which time he saw his authority in the Netherlands collapse and was forced to make an unfavourable truce with the Turks. But his hope to realize over 3,000,000 ducats from the *encabezamiento* proved vain: Castile was unable to pay. Faced with widespread opposition, Philip reduced the rate of increase. For the rest of his reign, the *encabezamiento* and 'Royal Third' brought him an average of 2,700,000 ducats a year.

Fortunately in these same years, the revenues from the Indies rose sharply. The Genoese bankers (who remained in his camp) and the Germans were soon back; and Castilian bankers, after a few good years, once more fell behind their competitors.

By the early 1580s, matters seemed to be running so well for Philip II that, upon his becoming king of Portugal, he abolished the customs barrier between Portugal and Castile. But the defeat in 1588 of the 'Invincible Armada', with the loss of half its ships, changed everything. In September 1588, Philip summoned the Cortes, informing them that the armada campaign alone had cost him 10,000,000 ducats. He asked for a special subsidy, above the customary extraordinary and ordinary grants, to see him through his difficulties, which by now included the running fifteen-year war against the Dutch rebels, a costly war with England, which turned the high seas into a battleground and endangered his treasure supply, and his deepening intervention on the side of the Catholic League into the civil wars of France. As usual, he claimed all of this had been forced upon him by his need to defend religion, his patrimony and his 'reputation'. (Even as the Cortes began its sessions, Philip borrowed a million ducats from the Spinola family of Genoa and 400,000 from the Fuggers of Augsburg.)

Early in 1590, after a year of haggling, the Cortes voted Philip the special subsidy (over and above the customary grants voted every three years), to be collected over a six-year period beginning the 1st of July, of 8,000,000 ducats, known as the *millones*, since it was reckoned in millions of ducats, rather than the traditional *maravedís* (which at 375 to the ducat would have given an even more astronomical figure).

Lifted by the *millones*, Philip's annual revenues from Castile peaked in 1592–93, reaching nearly 10,000,000 ducats; afterwards they began slowly to fall off, as the Castilian economy turned definitely downwards, after years of fitful stagnation, under the weight of war and taxation. In the same years, his expenditures averaged close to 12,000,000 ducats a year, and the considerable difference between them and disposable income had to be covered by further new loans, taken at 14 per cent and higher rates of interest.

The means of collecting the *millones* had been left to the municipalities, which more and more turned to the expedient of *sisas*, excise taxes on basic commodities such as foodstuffs. As a consequence, the poor and landless were hardest hit. Five years earlier, when preparing the Enterprise of England, Philip had rejected offers from towns to raise money by *sisas*, saying, 'we shall not tax the poor thus'.[30] Now his *corregidores* were arresting men for protesting the *millones*; in Ávila, a conspiracy to oppose the tax was uncovered for which several gentlemen were executed. The tax was collected, but dissent was not so easily stifled. In the Cortes new protests against the tax burden began to be heard, and delegates dared suggest that the king adopt a less expensive foreign policy, and spend Spanish money in the interests of Spain, not the dynasty.

But they could not affect the king, who in 1593 for the sake of religion and dynasty attempted to have his daughter, the Infanta Isabel, elected queen of France. By 1595, his heavy-handed diplomatic and military intervention in France had brought the French together behind Henri IV, who in 1595 formally declared war on Philip.

Thus Philip's reign drew to its close as it had begun, with war costs outpacing revenues. In November 1596, he again declared bankruptcy and suspended all payments on debts for the third time. It took another year before he had made satisfactory arrangements with his creditors. When he died, his long-term debts amounted to some 68,000,000 ducats, nearly three times what they were when he mounted the throne. In a last will and testament drawn up in 1594 when he feared he might die, Philip in clause after clause dealt with his personal debts and the mortgaging of the royal patrimony (which included selling to seigneurs 'temporary' jurisdictions over crown vassals) as securities to meet public expenses, 'because of great necessities and the obligation to defend the Church and my kingdoms and estates'.[31] He was not the first, however, to do this. The debts and mortgaging of crown rights (in effect the alienation of those rights to seigneurs, which had undermined the power of the Trastámaras, and which Ferdinand and Isabella, Charles and Philip wished to avoid) dated not only from his reign, but some also from his father's and others even from the reign of his great-grandmother, Isabella the Catholic. He had only continued to do what his ancestors had done – if on a larger scale – but he hoped that his successors might pay off the debts and redeem the pawned patrimony of the crown.

THE ADMINISTRATIVE COUNCILS

Though it was war that seemed to dominate his reign, and brought him to bankruptcy, Philip did not see himself primarily as a war leader, but rather as a dispenser of justice. Justice, both distributive and punitive, was the chief concern of the majority of Philip's administrative councils.

Since the institutions and laws of each of Philip's dominions were different, he, kept around him, in the tradition of his predecessors, expert legal advisers selected for their knowledge of any one of the monarchy's dominions. These experts sat on or advised councils, each of which had for its province a particular region of the monarchy, and provided a channel for correspondence between the king and local governments. Around Philip at Madrid were initially the council of Castile, the council of Aragon (which dealt with Aragon, Valencia, Catalonia, the Balearics and Sardinia), a newly formed council of Italy (for Naples, Sicily and Milan) and the council of the Indies. To deal with the Netherlands and the Franche-Comté, Philip brought with him from Brussels several 'Flemish' secretaries, and Charles de Tisnacq, keeper of the Netherlands' Seals. These men corresponded in French with the governor-general and the Netherlands privy council (which handled justice in Brussels). Not until 1588, after several petitions from the Netherlands, did Philip establish the council of Flanders. In 1582, Philip created the council of Portugal, through which he corresponded with the viceregal government in Lisbon on the affairs of Portugal and its empire.

Philip's establishment in 1558 of the council of Italy,[32] over the protests of the council of Aragon which had previously handled the business of the Italian realms, fits the pattern of reform of the monarchy's administrative organization (for the sake of efficiency) already encountered in the discussion of his reform of finances. It also underlines the importance of the Italian realms in the Catholic Monarchy. Yet the Italians saw it as a further attempt to Castilianize their lands; although of its six voting members, three had to be natives of Sicily, Naples and Milan respectively, the other three seats were usually given, whether by accident or design, to Castilians.

At the heart of this matter lay Philip's tendency to yield to convenience, appointing to office somebody competent who was close at hand or keeping in office men who had served Charles. In the case of the council of Italy, he appointed to it as treasurer the Castilian Don Pedro Fernández de Cabrera, second count of Chinchón, who was already treasurer of the council of Aragon, and therefore was familiar with the office. Though Chinchón had no vote in ordinary matters of justice, he naturally carried great influence on the council of Italy. When he died (1575), his offices were soon garnered by his son, Don Diego Fernández de Cabrera y Bobadilla, third count, through weight of tradition, efficacy of connections and proximity to the court. In 1585, Don Diego joined the council of state, and was a participant in the *junta de noche*.

State considerations powerfully influenced the appointment of presidents of the council of Italy, here as before to the detriment of the Italians. Though the presidents did not vote in ordinary matters, they enjoyed great influence; and most often, they were great Castilian nobles and prelates, who had some experience of Italy. And following the mechanics of bureaucracy and the logic of family connections, these Castilian presidents and treasurers of the council of Italy found places on it for their Castilian clients.

Philip as a Renaissance sovereign wanted his regional councils to do more than deal with local government and receive appeals-at-law: he wanted them to codify all extant law and to find out all they could about his subjects. The council with which he worked most closely, and which was the largest of them, the *Consejo de Castilla*, did in fact publish in 1569 a codification of Castilian laws, the *Nueva Recopilación*. It also began a sort of grand census of Castile, the *relaciones topográficas* (1575–78),[33] in which was collected according to a standard format the names of householders, their status, occupations, landholdings, whose immediate jurisdiction they fell under, and so forth. The project was only carried out in New Castile. The council of the Indies started a similar project, on which little progress seems to have been made, except in New Spain (Mexico).

However well intended, these tasks were generally beyond the means of Philip's regime, distracted by war and bogged down in the routine of ordinary business. The administrative councils daily dealt with bundles of appeals, reports, petitions and recommendations generated by Philip's dominions, and forwarded to the overworked monarch their opinions and recommendations for his decisions.

PHILIP II AND THE CHURCH OF ROME

Philip II's government was intrinsically bound up with the Roman Church, which served him as an instrument of government, and yet at the same time was his spiritual teacher and guide, and a great, international institution. In Philip's eyes the pope was simultaneously the vicar of Christ and a foreign prince.

In utilizing the Church for his purposes, Philip frequently came into conflict with the pope over the extent of each other's authority.[34] Such conflicts Philip submitted to his confessors and theologians for their judgment, which usually went in his favour. The link, however, between Philip's power in clerical appointments and the views of these men should not be drawn too tightly – the separation of temporal from spiritual authority was an issue with a long history. Philip naturally consulted Spaniards, who largely shared his belief in the mission of the Catholic Monarchy, and neatly separated the temporal sphere, best understood by secular rulers, from the spiritual, in which sphere obedience to the pope was limited.

Though the pope's theologians often disagreed with Philip's (and most others who served the growing national monarchies), the papacy in the late sixteenth century in its concern with Catholic Reformation and the struggle against Islam, had particular need of Philip II. The death of Henri II had thrown the other great Catholic state, France, into a generation of civil wars between Catholic and Protestant, so to wield the temporal sword for Rome there was none but Philip, who in his monarchy stood firmly against Protestantism, and possessed the resources and will to confront the Turks. This need of Philip posed an insoluble dilemma for each of the nine men who occupied in succession St Peter's Chair. Each wished to break the near-absolute control over Church institutions Philip enjoyed in his dominions, but each needed his cooperation. They found themselves constrained to grant Philip, however reluctantly, Church revenues for the common cause of Catholic Christendom, in which they found themselves yoked together.

Philip also needed the cooperation of the papacy. He could neither govern his own dominions easily nor conduct the foreign policy he wanted without some papal support, however obtained. The papacy could influence other Catholic rulers and sway public opinion in Catholic lands, including Philip's; it was an important factor in the secular affairs of Italy, and could help arrange alliances against the Turks. But most significantly, the pope, by honouring old concordats and making new concessions, allowed Philip to collect from ecclesiastical sources a sum of money, which according to a calculation made in Rome in 1565 came to some 2,000,000 ducats a year.[35]

What were these Church revenues that made Philip's relations with Rome so crucial?[36] Some of these revenues have already been mentioned: the Royal Third (of all tithes collected in Spain), the *subsidio*, generally 420,000 ducats, an annual clerical subvention known since the Late Middle Ages and by Philip's time virtually a routine matter, and the *cruzada*, first conceded by Adrian VI to Charles, an indulgence sold to raise revenue for the crusade against infidels and heretics, which brought Philip some 500,000 ducats a year. During a period of particularly sharp differences between Philip and Rome, Pope Pius V refused to renew the *cruzada* (1566), which he considered scandalous in itself. But soon after, he conceded to Philip the full tithe paid by the richest property in each parish in Spain – the *excusado* – to help pay for Philip's planned journey (never undertaken) to deal with heresy in the Netherlands. In 1571, Pius put aside his scruples and granted Philip the *cruzada* anew, in order to persuade him to join the Holy League he was forming against the Turks: it, along with the *excusado* which continued, and the *subsidio*, formed 'the Three Graces'. Retaining these 'Graces', which were subject to periodic renewal, was a prime aim of Philip's Roman diplomacy.

The issues over which Philip and the papacy differed fell largely into two categories: the first involved Philip's control of the institutional Church in his own dominions; the second, Philip's policies, domestic and foreign, aimed at defending Catholicism against heretics and Islam, for which Rome granted him the subsidies just discussed.

Philip's control over Church institutions was sanctioned by various concordats with the papacy, dating chiefly from the era of Ferdinand

and Isabella, which gave Philip the power to present (in effect to appoint) men of his choosing to bishoprics, to the supreme councils of the Inquisition in Spain and Sicily and to other major benefices. There were moreover certain medieval rights Philip enjoyed in Naples and Sicily which the papacy claimed he held of it as fiefs: the *Exequatur* in Naples, which permitted him to publish or withhold papal bulls as he saw fit, and the *Monarchia Sicula*, which permitted him as king of Sicily to act as papal legate to himself. In Spain, while he accepted a papal legate, he claimed under his sovereignty to enjoy the right of *Exequatur* and, moreover, permitted no appeal by his Spanish subjects to Rome from either the Inquisition or the councils of Castile or Aragon, which served in many instances as ecclesiastical courts.

Men said there was no pope in Spain, a remark endorsed by a recent scholar, who estimates that the crown's domination of the Church 'was probably more complete in Spain than in any other part of Europe, including Protestant countries with an Erastian system'.[37] Through his councils Philip in effect governed the Church in his dominions, and a large amount of his correspondence and memoranda concern Church affairs. Because of his power of presentation, clergymen seeking preferment looked to him, not to Rome, and once in office confronted the dilemma of having to please two masters, Philip and the pope. Philip enjoyed the revenues of vacant sees, and new appointees customarily thanked him for their appointments with some portion of their income. Individual clerics made contributions in times of need, as did Gaspar de Quiroga, cardinal-archbishop of Toledo (1577–94), both before and after the armada disaster of 1588. (However, all were not so accommodating: in 1556, Philip's former tutor Siliceo, when archbishop of Toledo, refused to contribute money for the war against Pope Paul IV, despite the support of Philip's position by the theologians of the Spanish universities.) Philip kept his finger on the pulse of the Spanish Church chiefly through his private secretary, Mateo Vázquez, who was officially secretary to the council of the Inquisition.

Philip tenaciously resisted all attempts by Rome to encroach upon his prerogatives in Church matters, and usually won. In one exception Pius V forced Philip to permit the case of Fray Bartolomé Carranza, archbishop of Toledo (1557–76), to be transferred from the Spanish Inquisition to Rome. Carranza had been arrested on charges of heresy in 1559; given his rank the papacy claimed prior jurisdiction. Philip refused the papal claim, on the argument that he could not guarantee the survival of the Catholic religion in Spain if he did not uphold the Inquisition in every instance. But in 1566, the *cruzada* came due for renewal, and Philip, at war with the Turks and facing troubles in the Low Countries, feared with good reason that Pius V might not renew it. Philip's ambassador to Rome, Don Luis de Requesens, warned Philip that Pius was a saintly man who paid little heed to reasons of state. Philip capitulated and permitted the case to be transferred to Rome a few days before he received from Pius a threat of excommunication. Carranza was acquitted in Rome in 1576, but died a few weeks afterwards.

To be sure, there were instances of significant cooperation, as in 1560–62, when Philip II and Pius IV worked together for the reconvention of the council of Trent. Initially, progress towards this end went slowly, partly because Philip and Pius had their differences over the council's purposes: Philip wanted the council to give final definition to the dogmas agreed upon in Trent's first two sessions; Pius wanted, beyond this, to define the Church's constitution in a way that clearly put the papacy above the episcopate as a final restraint on the Conciliar Movement.[38] Naturally Philip feared this as a threat to his own control of the episcopate in his dominions, but he feared spreading Calvinism more, against which the Roman Church needed to mobilize all its resources. Apart from this, there was a personal dimension to Philip's concern for Trent: he saw it as something begun by his father, which he as the son had the filial duty to see through.[39]

Philip and Pius, once agreed on the need for a council and committed to Trent, had to persuade the French and Germans to join them. These called for a new council, untainted by the hard-line dogmatism that characterized Trent's previous sessions, which would have a better chance to reconcile Protestants to Rome. In this regard, the question has been raised whether or not Philip, in differing with the Imperial court of his uncle, in fact differed from the position of his father.[40] Charles indeed had expressed doubts about Trent, whose decrees had made his political position in Germany difficult. However, in matters of religion Philip seems to have been more affected by Charles's later sentiments of bitterness and betrayal rather than his more politic and conciliatory pronouncements, made when he still hoped that concessions by the council would bring the Lutherans back to Rome.

Neither Philip nor Pius had much luck at first with the Germans or French; but the outbreak in France of religious civil war (1562–63), in which Philip aided the government of the queen mother Catherine de' Medici with a *tercio* of infantry, succeeded where diplomacy had failed: in November 1562, the French bishops appeared at Trent.

Ferdinand I was convinced not by his nephew Philip, but by Pius, to send the German bishops to Trent. Either before or during the council, for German backing, Pius agreed to support the election of Maximilian as king of the Romans, thus removing Philip from the place promised to him in the Imperial succession by the family.

By the time Pius's support of Maximilian became public, the papalists and Spaniards were in open conflict over the nature of episcopal authority. The papalists insisted that it was dependent upon the pope, the Spaniards that it came directly from God. With the aid of German votes, the papal faction (largely Italian bishops and members of the Curia) carried the council. For the rest, in matters of dogma, the papalists, whose theological experts were mostly Spaniards, including several prominent Jesuits, and the bishops from Philip's dominions were in full agreement, and combined to outvote the French and Germans.

Philip consequently had mixed feelings about the results of Trent: he approved Tridentine dogmatism, but feared the council's decrees on the episcopacy. When the papacy published the Tridentine decrees in January 1564, Philip withheld their publication in his dominions while his own canon lawyers studied them. They appeared at last in July with the proviso that in no way did they impair Philip's regalian rights.

But the matter involving Philip II and the papacy in the Catholic cause that carried the most profound consequences was the reform and enlargement of the Netherlands episcopacy (which included the intensification of inquisitorial activities under the jurisdiction of the bishops). Since the bishops were to be presented by Philip, his authority as well as the influence of the Church would thereby be extended. The Netherlands lay at the crossroads of north-western Europe, open to the Protestant currents running from Lutheran Germany and Calvinist Geneva. All seventeen provinces were embraced in only four bishoprics with antiquated organizations. Philip, putting into effect plans drawn up in Charles's time, in 1559 and 1561 obtained papal bulls authorizing the establishment of fourteen new bishoprics.

Philip's innovation raised widespread opposition: in brief, the Netherlanders saw the new bishops as agents of the central government, feared the Inquisition and did not wish to pay for an enlarged Church establishment. A struggle between the Brussels government and the local Netherlands authorities, including the stadholders, ensued immediately over the implementation of the bulls. The papacy urged Philip to travel north to settle matters, conceding to him the *excusado* for this purpose. Before he could go, the struggle erupted into open revolt. The papacy wanted Philip to brand the rebels as heretics. Philip hesitated because he did not want to provoke a war of religion which might draw into it German Lutherans, French Huguenots and English Protestants. But there was no disguising for long that the rebels were chiefly militant Calvinists, in receipt of both covert and overt assistance from other Protestants. Philip and his commanders soon routinely referred to them as 'rebels and heretics', and his army of Flanders, sent to suppress them, was called the 'Catholic Army'.

Ultimately, the revolt in the Netherlands so commanded Philip's attention and resources that, after he declared bankruptcy in 1575 because of his inability to sustain wars simultaneously against the Turks and the 'rebels and heretics', in 1578 he concluded a truce with the Turks. Gregory XIII, then pope, denounced it, while at the same time he vainly urged Philip to liberate Ireland and invade England. Rome always seems to have thought that Philip's resources permitted him to do far more than was in fact possible. 'He labours,' Philip commented about Gregory, 'under a delusion.'[41] All the same, Gregory grudgingly conceded to Philip the customary 'Three Graces'.

The Portuguese succession, which Gregory wished to adjudicate, created new diplomatic clashes. Philip pressed ahead with the conquest of Portugal in 1580 while his ministers slowed with ceremonies the journey of Gregory's special nuncio to his headquarters at Badajoz. By the time the nuncio arrived, Philip was able to present him with a *fait accompli*, and in turn demand the recall of the papal legate to Portugal, who personally favoured Dom Antonio, Philip's chief rival for the throne. Confronted with Philip's new accretion of power, Gregory yielded, but relations between Rome and Philip II, locked together in the same cause, became ever more embittered. In 1585, Sixtus V, who harboured a personal dislike of Philip, mounted Peter's Chair. He promised Philip money for the 1588 armada, to be paid, however, only when Philip's army had landed in England. At Rome it was said that Philip claimed to fight for the Church, but that his true goal was the security and aggrandizement of his own dominions.

Such a viewpoint seemed confirmed by his conduct in France after the assassination in 1589 of Henri III by a Catholic fanatic. He supported briefly a compromise candidate, who soon died, and then advanced the candidacy of his daughter Isabel for the throne of France, while his armies repeatedly intervened in the French civil war. He opposed all efforts to convert to Catholicism the Calvinist Henri of Navarre, who had the strongest legitimate claim on the French crown, and through his ambassadors in Rome, after the death in 1590 of Sixtus, hectored three successive conclaves to elect popes who would support his designs. None lived long, and in 1592 the cardinals rebelled against these heavy handed attempts of the ageing Catholic king to dominate the Catholic Church and direct its international policies. They elected the politic and independent Clement VIII Aldobrandini, who accepted the conversion of Henri of Navarre and in 1595 recognized him as king of France. It then took Clement three more years of effort and mediation to bring Henri IV and Philip II to the peace table; but from the point of view of Rome, in Henri the papacy had a powerful Catholic prince to whom it could turn to counterbalance Philip's long overweening power.

PHILIP AT WORK

We have discussed at some length the instruments used by Philip II in the government of his monarchy; now focusing once more on Philip himself, we must ask how he worked with his collaborators. Returning thus to the king himself brings to mind Professor Koenigsberger's imaginative remark, when he wrote of Philip's 'all but illegible, loopy handwriting – itself almost a visual image of the circles of command and power – endlessly returning back to the writer'.[42]

Philip's manner of dealing with his collaborators, whether ministers and secretaries at court or those serving him abroad, and his work habits in general, have fascinated both his contemporaries and all subsequent students of his reign.

Philip thought slowly, reflected on matters, and wanted to make his own decisions. He therefore generally dealt with his ministers in writing through a document called a *consulta*, essentially a minute of their discussions and recommendations kept by the secretary of the council concerned. A wide margin was left on the document for the king to jot down his observations and decisions. Letters from officials not at court were generally put in digest form by the secretary who received them – this depended on the subject of the letter, whether it was a matter of state, justice, religion, etc. – and sent to Philip. If there were a considerable number of letters, the digests would be put on a covering sheet, which would be forwarded to Philip with the relevant letters; if the letters were few, or urgent, the digest was written on an outer fold. Both correspondence and covering sheets carried wide margins for Philip's notations. A good amount of correspondence required deciphering, and what was not in Castilian, Latin or Portuguese had to be translated into Castilian. The originals were sent to Philip along with the deciphered or translated copies. Preparing digests and presenting papers to Philip personally gave the court secretaries almost daily access to the king; their cultivation by grandees suggests that they also enjoyed considerable influence with him (for example, the secretary Gabriel de Zayas in 1581 told the duke of Medina Sidonia that he would present the duke's plan to conquer Algiers to Philip when he sensed the moment was ripe).[43]

Philip pored over the *consultas*, correspondence and various memoranda assiduously, commenting on momentous issues of state and routine matters, such as providing pensions to veterans' widows or the costs of clothing soldiers. One gets the impression that he dealt with all matters with equal diligence as his pen scratched along the margins of documents and filled pages with remarks such as 'more study is needed', 'most important is the need for money,' 'I know him', or 'who is he?'

In regard to great issues, much of what came from Philip's pen strikes the reader not as the product of a ruler who wanted to direct the course of history, but of one who reacted to events in an attempt to hold matters together in the way he had found them. This is especially true in the first years of his reign and characteristic of the Philip II we find in Braudel's great study. There were, however, moments when he proved decisive: in 1566, after he learned of the image-breaking in the Netherlands; in 1570, when he agreed to join the Holy League; and in 1578 when he received the news that Dom Sebastian of Portugal had fallen in battle. Once he had won Dom Sebastian's crown (1580–83), he more often took the initiative and became more positive in his responses, in what appears to be the combination of a new confidence born in the aggrandizement of his power and resources and an ageing ruler's increasingly desperate determination to make things turn out the way he wanted. But despite a more active will, Philip's marginings generally continued to read the same, with laments over the everlasting lack of enough money and a growing lack of confidence in his agents becoming his dominant themes, even as his hand was beginning to fail and his notations became less frequent.

When Philip had perused a document he either made a decision, sent it to the appropriate council for review and its recommendation or to a particular minister for comment. If Philip's decision, whether taken at once or after consideration of various recommendations, required issuance of edicts, patents or orders, he worked on these with his secretaries or selected advisers. Ultimately a secretary drafted a fair copy for Philip's signature. Philip often added marginal notes and postscripts to letters and orders. The whole process was notoriously slow, and Philip's officials abroad, who waited not only on the king's decision but were also at the mercy of slow communications, used to say, 'If death came from Spain, we should all live to a ripe old age.'

With the volume of business handled by Philip's court, important documents meant for the king's attention sometimes went astray and others reached him too late for his liking, as his endorsement on a dispatch from Rome shows: 'The Cardinal [Espinosa], Ruy Gómez and the Prior [Don Antonio de Toledo] have seen this, and up till now I have known nothing of it.'[44] Philip wished every important dispatch to reach him first and he wanted to be the only one to know about everything. In general he succeeded in this aim till the last years of his life. His secretaries and ministers, however, though they admired his determination, did not always think the result justified the effort. Philip's secretary Gonzalo Pérez wrote to his cousin in 1566, 'His Majesty loses track of many things, and will continue to do so, by treating them with diverse persons, this time with one, this time with another, and hiding them from one, and revealing them to another; and thus it is not surprising that different orders go out, even contradictory orders.'[45]

Philip must have taken heed of what was being said, for in 1566 he gave to the indefatigable and brisk Cardinal Espinosa a general superintendency over government business, though he had no intention of permitting the cardinal to become a prime minister, or worse, favourite. The cardinal presumed on his authority and took to dealing with state matters with Philip so quickly that the king had no time to reflect on them; in effect, the cardinal was forcing his decisions. One day in 1572 Espinosa so exasperated Philip that he ordered him from his bureau.[46] Soon after, the story goes, Philip in effect called the cardinal a liar in front of several other councillors, and the cardinal withdrew from government.

Espinosa's disgrace (which he did not long survive) threatened to leave the administration of the monarchy in a chaotic state. To avoid this, Philip took into his service Espinosa's secretary, Mateo Vázquez de Leca, who had handled the late cardinal's business.[47] Vázquez provided Philip with what he needed: someone who would supervise matters, but who lacked the status to assume the role of a prime minister. A hard-working, self-effacing priest, Vázquez worked quietly behind the scenes and became, as Cabrera de Córdoba put it, Philip's 'arch-secretary'.

Yet despite the aid of his 'arch-secretary', Philip persisted in his habitual ways of handling business. In 1576, Alba, in a conversation with Vázquez, made much the same point as had Gonzalo Pérez:[48] the king tried to do far too much, and worked chiefly through secretaries so that the councillors were not sure what resolutions had been taken; correspondence was referred to some councillors and not to others; there was no regularity, much of the correspondence was out of date and some matters debated in council had already been resolved without the councillors' knowledge; sometimes matters were submitted to the council at the last moment, with little time left to make proper recommendations, thus risking a wrong decision. Alba suggested that a routine be established in which correspondence was routed to the councillors early enough so that they had time to weigh matters carefully, before being called upon to make recommendations to Philip.

Philip expressed his reaction to Alba's suggestions in the margin of Vázquez's memorandum of the conversation as follows: 'Of the zeal of the Duke I am very sure; about the rest, although he is often right about many things, still in some instances perhaps not, and therefore I do not expect to look into all [he says] in order to arrange matters suitably, unless there is more time for it, but for now I will go on thinking about it. In order to take care of this it is necessary to look into other matters, but as I said, all will be studied in order to do what I believe is suitable.'

Looking at the complaint and the reaction, one wonders if indeed much of the problem in Philip's relationships with his councillors lies in the slowness of his thought processes. Sixteenth-century Spanish governmental correspondence usually lacks the virtue of getting quickly to the point, but Philip's marginings here and elsewhere seem to suggest that he did not easily and instinctively impart precision and organization to his thoughts.

The Espinosa episode suggests that Philip was probably aware of the shortcomings of his thought processes, which may well have played an important part in another aspect of his relations with his collaborators that attracted much attention: his suspiciousness. Certainly experience, whether acquired through reading histories or from Charles's warnings, gave Philip cause to be suspicious, but his contemporaries found him extraordinarily so. He consciously refrained from giving anyone his complete confidence, and turned, so to speak, the constant testing of his ministers' loyalty and reliability into a technique of government. He encouraged ministers, secretaries and officials to make reports on each other and sent agents to investigate their conduct while *in* office – not *after* their tenure as prescribed by law. For instance, when he sent the biblical scholar Arias Montano to Antwerp for the publication of the *Poliglota Real* (1568–72), he asked him for comments on Alba's conduct of the Netherlands government. Indeed, Philip was prepared to receive, and even reward, information about his subordinates from any source, official, unofficial or thoroughly disreputable. However, receiving information did not mean that Philip was ready to act on it. He first carefully evaluated it, always trying to be fair. When complaints of a man's conduct of office did lead to his removal by Philip, it was usually with good reason; either the complaints were true or came from so many and such influential persons that the office holder clearly could no longer effectively discharge his office.

Philip's methods, however, encouraged intrigue in his already factious court. Men often felt driven to act secretly, whether in their own interests or the king's, and disregarded normal lines of communication and the ordinary chain of command and responsibility.

Those who served Philip, though sometimes personally offended by his suspiciousness, seem not to have been surprised. They understood the complexity of his task and assumed that intrigue, which provided much of the stuff of Roman history and Renaissance political theory, was natural to any court. In general they showed amazing loyalty to Philip II and his mission; despite the vicissitudes of his confidence in them and their employment in his service, persons such as Granvelle, the duke of Alba and Margaret of Parma stayed faithful till the end. Just before he died in 1592 Alexander Farnese, Philip's governor-general of the Netherlands (1578–92), instructed his son Ranuccio to go to Philip, 'who is so good, and assure him of your desire, like mine, to sacrifice yourself and all you possess in his royal service, the thing I most care for in this world'.[49]

Ironically, Philip had just then finally succumbed to the insistence of his Spanish ministers that Farnese be recalled from his office. Moreover, he allowed himself to be persuaded by them that Farnese might disobey, and therefore made provisions for his arrest. Had Farnese known this, his remarks may have been different, but in the tradition of most of Philip's servants, he would probably have resigned himself to his disgrace and remained loyal.

Shortly before Philip had decided to recall Farnese, his fear of being betrayed had been given a frightening reality when his former secretary Antonio Pérez led a revolt in Aragon against him. The Pérez case provides perhaps the most interesting example of Philip's suspiciousness and its consequences to himself, others and the monarchy.

Antonio Pérez, the son of Philip's first secretary and a protégé of Ruy Gómez, enjoyed extraordinary confidence with the king, capturing with brilliance and charm, Gregorio Marañón suggests, the prosaic Philip's favour.[50] After Ruy Gómez's death, Pérez assumed responsibility for holding his faction together, advocating the policies and promoting the interests of the late prince of Eboli. This required that he play court politics, for which he had a flair, but through his conducting himself, a commoner, like a lord, he earned the resentment of his peers among the royal secretaries. Philip, in the meantime, as he promoted his half-brother Don John of Austria to ever higher posts, had reason to worry about his brother's ambitions. Don John sought support in Rome for his becoming king of Tunis, which in 1573 he had captured for Philip. The same year Philip, on the advice of Pérez, posted as secretary to Don John a protégé of Pérez, Juan de Escobedo. Escobedo was captivated by Don John and broke from Pérez's leash.

None the less, Pérez tried to keep himself and Philip informed of Don John's activities by making sure that his correspondence passed through his hands. When in 1576 Philip appointed Don John governor-general of the Netherlands, at a moment when the provinces had broken into full rebellion, Pérez retained his control over Don John's and Escobedo's correspondence, to the irritation of Zayas, secretary of state for the North, and the 'Flemish' secretaries.

Don John's ambitions continued to run high. From the Netherlands he wished to lead an expedition against England, depose Elizabeth, and rescue and marry Mary Queen of Scots, with whom he would mount the English throne. Such ambitions seemed far-fetched to Philip, but to improve Don John's disposition towards his new office, which he did not want, Philip gave his consent to his half-brother's plan, but hedged it in with preconditions, most especially that no invasion of England be undertaken before the Netherlands had been brought under control.

In the Netherlands Don John only made matters worse by resorting to arms, when Philip and Pérez, in line with Ruy Gómez's policies, had wanted him to pacify the provinces through diplomacy and, if necessary, dissimulation. Don John sent Escobedo to Madrid to explain why he had resumed the fighting, but Escobedo found little sympathy for Don John's position. Philip believed that Don John had forced his hand, and resignedly ordered troops to the Netherlands; but he was hard put to find the necessary funds so soon after his declaration of bankruptcy in 1575.

For reasons that are not clear, but probably involved in his desire to

hold Philip's favour, Pérez criticized Don John's conduct, thus helping
to undermine Philip's confidence in his half-brother. In response,
Escobedo decided to undercut Philip's confidence in Pérez by revealing
how Pérez had been getting rich from Philip's transactions with Genoese bankers. Pérez got wind of this and insinuated to Philip that Don
John was behaving in a disloyal manner. He produced Don John's
correspondence to him expressing a desire to serve Philip at court and
implied that Don John meant to take the reins of government from the
ageing and often ailing king. He also reported rumours that Don John
intended to make himself ruler of the Netherlands and marry Queen
Elizabeth. The evil genius behind such schemes, Pérez stated, was
Escobedo, who for the sake of the monarchy and Don John should be
removed. After some discussion of the matter with Pérez and the
marquis of los Vélez, one of Pérez's allies, Philip seems, as best we can
tell, to have accepted Pérez's argument that Escobedo was dangerous,
and that it would be unwise to try him in a court of law, since he might
reveal embarrassing matters. On the other hand, he did not authorize
Escobedo's assassination. Pérez, certain that the king would back him,
took matters into his own hands and ordered Escobedo's murder.

On 1 April 1578 Philip heard from Mateo Vázquez that Escobedo
had been shot dead in the streets of Madrid. None doubted that Pérez
was behind the deed, but Philip chose to ignore the matter. Neither did
Philip reveal his thoughts about Don John's conduct or loyalty. His
behaviour, however, indicated that he was perplexed and consequently
unusually indecisive, which hardly helped Don John, desperately writing
for more men and money from the Netherlands battlefields, where he
died in October.

Pérez enjoyed extraordinary influence with Philip in the months
after Escobedo's death. He must have thought that hoodwinking him
was no difficult matter. In addition to abusing Philip's confidence in
monetary transactions and even in regard to state secrets, Pérez began
to exploit the possibilities opened by the Portuguese succession question,
with the death in August 1578 of Dom Sebastian. The princess of
Eboli, widow of Pérez's late patron, wanted to marry her youngest
daughter to Dom Theodosio, duke of Barçelos, the eldest son of the
duchess of Bragança, a rival of Philip for the Portuguese crown.
Dom Theodosio, aged twelve, had been captured at the battle of
Alcázarquivir, in which Dom Sebastian fell, and was a prisoner of the
sherif of Morocco, who was using him as a pawn in his diplomatic
dealings with Philip II. Pérez kept *La Eboli* informed of Philip's activities,
and she in turn seems to have relayed what she learned to Portugal.

But in the spring of 1579, Philip received all of Don John's private papers from the Netherlands, and after looking through his half-brother's most confidential correspondence, he realized that Don John, however wild his dreams, had been utterly loyal to the monarchy and had tried his best to carry out Philip's policies. He found nothing to support Pérez's insinuations. Philip had yielded overmuch to his suspicions; now he determined to right things as much as he could.

He decided that Pérez had to be arrested, but before he could do this, he needed a strong minister to take over the future direction of foreign policy, Pérez's main province. Alba was out of the question, since he had been sent from court and put under house arrest for disobedience in a family matter[51] – Philip wanted none to appear indispensable, especially the seventy-year-old duke, whom the fifty-two-year-old Philip found increasingly insufferable. He therefore summoned Cardinal Granvelle from Rome, and in the meantime put Mateo Vázquez to preparing a dossier on Pérez's conduct of office.

Vázquez, who like the other secretaries resented Pérez's aristocratic airs, soon had evidence of Pérez's widespread peculations and trafficking in state secrets. He also got in touch with Escobedo's family, which had already taken the case to the law courts. The widow petitioned Philip for an interview, which he granted her in April. He excluded Pérez from the interview, but later told him that she had implicated him in the crime.

When Granvelle arrived in Madrid at the end of July, Philip ordered Pérez's arrest. On the night of 28 July, he worked late with Pérez, then at ten gave him the Italian correspondence to take care of; the Portuguese papers he kept himself, since he had not as yet read them. As Pérez departed, Philip remarked, 'Your business will be taken care of before I am finished.'

An hour later, Pérez was arrested in his home. At the same time, guards arrested the princess of Eboli. Philip, according to letters sent to her powerful kinsman, the duke of Infantado, and her son-in-law, the duke of Medina Sidonia, ordered her arrest because of her interfering with the work of Vázquez and Pérez, and her refusal to desist when asked. Vázquez's investigations had probably revealed something most serious, most likely her intrigues to marry her daughter to Barçelos.

The story of the episode in subsequent years took on amorous embellishments, suggesting that Philip and Pérez were rivals for *La Eboli's* love. Yet, according to the best evidence, Philip never had an affair with his closest friend's widow, and the only passion certainly shared by Pérez and the princess, no matter what he boasted later in life, was a lust for power and position.

Pérez was stripped of his offices and subjected to questioning after his arrest, but Philip was hardly anxious to press the case, since he himself was implicated in Escobedo's assassination. Moreover, as was the custom of the age, a secretary's state papers were his own property, and Pérez kept large quantities of drafts of documents, correspondence and memoranda relating to the affairs of state in his home, and Philip had no quick means within the law of getting at them. Philip permitted Pérez to return to his home, still under arrest, and even let him handle some royal correspondence. Pérez was thus quieted, but the problem remained unsolved.

The wheels of bureaucracy were grinding in the meantime, and by 1585 Rodrigo Vázquez de Arce, of the council of Castile and no friend of Pérez, had made out a legal case against Pérez's venality. Pérez was hauled once more to prison, while guards, with proper warrants, searched his house for state papers. Not getting all the papers he wanted, Philip played a sort of cat and mouse game with Pérez, alternating rigour and relaxation to gain from the secretary and his wife still more documents – but still not all.

In the meantime Escobedo's son pressed for Pérez's trial for murder, but was persuaded after some time by Pérez and Philip's confessor to withdraw his charges for a cash indemnity, in order to spare Philip embarrassment in court. But Pérez's small cooperation in this matter spared him nothing. The whole affair had become an intolerable burden on Philip's conscience, and after the defeat in 1588 of his armada against England, Philip, who took defeat as God's punishment for his sins, resolved to clear it by wringing from Pérez a confession of full responsibility. He ordered his judges to have Pérez explain once more the reasons, and offer proof of them, why Escobedo had to die. Under torture, Pérez went through the stories of Escobedo's double-dealings, and his encouraging of Don John's hankering for a crown; he believed then for the sake of the monarchy that some drastic step had to be taken. It was, however, Pérez claimed, los Vélez (already dead) who first advocated the assassination of Escobedo.

When the judges informed Philip of Pérez's explanations, Philip found them vague and unconvincing. Pérez offered no proof, and Philip had seen a good deal of evidence, including Don John's papers, which contradicted Pérez's allegations. In effect, Pérez had ordered Escobedo's execution, on inconclusive evidence, with neither due process of law nor the express order of the king.

Pérez, correctly sensing that he was doomed, arranged to escape from his Madrid prison with the help of his wife and friends. He fled to Aragon, where, once across the border, he claimed the right of an Aragonese subject to have his case heard in the court of the *Justicia*. The rest of Pérez's story is deeply involved with the altercations of 1590-91 in Aragon, and the wars of the 1590s.

Seeing what could happen when confidence was betrayed, what kind of character did the men Philip chose to serve him have? The allegation has been frequently made that he favoured men who were soft-spoken and colourless, and rejected men who were outspoken and strong. This is largely wrong. Certainly both types of men served him. He had a limited number of men willing and available to serve and many offices to fill. He often had to employ whoever was at hand, and as he grew older, he feared that the quality of those willing to serve was declining. Whether strong or weak, they customarily presented their opinions to him on paper, where one was no louder than another. Philip sought Alba's opinions on all matters of war and most matters of state, even when Alba was in disgrace. He maintained a steady correspondence with Granvelle from 1559 when he left the Netherlands until Granvelle's death. And though he avoided situations in which he felt pressured by his ministers, he was always the king, and when he needed their advice, he called them to him. Many of the noblemen, who complained of his conduct of business through secretaries, had access to him anyway, through their positions in his household. In general, fewer great nobles served the serious and bureaucratic court in the latter part of his reign; it did not suit them. Much of the problem in reality lay in the nature of bureaucracy, which has lately been much studied. We now realize that the organization itself had ways of destroying or stifling its most outspoken and energetic members. There was no need for the king to do so.

Towards the end of his life, Philip seems to have conducted less business working alone with his papers and more in conference with his two chief ministers, Moura and Idiáquez. Both seem to have been soft-spoken and had made their mark in diplomacy, but neither was weak. Each had proved himself in an important situation, Idiáquez in Genoa during the financial crisis of 1573-77, and Moura during the Portuguese succession struggle, 1578-81.

Nor did Philip favour weak men in positions abroad, although his suspiciousness caused him to recall men who were in fact strong. His replacement of Juan de Vega in 1558 with the duke of Medinaçeli in the viceroyalty of Sicily, often used to support the contention that Philip feared strong viceroys, is easy to explain. Vega had been appointed by Charles, and Philip was, in Sicily as in other dominions, in the process of replacing Charles's appointees with his own. However, Philip respected the men Charles had employed and usually found other places for them. In Vega's case, Philip immediately appointed him president of the council of Castile, the most important office in that kingdom, at a time when Philip's sister Juana was acting as regent and needed the best assistance she could get. This does not seem to reveal a fear of the strong.

Another case raised to show Philip's favouring the weak over the strong is his appointment in 1588 of the duke of Medina Sidonia to command the armada.[52] None then thought the duke weak, though it was admitted that he lacked experience in commanding ships and fleets. He had for some years assisted in getting the Indies fleets under way and had acted as an adviser to Philip on maritime strategy. He was closely involved in the planning and preparation of the Enterprise of England.

In 1596 Philip appointed to the command of the ocean armada the fiery Don Martín de Padilla, *adelantado mayor* of Castile, who gave evidence of the king's conviction that he could control strong men as well as weak ones, when he exclaimed on the king's death, 'Men will see what Spaniards are worth, now that they have a free hand and are no longer subjected to a single brain that thought it knew all that could be known, and treated everyone else as a blockhead.'[53]

Though Philip was determined to control all the men who served him, and meant to know all he had to know to rule his dominions, did he presume that this could be done? Professor Koenigsberger in his recent essay seems to think so, and labels Philip's presumption *hubris*. However, in my view Philip's pessimism about controlling events seems to hold him short of *hubris*; it rendered him frequently indecisive and affected his decisions. When he was a young man, he seems already old; within himself he carried all the disillusionment with men and uncertainty about the course of events which characterized Charles V in his old age. He also had Charles's sense of obligation, and he was willing, if often hesitant, to risk all. Step by step, Philip II committed himself to courses of action which by temperament he would have preferred to avoid, raising within him contradictory impulses and causing his indecision. He was acting most often, as he well knew, under circumstances allowing little margin for error and giving much reason to pray.

V

Philip II, Europe
and the World

Philip II's reign covered more than forty momentous years of history, during which Catholics fought Protestants, the old medieval order, with its religious and feudal values, struggled to survive, and new order we call modern, with its rational, burgher and self-consciously secular mentalities, at the same time struggled to emerge. Philip II clearly championed the traditional order of Catholic Christendom, monarchy and nobility, however much the exigencies of war and his sense of justice brought him into conflict with the Church or the nobility, and led him to introduce certain 'rational' reforms into his regime.

In studying Philip in the history of his times, the modern historian is tempted perhaps to follow the lead of Cabrera de Córdoba (Philip's contemporary biographer) in examining Philip's reign chronologically. One could thus age with Philip, sensing, almost existentially, the impact of the chaotic occurrence of events upon him, and emphathizing with him as he reacted to news and made the necessary decisions. Unfortunately, none but scholars immersed in the study of the late sixteenth century could hope to follow Cabrera's pace and style with understanding, as he hops back and forth across the map of Europe and the world from chapter to chapter, and even within chapters, packing in event after event, involving all the ministers of Philip's regime, the grandees and foreign princes. The edition of 1876–77 published by the *Academia Real de Historia* consists of four folio volumes. Within the more limited compass of this work, five broad issues, agreed to be the most consequential of Philip's reign, have been isolated for study in turn, rather than attempting any chronological approach. A few brief 're-minders' have been included to clarify the inter-relationships and simul-taneities of these issues which all confronted Philip throughout his life, often at the same time, with resulting profound effects on each other.

After a study of the basic considerations of Philip II and his ministers involved in the formulation and execution of policies relating to foreign powers and the defence of the monarchy, in part or as a whole, we can, in the light of this, then deal with five issues: (1) unity and disunity in the Iberian peninsula; (2) the peace of Italy and the defence of the Mediterranean; (3) the revolt of the Netherlands; (4) the emergence of England as a world power and, closely related to this, (5) Philip's attempt to control developments in France, torn by religious strife. Since Philip gave these European problems clear priority, the problems of his overseas dominions will here be treated only as they relate to them.

GENERAL POLICY CONSIDERATIONS

Philip's activities during his father's reign and in the administration of his dominions reveal some of the chief considerations in the making of higher policy. For Philip, when he mounted the throne, thought in terms of the foreign relations and domestic policies of his predecessors, which to him and his subjects were familiar. Moreover, Philip was hardly one to take great initiatives of his own volition. He and the statesmen of his generation seem diffident and rather demoralized, given to half-measures and last minute expedients, and always slightly puzzled by, sometimes fully resentful of, the religious fervour which drove some of their more zealous contemporaries, and often upset their more rational and worldly calculations. Philip II taking the sort of confident initiative, with its almost gay abandon, which characterized Charles VIII of France when he invaded Italy in 1494, or Frederick the Great when he pounced on Silesia in 1740, seems almost unthinkable. Renaissance trust in *raggione* had passed and the Enlightenment's faith in Reason lay far in the future: Livy had yielded to Tacitus (Philip's favourite) as *the* historian. The temper of Philip II's times was a stubborn stoic fatalism and sense of obligation, or resignation to the will of God. Indeed, a few zealots such as Pius V or Philippe de St Aldegonde confidently saw themselves as instruments of God's will, as did Philip, but his diffidence belied his trust. There were also a few left-over knights-errant such as Don John of Austria, and a handful of desperate men matured by adversity, who risked all and became great, men such as William the Silent and Henri of Navarre. Every age has some variety. But those born to power and responsibility and those who served them were conservative, cautious and hesitant; they were parsimonious; they frequently seemed timid and lacking in energy; they exasperated their more zealous contemporaries. Philip II comes first to mind, but one need only think of Elizabeth and Cecil; Maximilian II and his morose sons Rudolf II, Matthias, Ernst and

Albert; the last three Valois kings of France, Francis II, Charles IX and Henri III and their mother, Catherine de' Medici; the pathetic Mary Queen of Scots and her son James VI; Cardinal Henry, regent (1562–68) and briefly king (1578–80) of Portugal.

Philip II's policies were generally regarded as conservative. The Venetian ambassador Michele Suriano in 1559 reported perceptively that Philip's aim was 'not to wage war so that he can add to his kingdoms, but to wage peace so that he can keep the lands he has'.[1] Philip's assessments of those who opposed him reflects his conviction of the divine ordination and therefore the fundamental rightness of the existing religious, political and social order of his realms. Like most statesmen of his age, he did not see political behaviour as motivated by abstract objective criteria, such as 'interests' or 'reasons of state', as much as by personal reasons or drives. When a man said 'Spain' or 'France' in regard to state policies, he was not thinking in terms of an abstraction, which summed up a congeries of objective interests and potentialities, but rather of the person of the king of Spain or the king of France.

Since the prevailing views of the court most often reflect – and help form – the views of the prince, we can assume that the views of Cabrera de Córdoba, who served Philip's government as a secretary, probably reflect Philip's. Cabrera depicted the prince of Orange as an ambitious, unprincipled man, Count Egmont as Orange's dupe, Calvinists as wrong-headed heretics and traitors to their sovereigns, the king of France ('the enemy of our House', Charles V had called him) as covetous of Philip's possessions, and the Grand Turk as doing the work of the devil. Philip's ambassador to France, Don Francés de Álava, in 1565 referred to a Turkish envoy who had landed at Marseilles as 'the ambassador of Satan, sent from Hell'.[2]

In formulating policy, Philip tended to refer to the motivating assumptions and understanding of history of his father and the confidential advisers of his late reign, many of whom, like Alba, Manrique de Lara and Granvelle, continued to serve Philip. Charles saw himself as the bulwark of Christian Europe against the Ottoman Empire, as the sword of Catholic civilization against the spread of Protestantism, and as a brake on the ambitions of the king of France, who perversely threatened the peace of Christendom, made alliances with the Turk, and refused to take his place – after the Emperor and the king of Spain – in the defence of the Church and Catholic Europe. He tried to forge his dominions and allies into an interrelated system to realize these purposes. After Charles's death and the division of his dominions and dignities between Philip and Ferdinand, his grander imperial designs were abandoned, but the courts of Madrid and Austria maintained close ties, and the heirs of Charles and Ferdinand customarily intermarried, in order to ensure that Charles's patrimony would always remain in the hands of the Habsburg dynasty. The two courts had, however, their own interests and developed different attitudes to both particular and common problems. Despite protestations of brotherly affection, the heads of each branch of the family often differed strongly. Philip believed that Maximilian II (reigned 1564–76), who was tolerant of Protestants and sympathetic to the dissident magnates of the Netherlands, needed to be 'undeceived' about those matters.[3] Maximilian's son Rudolf II (reigned 1576–1612), whose education Philip supervised in Madrid, proved too lethargic to support effectively Philip's policies in the Netherlands and neighbouring German lands, and though a devout Catholic, he dabbled enough in the occult sciences to lead Philip to worry about his orthodoxy.

Philip, as Charles's son and the most active, wilful and wealthy member of the dynasty, took the lead in preserving and directing the system Charles had forged. He considered Austria, Bohemia and Habsburg Hungary as its components, regardless of the dignity implied by the Imperial crown, worn in succession by his uncle, his cousin and his nephew, which they – and the Germans – denied him.

Philip viewed the system from Madrid, unlike Charles who shifted his court from place to place, and Castile was in every sense its cornerstone. One can then envision the bulwark against the Turks, extending from Spain across the western Mediterranean via the Balearics to Sicily and Naples, with Oran, Malta and La Goleta its outposts; from Naples it ran north, embracing the lands of the pope and Philip's allies, Tuscany, Parma, Mantua, Genoa and Savoy, held firmly in line by Milan and the Tuscan *presidios*; from Milan it ran along the line of the Alps, from the Tyrol to Styria and the fortified frontier of Habsburg Hungary, and thence to the mountains of Bohemia. To be sure, Venice, Ferrara, Ragusa (Dubrovnik) and to an extent the Papal States, were not allied to Philip, but they were Christian lands opposed to Ottoman aggression and would stand with Philip's dominions. The bulwark did not stop with the Habsburg lands on the Danube, but continued through Poland, and even to Muscovy. In 1572 Philip II through his embassy to the Empire tried to arrange the election of the Archduke Maximilian as king of Poland, without success; and considered sending an envoy to Moscow to make an alliance with the grand duke against the Turks.

To hold in line those pieces of the system lying between Spain and Austria, there was the closest possible cooperation between Philip and his viceroys, governors, commanders and ambassadors. The governor-general of Milan dealt with Savoy-Piedmont, Tuscany, Genoa, Parma, Mantua, Venice and the Swiss, and kept open communications across the Alps. The viceroy of Naples kept a watch on the papacy and on developments in the Ottoman Empire. The viceroy of Sicily maintained correspondence with Naples, the knights of Malta and La Goleta on defence against the Turks, and paid close attention to the affairs of the Barbary States of Tripoli, Tunis and Algiers. Algiers also interested the viceroy of Valencia and the captains-general of Granada and Andalusia. The duke of Medina Sidonia combined the captain-generalship of Andalusia with that of the Ocean-Sea; he not only attended to the defence of Andalusia but handled relations with Morocco and supervised the sailings of the Indies convoys.

The role of Philip's embassies and ambassadors in the functioning of the system was to deal directly with those components not ruled by Philip himself. Philip inherited a fine diplomatic service whose traditions went back to the reign of Ferdinand the Catholic.[4] In making policy the actual intentions and activities of foreign rulers, in addition to the histories of their dynasties and dominions, had to be taken into consideration, and it was up to Philip's embassies, aided by informers and spies, to provide Philip and those who advised him with the necessary intelligence. Philip's ambassadors moreover had to relay his intentions – or what he wanted others to believe were his intentions – to foreign governments. And if embassies were important to preserve the bulwark against Ottoman aggression, they were equally so in dealing with courts in north-western Europe, where statesmen less apprehensive of the Ottoman menace (and therefore less inclined to band together for the common defence of Christendom) had views different from Philip's, and little appreciation of his claim to leadership in Christendom. In fact, in the view of Protestant statesmen Philip was the chief threat to Christian truth, whence the *bon mot* 'rather the Turk than the Spaniard'.

But what ran in Philip's favour was the general tendency of statesmen, Catholic or Protestant, to maintain the *status quo*, largely as defined in the Peace of Câteau Cambrésis, after Europe had been troubled by a generation of religious reformers and ambitious dynasts. But if the dynasts were prepared to be quiet, the reformers were not finished. The Calvinists, who had not been recognized in the Peace of Augsburg, were busy proselytizing in the fertile fields of the French-speaking lands, where Catholic reform had so far been minimal, while the Counter Reformation, spearheaded by the Jesuits, meant to check the Calvinists and go on to recover for Rome all lost peoples. These religious zealots on both sides were prepared to make common cause with those who, for whatever reason, were discontented with the existing political and social order, which, given the respite of peace provided by Câteau Cambrésis, rulers meant to reinvigorate and refine.

Looking northward then from Madrid, Philip saw a delicate and disturbing situation which demanded of him just the right combination of force and finesse if he were to maintain the *status quo*. Most alarming, of course, was the isolation of his Netherlands, flanked after 1559 by Protestant powers: England across the Channel, and Denmark and the Lutheran German principalities, most importantly Saxony, to the east. For Philip, keeping the archbishopric of Cologne Catholic was vital: it commanded the Rhine as it flowed into the Low Countries. The Lutheran princes of Germany, however, had become after 1555 largely conservative, and being guaranteed by the Peace of Augsburg the right to determine the religion of their subjects, they had no wish to disturb others or risk being disturbed. England proved another case.

Between Philip's southern lands and the Low Countries lay France, whose kings had battled with Philip's Burgundian, Habsburg and Trastámara predecessors for generations. Philip's communications with the Netherlands perforce had to go around France, and were affected, as we shall see, by the intensifying religious–civil wars that rent France between 1562 and 1598.

Sea communications even in peacetime posed problems; to the ordinary matters of wind and water was added the menace of piracy. After 1568, occasional piracy was in effect replaced by an undeclared war by Protestants, sailing from France and England, against the shipping of Philip's subjects, purportedly in response to Philip's attempts to repress Protestantism in the Low Countries. Philip had little luck in forcing the Channel passage to the Low Countries with armadas (1572, 1574, 1575, 1588, 1598), all but the last of which were broken up by storms or battles.

Far more dependable was the overland route to the Netherlands from Genoa and Milan through Savoy, the Franche-Comté and Lorraine, the famous 'Spanish Road'.[5] The sea legs of the journey, from Naples and Sicily, or Spain, were easy, requiring only coasting under the protection of Philip's galleys. The troops and supplies landed in Liguria got into marching order in Savoy or Milan, drawing heavily from the Milanese arsenals, and then proceeded north, often escorting trains of pack animals carrying the gold and silver, hauled from Mexico and Peru, to pay them, their suppliers and the bankers in the Netherlands.

The 'Spanish Road' came into steady use by Philip's armed forces in

1567, when the duke of Alba led 10,000 crack troops northward to deal with the disturbances that gripped the Netherlands. The diplomacy of keeping the road open subsequently kept Philip's envoys busy, since much of it lay not in his lands, but in those of his allies, who were therefore threatened by his enemies.

The hub of the whole route was Genoa, in whose ports – Genoa, Savona, La Spezia – the overland road began. The politics of Genoa had been historically stormy, and it was only in 1528 that Andrea Doria had allied the republic to the Habsburgs. Before that, Genoa had been closely bound to France, and a powerful pro-French faction survived, causing Philip II considerable anxiety during the financial crisis of the 1570s, when they challenged the rule of Gian Andrea Doria and the big bankers, who were growing rich from the Spanish connection.

Milan of course was Philip's, and from it he could put pressure on Genoa and Savoy. It was through Savoyard territory during Philip's reign that the road wended its way across the Alps to Philip's Franche-Comté. The successive dukes of Savoy, Emmanuel Philibert (1553–80) and Charles Emmanuel (1580–1630), were Philip II's faithful allies and, for the sake of the security of the 'Spanish Road', refrained – reluctantly – from trying to reconquer Geneva, which would certainly have provoked a war with the Swiss and the French Huguenots. (With the death of Henri II of France, who wanted to destroy the 'hotbed of heretics', Geneva was in effect secure: Philip II, who approved Henri's plan, could afterwards not afford the risk, since he could not count on French support.) The Swiss confederacy moreover provided security for the Franche-Comté, which they viewed as a buffer zone between Switzerland and France.

Likewise essential to the security of the Franche-Comté and the road was a close alliance with the duchy of Lorraine. Philip's cousin, Christine of Denmark, dowager duchess of Lorraine, was fortunately dedicated to the Habsburg interests, and carried great influence with her son, Duke Charles III, until her retirement in 1578 to her estates in Milan. Charles proved a staunch Catholic, and was closely associated with his French cousin, Henri of Lorraine, duke of Guise, with whom in 1584 Philip signed a secret treaty for the support of Guise's Catholic League and the preservation of Catholicism in France. The Guise estates (and those of his brothers and kin) in north-eastern France formed with the duchy of Lorraine one of those extensive family feudal domains that overlapped the boundaries of states, that state-builders of the next century worked so hard to suppress, to prevent the very sort of alliance Philip made with Guise.

Once through Lorraine, the road lay in Philip's territory, Luxemburg, which, under the firm government of Count Peter Ernst Mansfeldt, did not undergo the tumults which disturbed the other provinces of the Low Countries. The passage of the road thence through the independent bishopric of Liège was unhindered; arriving in Brabant, the road terminated at Brussels.

A view as disturbing apparently to Madrid as that towards the Low Countries lay across the Atlantic: the seaways along which the gold and silver of the New World flowed into Philip's treasury. Philip's credit and thus war-making ability depended upon them. Philip and his maritime strategists such as Don Alvaro de Bazán, marquis of Santa Cruz, Pedro Menéndez de Avilés, *adelantado* of Florida, and the duke of Medina Sidonia, and Philip's European enemies, all knew that the routes were vulnerable. The possible loss of a treasure fleet, upon which the king's creditors waited like vultures, was a recurring nightmare in Madrid. The nightmare grew more frightening after 1580, when Portugal and its seaborne empire were added to Philip's responsibilities. During the Habsburg–Valois wars of the 1550s, Bazán put flotillas of galleons to sea and improved the convoy system, thus checking the mounting losses of ships to French privateers. Menéndez de Avilés further refined the convoy system, and in the late 1560s built the Indies armada to patrol the sealanes to the New World, escort the Indies fleets, and chase pirates from the Caribbean. Menéndez died in 1574 and his armada was dissipated in futile missions or lost to storm and neglect. (Bazán, who had been in charge of the ocean defences before Menéndez, was until 1578 employed in the Mediterranean, and not much concerned with Atlantic problems.)

The convoys, however, made their annual voyages, one getting underway from the Guadalquivir for Mexico in late spring – with luck – and the other for Tierra Firma (northern South America) in late summer or early autumn. In the Caribbean, having done their business and picked up the treasure and other cargoes, the two fleets joined at Havana early the following summer, and tried to get underway for Spain before the end of July in order to avoid hurricanes. If they weighed anchor on schedule, they were home in September; fleets often arrived, however, in November or December, running before wintry gales.

After Philip took over Portugal, a *junta* of his military advisers, including Santa Cruz, Medina Sidonia, the duke of Alba, and the secretaries for war and the Indies assembled in 1581 in Lisbon to discuss the defence of Philip's vastly extended empire, which Drake's round-the-world marauding expedition had proved vulnerable. Of their recommendations, to reconstitute the armada of the Indies route, to fortify the chief ports of the Indies and to provide galleys and frigates to patrol the Caribbean and the Peruvian coast, only the first was expeditiously undertaken. A new Indian Guard sailed in 1584. However when Drake raided the Caribbean in 1586, he found the towns still unfortified and only two tired galleys to oppose him at Cartagena, while six were still being outfitted in the Guadalquivir. The raid provoked a vigorous response: stone walls went up around the chief towns, frigates were built at Havana, and fleets brought munitions to the Indies from Seville.

Yet despite improved defences in the Indies, and the strengthening of the ocean armada and the armada of the Indies route in the 1590s, the situation of the treasure routes appeared so desperate from Madrid that the safe return of the fleets each year was regarded as nearly miraculous. The duke of Medina Sidonia in 1598 urged Philip not to ruin Spain's trade relationships with the Dutch rebels, lest the rebels join the English in attacking the sea lanes and making it entirely impossible to sail them, instead of just nearly so.[6]

Beyond these major concerns of Madrid, there were other problems of war and foreign relations involving the empire. The New World, of course, was a zone of conquest, and the Spaniards reduced the Indians to their rule as they could. But the world surrounding the Philippines was another matter, and there Philip's officers had to consider strong native sultanates and kingdoms, and to the north Japan and the great empire of China. In 1596 and 1598, expeditions were sent from Manila to assist the king of Cambodia against the king of Siam, but no tangible gains resulted.[7] Until 1580, the Spaniards and Portuguese were rivals in the Pacific in expanding their commerce and missionary activity. Philip II, after he became king of Portugal, carefully tried to separate clearly by edict the spheres of activity of his Portuguese and Castilian subjects in order to prevent friction. In general, Philip instructed his governors in eastern Asia, as elsewhere, to be prudent and avoid risks.

Added to the anxieties of Madrid over defence against the Turks, the preservation of the Netherlands and the security of its sealanes and overseas empire, was a growing fear for the safety of Spain itself. Alba told Catherine de' Medici in 1565 that he feared the Huguenots in France would stir the *moriscos* to revolt. (The *moriscos* in turn would call in the Turks.) In 1576 he told Mateo Vázquez that even Madrid was not safe.[8] And in 1590, the secretary of war Andrés de Prada lamented to the duke of Medina Sidonia about the 'miserable state of the monarchy, for the which the only remedy and hope is to fortify Gibraltar, Perpignan

Navarre and the other frontiers ... and to surround Madrid with
fortresses, praying to God to give us the time, and in his mercy not
punish us for our sins. ...'⁹

This sense of peril in Madrid we must bear in mind, along with the
policy considerations discussed, while remembering that Philip, in
responding to issues, usually had to respond to several simultaneously.

In sum, Philip II's foreign policy was essentially defensive and conservative. He had no universal plan for extending his power, or even the
sway of the Church of Rome. In general he reacted, with varying degrees
of decisiveness, only to particular situations rather than implementing
some grand design, which leaves the student of his reign looking at a
seemingly disjointed series of events with no unifying thread save for the
universal consideration of cost, which from time to time forced Philip to
reassess each course he was pursuing and give some one of them priority.
The old argument of Protestant historians that the apparent disorder of
his policies was the result of his clever dissimulation holds no truth.
Philip was in fact frequently confused, and his policies were as often the
result of his confusion as of his designs.

UNITY AND DISUNITY IN THE IBERIAN PENINSULA

The union of the peoples of the Iberian peninsula under a single regime
would seem from a glance at the map an obvious thing. And so it did to
the Christian ruling houses of the peninsula (Castile, Aragon, Navarre
and Portugal), as demonstrated by their policy of almost constant inter-
marriage from at least the end of the fourteenth century. In this tradition
Charles V, the heir of the realms brought together in dynastic union by
the Trastámaras (Castile, Aragon and Spanish Navarre), married Isabel,
the oldest daughter of Emanuel the Fortunate, of the Portuguese House
of Avis; and Philip while a prince married Maria Manuela, the eldest
daughter of Emanuel's heir, John III, and after her death was betrothed
to her aunt Maria, sole daughter of Emanuel's third marriage to Charles's
sister Eleanor. Significantly, in the interests of the Netherlands, not
of the Iberian peninsula, negotiations for this marriage were broken
off in 1553, when Charles decided that Philip should marry Mary
Tudor.

Each dynasty, of course, hoped that the rule of the entire peninsula, the
recreation of Roman and Visigothic *Hispania*, would fall to it. But this
required that the primogenitural line of one of the houses die out, which
in fact began to happen to the descendants of Emanuel.¹⁰ Only one
of John III's sons reached manhood, and he died a few days before

the birth of his only child, Dom Sebastian, sole grandson and heir to John III.

Supporting the aims of the dynasts to bring the peninsula under one sceptre were the marriage policies of their nobles, who married their children into the great families of the neighbouring kingdoms as well as their own. Likewise the merchants of Seville and Lisbon found much in common, and Lisbon became dependent upon New World silver to conduct its spice trade with the Orient.

Yet to offset these forces were the centrifugal forces of geography, which divided the peninsula into zones among which communications were rudimentary, of the history and growth of vested interests around each court and provincial capital, and certainly of rivalries of noble houses and merchant companies, which often contradicted their efforts to find common ground.

Among the common folk there were language and ethnic differences. While most Iberians spoke a Romance language or dialect, a significant minority in the north spoke Basque, and in the south and along the east coast lived the *moriscos*, who spoke Arabic. And even the Romance languages and dialects were developing separately, with no effort being made to establish one of them as the standard, although for historic reasons, Castilian did predominate and was the language of the court. These differences in language, regional customs and varying lifestyles, and the fact of relative isolation and attendant xenophobia, provided real and basic obstacles to unity, as the history of the peninsula, not only before and during Philip's reign, but afterwards, attests.

Religion also provided grounds for unity and disunity. The rulers saw it as something which might bind together their diverse subjects, and from the beginning of the sixteenth century, Roman Catholicism, the ancestral faith of the majority of its peoples, was the sole religion tolerated in the Iberian peninsula. Each kingdom had its Inquisition to prevent *conversos* and *moriscos* from backsliding and to suppress any foreign heresies that might try to enter the peninsula. In Portugal, it must be said, the powerful *converso* community of Lisbon prevented the Inquisition from becoming quite so oppressive as that of Spain.

More divisive than unifying seem the statutes of *limpieza de sangre* (purity of blood) which reflected the fears and prejudices of the Old Christian majority. These excluded New Christians from many government and ecclesiastical offices, colleges, corporate bodies and confraternities, and led to endless litigations and the manufacture of falsified genealogies by those seeking entrance, since in the past the racial climate of the peninsula had been freer, and the bloodlines of many were 'tainted'. These statutes tended to hit the *conversos*, who aspired to enter the professions, harder than the *moriscos*, chiefly agricultural labourers on the estates of great nobles, who afforded them some protection. The Old Christians generally viewed the *moriscos* as an 'Ottoman Fifth Column'[44] and the *conversos* as their allies. The *conversos*, moreover, were suspected as being in sympathy with Protestantism, which in the peninsula was regarded not so much as an alternative Christian experience, but rather a means of restoring Judaism and Islam. Philip's tutor Siliceo claimed that all the heresiarchs ruining Germany were descended from Jews.[12] Philip shared this opinion.[13]

For the religious, cultural, economic and political factors which contributed to the unity or disunity of Hispania, Philip's reign was a crucial period. For during it, his attempts to force the assimilation of the Granadine *moriscos* into the religious and cultural norms of the Castilian Old Christians provoked their rebellion, which many feared would bring about Ottoman intervention. The luck of his dynasty in accumulating possessions through marriage continued when, upon the death of Dom Sebastian, he successfully claimed by right of descent (through his mother, from Emanuel the Fortunate) the crown of Portugal. Finally, the absolutist tendencies of his regime, centred on Castile, provoked a rising against him in Aragon.

THE REVOLT OF THE GRANADINE MORISCOS (1568–71)

The *moriscos* of Granada formed about a fourth of that kingdom's population, but they were chiefly concentrated in the valleys just south and east of the capital, where they formed an absolute majority. They had been under Castilian rule, which in many ways was colonial in character, for only two generations when Philip II became king of Castile. When Granada fell to Ferdinand and Isabella in 1492, the Moors had been guaranteed the practice of Islam; but their revolt in 1499 cost them this right, and they were given the choice of conversion to Christianity or emigration. Those who chose conversion, becoming *moriscos* instead of *moros*, were soon ordered by royal edicts to change their language from Arabic to Castilian, change their old lifestyle and give up Moorish dress. Enforcement of the edicts proved lax, and Charles V suspended their operation in 1527 for forty years following problems with the *morisco* community. When the forty years were up in 1567, the anti-Islamic and crusading fervour of Spain was at a high pitch. Philip II was at war with the Turks in the Mediterranean and about to send a military expedition to the Netherlands to suppress religious dissent.

On 1 January 1567, Philip reissued the edicts forbidding the *moriscos* their language, dress and lifestyle, and put the president (of the council) of Castile, Cardinal Espinosa, in charge of their enforcement.

There was, however, opposition to the edicts, and not only from the *moriscos*. The captain-general of Granada, the marquis of Mondéjar (whose father had preceded Espinosa as president of Castile), and many noblemen who employed *moriscos* on their estates, petitioned the court not to enforce them, but to no avail.

Espinosa sent as his agent to Granada Dr Pedro Deza, a man whose family had a feud with Mondéjar's, and secured his appointment as president of the chancellery of Granada, the high appellate court for New Castile and Andalusia. Between the legists of the chancellery and the office of the captain-general there were constant jurisdictional disputes. To complicate matters, the archbishop of Granada, who had returned from the Council of Trent inflamed with zeal, had his interests in the *moriscos* who formed his flock, while the various municipalities of Granada had their interests too.

All these men and their supporting institutions were involved in varying ways with the enforcement of the edicts, and frequently managed to work at cross-purposes,[14] generally to the detriment of the *moriscos*, who suffered countless abuses against their persons and property.

The *moriscos*, already suffering hardships related to a depression in the silk industry from which many earned their livelihoods, were driven to desperation. Several leaders of the *morisco* community formed underground bands, dropped their Christian names for traditional Moorish ones, and sent agents secretly to Constantinople and Algiers to seek assistance, which they were promised, for a rebellion. On Christmas night 1568 a group of armed *moriscos* tried to seize Granada by main force and called upon their fellows to rise in revolt.

The attempt on Granada failed, but the revolt spread, and required two years of hard fighting on the part of government forces before the last *morisco* rebels were burned out of their caves in the Granadine sierras. The feared intervention by the Turks did not occur. The task might have been accomplished sooner had it been left in Mondéjar's charge, but Deza complained to the court that the marquis was treating the *moriscos* too leniently and called in from nearby Murcia the marquis of los Vélez with his militia. Confusion in command led to a lack of discipline among the soldiers, and their mistreatment of loyal *moriscos* caused the revolt to intensify and grow. Philip, who listened to too many persons, tried to clarify the command situation by appointing his twenty-two-year-old half-brother Don John commander-in-chief. He assigned the duke of Sessa and Don Luis de Quijada to assist the young man, who proved himself a brave and intelligent commander.

Philip and his councillors for a moment considered expelling the *moriscos* from Spain, thus achieving the unity they thought essential to Castile by ridding it of a people who did not conform to the norms of Old Christian society, but rather to those of the Muslim enemy. However they decided to try once again to force their assimilation by breaking up the concentration of *moriscos* in Granada and dispersing them throughout Castile.[15] From detention camps in Granada, the *moriscos* began to march in the winter of 1570–71 to the inland towns and villages designated to receive them. The operation was poorly organized by the council of Castile. Local authorities often proved unprepared or unwilling to accept them, and their reception everywhere was less than warm. The forced dispersal, with all its attendant hardships, continued through 1571 into a second winter before it was completed. More than 80,000 persons altogether were relocated. With great resourcefulness the *moriscos* improved their lot, but remained an alien race in their native Spain. In 1609 Philip III implemented the 'final solution', the forced expulsion of all *moriscos* from the Iberian peninsula.

THE ANNEXATION OF PORTUGAL (1578–83)

The same climate of crusading fervour that prompted the repression of the *moriscos* in Castile drove Dom Sebastian, king of Portugal, to undertake the campaign which cost him his life and brought his uncle, Philip II, the crown of Portugal.

Dom Sebastian, aged twenty-three in 1578, showed interest in little but martial exercises, the hunt and pious devotions. His indifference to women was taken as a sign of impotence, and the schemes of Philip and others for his marriage had tapered off. Philip, with his own claims to Portugal, was hardly averse to Sebastian's self-willed celibacy.

Philip, on the other hand, was opposed to Sebastian's dream of a crusade against Morocco in order to recover the Portuguese fortresses lost to the sherifs of the Saadien dynasty during the preceding generation, and to convert Morocco into a client state of Portugal, under Muhammad el-Motawakkil, the former sherif (deposed in 1576 by his uncle Abd el-Malik, with Ottoman support), who had fled to Lisbon. Philip at the beginning of 1578 was on the verge of obtaining a needed truce with the Turks and wanted nothing to disturb this prospect.

Philip could not dissuade Dom Sebastian from his venture, and was finally constrained to assist his nephew with supplies, ships and Castilian 'volunteers' (though more than half of these were not ready to join Sebastian in time). In June 1578, Sebastian sailed from Lisbon for Morocco.

On 13 August 1578, Philip learned that Sebastian and his army had been annihilated by the Moroccans at Alcázarquivir. In a burst of decisiveness, he ordered his ministers and commanders to stand ready to aid the last Portuguese outposts in Africa (Ceuta, Tangier, Mazagán and Arcila) and to prepare for the eventuality of the death at any time of Sebastian's successor, Cardinal Henry, aged sixty-six and bound by vows of celibacy. By his own reckoning and that of his legists, Philip, as the oldest male descendant of Emanuel the Fortunate, was next after Henry in line for the Portuguese Crown.

Philip's chief rivals for the Portuguese crown were Catalina, duchess of Bragança, the only surviving child of the Infant Dom Duarte, and Dom Antonio, prior of Crato, the bastard son of the Infant Dom Luis by a woman of *converso* stock. The queen mother of France, Catherine de' Medici, unearthed a claim of her own, dating back to the Tuscan Middle Ages, which was flimsy in itself and succeeded only in confounding the aims of French diplomacy in Lisbon. Another candidate, whose claim was perhaps best in strictest terms of legitimacy, was Ranuccio Farnese, the son of Alexander Farnese, prince of Parma (duke in 1586) and Maria of Portugal, Dom Duarte's eldest daughter, who had died in 1576. Ranuccio's claim was not pressed, though none were ignorant of it. His father took command of Philip's army of Flanders in the autumn of 1578, and became acting governor-general of the Netherlands. Farnese, a grandson of Charles V, was dedicated to the cause of the House of Habsburg, embodied in Philip.

The King-Cardinal Henry, fond of the Duchess Catalina but fearful of Philip's power, refused to designate a successor, although he did try to bar the path of the bastard Dom Antonio, whom he loathed. To settle the succession question, he convoked the Portuguese Cortes.

Philip, watching developments in Portugal, prepared both a diplomatic and military offensive. He sent a special embassy headed by the duke of Osuna and Don Cristóbal de Moura to Lisbon to build a party in his favour, and arranged with the sherif of Morocco for the ransom of Portuguese nobles captured at Alcázarquivir, among them the duke of Barçelos, the young son of the duke and duchess of Bragança, whom Philip briefly used as a pawn to induce his mother to drop her claim. The duchess exclaimed that she would prefer the boy in the hands of the Turk, from whom she could rescue him with money alone. Philip, after having the duke of Medina Sidonia entertain Barçelos for some two months, sent him home in March 1580.

In the event that diplomacy would not succeed in winning him the Portuguese crown peacefully, Philip assembled a powerful army in Extremadura, collected an armada at Cadiz and ordered the towns and seigneurs along the frontier to muster their militias. His need of vigorous assistance in preparing for war was a prime factor in his decision to bring Granvelle to Madrid from Rome. Granvelle and the council of war in turn persuaded Philip to bring Alba out of disgrace and put him in command of the main field army.

In January 1580 King-Cardinal Henry died. The Cortes had not yet designated a successor and broke up in confusion. The five governors provided by Henry's will, three of whom favoured Philip, summoned the Cortes to meet again in May. Their sessions opened at Santarém, but were soon transferred to Setúbal because of pestilence and popular disturbances excited by the supporters of Dom Antonio.

Dom Antonio had emerged, despite the late king's efforts to block him, as Philip II's strongest rival. The duchess of Bragança's cause, on the other hand, was ruined by the ineptitude and unpopularity of her husband. Dom Antonio found his chief support among the commons, the Lisbon *conversos* and the lower clergy; Philip found his among the nobility, indebted to him for their ransoms from Morocco, and rich merchants (except for the *conversos*) whose business interests were linked with Seville's.

Dom Antonio and his followers used the confusion caused by the transfer of the Cortes to Setúbal to seize Lisbon, the royal arsenals and the crown treasury. The commons proclaimed him king, while the three governors who favoured Philip fled to Spain, where they proclaimed Philip king and outlawed Dom Antonio.

Philip on hearing the news ordered his armies and armadas forward. In a sharp, brilliantly conceived campaign, the armada, under the marquis of Santa Cruz, joined with the land forces to complete the conquest of Portugal by late autumn. Alba occupied Lisbon, Medina Sidonia overran the Algarve and Sancho Dávila, striking north from Lisbon, occupied Oporto. Philip's diplomacy proved its effectiveness by minimizing resistance. Dom Antonio's one stand, at the head of an army described by Spanish sources as a rabble of artisans, shopkeepers and Jews, led by friars, was quickly crushed by Alba, and Dom Antonio and his chief lieutenant, the count of Vimioso, both wounded, became fugitives, hounded by agents and soldiers directed by Medina Sidonia. In early 1581, they fled to France.

The queen mother, Catherine de' Medici, decided at this point to drop her own fatuous claim to Portugal and support Dom Antonio, with some encouragement from Queen Elizabeth of England. The reasons for this are complex, being involved as they were in Philip's relations with France and England over the revolt of the Netherlands. Dom Antonio thus remained a thorn in Philip's side, working until his death in 1595 to topple Philip from the throne of Portugal.

Between 1580–83, Antonio's supporters held Terceira in the Azores, which threatened the treasure routes from the Indies and India, the lifeline of Philip's empire. Two expeditions, commanded by Santa Cruz, and his naval victory over a Franco-Portuguese fleet outfitted by Catherine de' Medici and Dom Antonio, were required before Terceira was brought forcibly under Philip's sceptre in 1583. Santa Cruz's execution of French captives as pirates and interlopers put a serious strain on Philip's relations with France.

In 1589, Dom Antonio again threatened Philip seriously when he sailed in an English expedition, commanded by Sir Francis Drake, to liberate Portugal. Quick Spanish military response, the loyalty to Philip of the Portuguese magnates (led by the duke of Bragança, the onetime pawn Barçelos) and the indifference of the Portuguese people, who had found Philip's government, left in the hands of Portuguese, to be benign, all worked to frustrate Dom Antonio's hopes. After a few futile weeks near Lisbon, the expedition returned to England, its ranks decimated by skirmishes and disease.[16]

Philip made his formal entry into Portugal in December 1580, accompanied by his favourite nephew, the Archduke Albert. (Ana, his queen, had died that October.) He dressed in Portuguese fashion and tried his best to use the language of his mother. In April 1581 he received the homage of the Portuguese Cortes as King Philip I and swore to uphold the liberties of the kingdom. Since there was no need for Church reform, little heresy and an active Inquisition in Portugal, Philip needed to undertake no major innovations. The institutions of government in Portugal were well developed, especially in the administration of maritime matters. For the sake of good will, he abolished the customs barrier between Castile and Portugal, and wedded the high nobility to his monarchy in the Burgundian manner with collars of the Golden Fleece. In a *carta patente* of 1582, made in response to petitions from the Cortes, he announced that Portuguese alone would administer, under his sceptre, their realm and its overseas possessions, and would continue to enjoy, in line with existing treaties, their traditional monopolies in commerce and fields for missionary and colonizing endeavours. He promised never to summon their Cortes outside Portugal and to establish at his court a *conselho de Portugal* to advise him on Portuguese affairs. The viceroy of Portugal would be a native or a member of the dynasty. When Philip left Portugal for Castile in February 1583, he appointed his nephew, the archduke, and now cardinal, Albert of Austria, his first viceroy of Portugal.

PHILIP II AND THE 'LIBERTIES' OF ARAGON

The generous recognition of customary privileges made by Philip to Portugal suited his temper. He expected the Portuguese and his other subjects to be equally generous towards him and, of course, to share his views. But in Aragon, instead of generous understanding, he found a spirit of contention, especially among the generally poor but numerous nobility. In Aragon and Catalonia, unlike the other parts of Spain, there had been a well-developed and highly articulated feudal system, with its maze of privileges and mutual obligations, which placed the nobility in a privileged position against the crown and over the peasantry. The matter of the *Justicia* is a case in point. Every move by the crown was looked upon by the Aragonese nobles as a threat to their privileged position.

After becoming king, Philip did not visit Aragon until 1563, when he came to swear to uphold the 'liberties' of the kingdom. He next appeared in Aragon in 1585. The Aragonese resented these infrequent appearances, and in 1585 resisted Philip's attempt to incorporate into the royal domain the county of Ribagorza, which stretched into the Pyrenees and was seen by Philip and his advisers as vital to Spain's defence against French Huguenots from neighbouring Béarn and Languedoc.

Philip decided in 1588 to appoint a viceroy who would press the Ribagorza matter, and designated a Castilian, the marquis of Almenara, cousin of the treasurer of the council of Aragon, the count of Chinchón, to procede to Zaragoza and obtain the approval of the *Justicia* to his taking office. The Aragonese claimed that Philip could only appoint an Aragonese as viceroy; Philip insisted that it was only logical that his person should be represented by 'a person of his choice, not of his subjects'.

In May 1590 the *Justicia* accepted Philip's argument, but the younger nobility of Aragon did not. At this precise moment, Philip's problems involving Ribagorza and Almenara's appointment were exacerbated by the case of Antonio Pérez, who arrived in Zaragoza after his flight from a Madrid jail, and claimed the privilege of an Aragonese subject to be tried in the open court of the *Justicia* rather than a closed court in Castile. With him he brought secret state papers, which he began to broadcast, creating a sensation. The defenders of the 'liberties' of Aragon rallied to his cause, and threatened Philip with another 'Flanders' if he did not back down.

Philip, not wishing to proceed against Pérez in the *Justicia*'s court, had the Inquisition charge him with heresy, blasphemy and sodomy, crimes which came under its jurisdiction (and given Pérez's Renaissance life-style were not without foundation). The attempt to remove Pérez from the custody of the *Justicia* to that of the Inquisition, which had prior jurisdiction, led, however, to rioting. Almenara was injured and died. Philip and his advisers, in response, moved a Castilian army, which they had meant to use against Henri of Navarre in France, to the Aragonese frontier, while they successfully persuaded the majority of Aragonese to shun the commotion in Zaragoza. A second altercation in Zaragoza in September, caused by a second effort to move Pérez, brought this army across the border. Zaragoza was speedily occupied and the ringleaders of the tumults summarily executed, including the young *Justicia*, Juan de Lanuza, who had succeeded his father in the middle of the unrest and had been persuaded by his peers to take charge of the defence of their 'liberties'. Pérez fled to France, where he began his life in exile. Aided by French Huguenots, he tried in 1592 to raise Aragon in revolt, but failed. He then turned to the pen as a means of attacking his former master.

Late in 1592 Philip convoked the Cortes of Aragon at Tarazona to have them revise their constitution, so that a wilful few should no longer be able to oppose royal authority successfully and within the law. The *Justicia* would henceforth serve at the king's pleasure; a majority, not unanimity, would henceforth suffice to carry each chamber; and – underscoring the role of adolescents in the commotions – nobles under twenty could no longer sit with their estate. For the rest, Philip left the Aragonese constitution as it had been. Only a minority had participated in the altercations, and Philip wanted to keep the majority content. He also wanted to show the Catalans and Valencians, who had watched events in Aragon closely but had not stirred, that he meant to do no more than was reasonable. He did not want to appear the tyrant des-cribed by Pérez, a dissembler who used murder and poison in politics and rode roughshod, with the aid of his Castilian henchmen, over the liberties of his subjects.

In dealing with the problem of unity and disunity in the Iberian peninsula Philip worked hard for unity. Bringing Portugal (with its empire) into dynastic union with the other kingdoms of the peninsula was in fact the greatest triumph of his reign. On the other hand, his

solutions to the *morisco* and Aragonese problems proved in the long run
to be failures. The repression of Aragon was looked upon as much as a
Castilian act as a royal one and helped to further resentment of Castilians
throughout the peninsula, which led to the revolt in 1640 of Catalonia
and Portugal, and has continued since to plague the history of Spain. Yet
in both cases, the failures are of the people and, to an extent, of the rulers
who succeeded Philip. Philip II had realized the dreams of his ancestors
of recreating Visigothic *Hispania*; he had changed the constitution of
Aragon with the ideals of justice and the common defence in mind, and
had not expelled the *moriscos*, but had sincerely tried to provide for their
assimilation into the Old Christian society he thought best for them.

THE PEACE OF ITALY AND THE DEFENCE OF THE MEDITERRANEAN

In a classic study the great nineteenth-century historian Leopold von
Ranke perceptively linked the Spanish and Ottoman empires, the two
great state complexes which dominated Mediterranean history in the
sixteenth and seventeenth centuries.[17] His study dealt chiefly with political institutions, diplomacy and war, in the 'scientific' manner that he
pioneered, working critically with original sources yet illuminating
everything with brilliant flashes of insight. In 1949 Fernand Braudel
published a new study, *La Méditerranée et le monde méditerranéen à
l'époque de Philippe II* (second ed. 1966), again dealing with the two state
complexes and their world, in which he has utilized in masterly fashion
all the new techniques developed by the historical, social and geographic
sciences since von Ranke's time, giving us a study far larger in scope than
von Ranke's, and at least equally full of provocative analyses and
conjectures.

Braudel finds the conflict of empires overriding in a seemingly contradictory fashion, a world and its peoples which had much in common:
climate, the lie of the land, basic economies, social structures, lifestyles
and, above all, the great Mediterranean Sea which touched all their
shores and served as a bond among them.

What divided them was history, and the force which held the Mediterranean peoples in two fundamentally irreconcilable camps was religion:
Christianity and Islam, each with its values and beliefs, and attitudes
towards those who did not believe in them. Each had its 'Holy War':
the crusade; the *jihad*.

Whatever material motives were involved in the developments of the
Spanish and Ottoman empires, religion served as their justification.
Religion and opposition to the Turks provided the most widely felt and

popular bonds which held the peoples of Spain and southern Italy together, and the tradition of holy war gave a *raison d'être* for a top-heavy Church and nobility (the 'military' estate, *brazo* or *braccio militar*). The tradition of the crusade was a powerful part of the mentality of Philip II, his associates and his subjects, who regarded the Turks, and Muslims in general, as their natural enemies. It took compelling reasons of state and considerable soul-searching for Philip II to consider even an armistice with the Turks.

In the struggle with the Turks, Philip's south Italian dominions were viewed from Madrid as Christendom's front line, from which projected the bastions of Malta and La Goleta (controlling the harbour of Tunis), and from which ventured Philip's galleys, generally mustered at Messina, towards North Africa and the Levant. Alongside Philip's own squadrons (of Spain, Naples and Sicily) the warships of his allies – Genoa, Savoy, the papacy, Tuscany and Monaco – usually sailed, often subsidized by Spain.

Despite a need for cooperation, there was a fierce competition among the Spaniards and Italians for command of Philip's Mediterranean armada and some differences over how it should be employed, though generally the allies agreed that control of the western Mediterranean took first priority. The supreme command after the death in 1560 of Charles V's admiral, Andrea Doria, was taken in succession by the Castilian Don García de Toledo (1564–68), Don John of Austria (1571–78) and Doria's grand-nephew, Gian Andrea Doria (1583–1606).

The appointment of the second Doria, at the instigation of Granvelle, who was trying to preserve the monarchy's multinational character, precipitated a clash at the court of Madrid with Philip's Castilian ministers which cost the cardinal much of his influence. Philip tried to placate the Castilians by making their candidate for the post, Santa Cruz, a grandee of Spain and captain-general of the Ocean-Sea (Atlantic). This did not stop the marquis from snubbing the cardinal, nor the struggle for office between Spaniards and Italians, which went increasingly in favour of Spaniards. Italian resentment was neatly summed up in a remark about the defeat of the 'Invincible Armada', largely an Iberian production, by the Venetian ambassador, who attributed it to 'the want of experienced Italian men and officers, of whom there were none aboard the fleet'.[18]

Command rivalries in the Mediterranean fleet were hardly Philip's only problem in holding together the Hispano-Italian coalition against the Turks. Keeping the independent Italian states in the coalition and maintaining the *Pax Hispanica*, by preventing them from renewing ancient quarrels among themselves, were constant tasks of his diplomacy. The papacy, despite differences between Philip and succeeding popes, was morally committed to a leading role in the crusade against Islam. The papal commander, Marcantonio Colonna, was a staunch supporter of Philip and his house, and advocated Italian participation in shaping the policies of the monarchy. In the crusade, however, which gripped the imagination of Counter Reformation Rome and Italian fighting men, Philip often seemed a reluctant partner, especially after the troubles in the Netherlands forced him in 1578 to make a truce with the sultan, which he subsequently renewed.

The other Italian states did not have a moral commitment to the crusade equal to that of the papacy. Nor were they, in Philip's view, dependable, with the exception of Genoa, whose bonds to the Monarchy were not moral, but monetary. Of his customary allies, Tuscany proved the most difficult. In 1557 Philip had bought the allegiance of Duke Cosimo I by ceding him Siena; but in the 1560s Cosimo fished in the troubled waters of Corsica, where rebellion had broken out against Genoese rule, and Philip had to use threat to restrain him. Then in 1567 Cosimo accepted from Pius V the title grand duke of Tuscany, which irritated both Philip and Maximilian II, who resented papal intervention in the affairs of the Holy Roman Empire, of which Tuscany was still considered part. On Cosimo's death in 1574, however, Philip and Maximilian recognized the title grand duke for his heir Francesco I (ruled 1574–87) who in his turn proved a faithful servant of Habsburg interests and a source of loans for Philip. Francesco's brother, Piero de' Medici, looked after Tuscan interests at the court of Madrid, and in 1580 commanded the Italian contingents in the invasion of Portugal. Grand Duke Ferdinand (reigned 1587–1609) broke the bonds with Philip II and set his own course, when in 1589 he recognized Henri IV as king of France.

Philip's full intervention in the French civil wars in 1590 represented a turning point for the *Pax Hispanica* in Italy. The Turks began to stir in the Balkans and in 1593 attacked Habsburg Hungary. But Philip had committed his forces to the French civil wars, the Netherlands and the Atlantic, and had little to spare for the Mediterranean. In 1595 he refused to recognize Rome's absolution of Henri IV. Henri's Protestantism had been Rome's and Italy's only reason for respecting Philip's intervention in France; now Italy and the papacy became exasperated with the ageing king who had long dominated Italian affairs. Doria's cautious foray towards the Levant in 1596 accomplished nothing and failed to placate the Italians. A papal diplomat remarked bitterly that with a quarter of the troops Philip mobilized in northern France and Flanders great things could be done against the Turks.[19] Philip's power position in Italy shrank to include no more than his own dominions, Savoy (his ally in invading France) and Genoa. Even Parma, long loyal under Duke Ottavio (d. 1586), the Duchess Margaret, Philip's half-sister (d. 1586), and their son Alexander (d. 1592), began to go its own way under Duke Ranuccio (1569–1622), who resented Philip's interference in his marriage plans.

Venice was not Philip's ally, but rather stood deliberately independent of the Catholic Monarchy and the coalition it headed. Philip, however, maintained respectful relations with the Serene Republic, and its ambassadors to him have provided us with perceptive and generally favourable observations on his statecraft. Venice was the greatest Italian naval power, possessing more war galleys than Philip, but because of difficulties in manning and maintaining them, kept only part of them in commission, save during emergencies. The republic did not want war, especially not a crusade against the Turks, because of its business interests in the Levant.[20]

Like Venice, the Dalmatian republic of Ragusa (Dubrovnik) preferred to do business with the Turks than to fight them. The Ragusans' pursuit of profit, however, led them in 1590 to sign a contract with Philip II to provide him with a dozen galleons to help him rebuild his armada, despite protests and threats by the sultan.[21] The galleons, which arrived in Cadiz in 1595, sailed against Ireland in 1596. Half were lost in the storms which drove the armada back to its ports.

Philip II understood the commercial interests and exposed situation of the Adriatic republics, even though his own attitudes and positions committed him to at least an aggressive defensiveness if not to an outright crusade. Yet in 1558, when he was battling Henri II of France in western Europe, and the French and Turks had landed an army on Corsica, he discussed with his uncle, the Emperor Ferdinand I, the possibility of being discreetly included in a truce which Ferdinand found it necessary to make with the Ottomans. The sultan, however, rejected Philip's inclusion.

With the signing in 1559 of the Peace of Câteau Cambrésis, Philip ordered an end to explorations for a truce with the Sublime Porte, and instead gave his assent to a proposal of the duke of Medinaceli, viceroy of Sicily, and the grand master of the knights of Malta for the recapture of Tripoli, lost in 1551 by the knights. Should this succeed, the recovery of Bougie (lost in 1555) would follow, the Monarchy's barrier across the central Mediterranean would be restored, and Algiers would become isolated. The 'Enterprise of Algiers' could then proceed, avenging Charles V's defeat of 1541 and turning the western Mediterranean into a corsair-free lake, dominated by the Catholic Monarchy.

But the proposed expedition turned into a disaster. Medinaceli, after wasting time in its preparation, sailed early in 1560 to the island of Djerba, rather than to Tripoli, and began to build an advance base. The Turks caught him there, sunk twenty-eight of his galleys, and in July forced the surrender of 10,000 troops left stranded on the island. The duke and his admiral, Gian Andrea Doria, barely escaped with their lives.

Nearly half the galleys available to Philip were lost at Djerba, and in 1562 twenty-five more sunk in an autumn storm off Málaga. Philip dunned money from his Cortes, *parlamenti* and the papacy to make good his losses, and by 1564 Don García de Toledo had ninety galleys at sea. Fortunately the Turks had allowed Philip time to recover, having other matters to contend with. The Barbary corsairs were not so generous, but neither were they so formidable. None the less, they raided the coasts of Philip's dominions with impunity and in 1563 Hassan Pasha (son of the famous Khair ed Din-Barbarossa) led a massive Algerian attack against Oran.

It was against the corsairs that Don García struck when in 1564 he occupied Peñón Vélez de la Gomera, a massive rock off the African coast opposite Málaga, used as a corsair haven. Pope Pius IV, however, was not impressed: 'What is Peñón,' he asked Don García that winter, 'compared to Algiers?'[22]

On the margin of Don García's report of the audience with Pius Philip wrote, 'The Pope has his eyes on us.' Philip knew that his performance was being constantly judged by the Holy Father, the moral leader of Catholic Europe, who granted Philip vital revenues, despite their many differences.

But attempting to satisfy the papacy with the kinds of crusade it repeatedly called for – something grand to liberate Constantinople or the Holy Land from the heathen – was, however, out of the question. For one thing, even had Philip commanded the necessary resources, he faced too many problems at once to commit all of his resources to one. Above all, he was concerned about the growth of Huguenot power in France, which threatened the security of the Netherlands where, more-over, he was forced to make one concession after another to opponents of his policies, because he was engrossed in Mediterranean problems and could spare neither sufficient money nor soldiery to use force. Since he could not ignore this situation, he dared not commit his forces too deeply to fighting the Turks, but rather had to keep them on the defensive in the western Mediterranean. The initiative in the Mediterranean, which Philip had tried to seize with the expedition against Tripoli, therefore remained with the Ottomans, and permitted them to shift their attention at will from east to west, from the Balkans, the Mediterranean and North Africa to Persia, the Caucasus and the Red Sea, without being disturbed by Philip.

In 1565, the Ottomans turned west and in May struck at the Catholic Monarchy's central Mediterranean barrier with an invasion of Malta. It was September before the relief force, organized by Philip II and his commanders, appeared off the island. The knights had held out and the Turks, suffering from disease, had already begun to withdraw. In Rome Philip's efforts were derided, yet in truth Philip's forces had mobilized as quickly as distance and the demands of defending many shores permitted. Having had to repair over the past five years so many galley losses, Philip did not want to risk his forces in battle before they had all assembled and looked superior to those of the sultan.

The repulse of the attack on Malta brought no respite in the war. Intelligence received in Madrid during the winter of 1565–66 revealed to Philip and his councillors Suleiman's design for a massive two-headed offensive against Christendom: the sultan himself would lead an army against Austria, while the fleet would sail into the central Mediterranean to avenge its defeat at Malta. Philip, who was now contemplating sending an army to the Low Countries to deal with dissent there, had to hold his available forces on the alert in the Mediterranean, while finding money to aid Maximilian II. The feared offensive in fact achieved little, and in September Suleiman died in Hungary. For the next three years, while Selim II, aided by Suleiman's grand vizier Mehemet Sokoli, assumed power in Constantinople and prepared for his own campaigns, the Turks did little to disturb the Mediterranean.

This gave Philip the respite needed to dispatch an army under Alba to the Netherlands, and a free hand in subduing the revolt of the *moriscos*. For the second time in his reign, he sent out peace feelers to Constantinople through third parties, but for the second time the sultan rejected them, insisting upon open and formal negotiations.

In 1570 the Turks renewed their belligerent activities in the Mediterranean. In January, the Ottoman beylerbey of Algiers, Euldj Ali, seized control of Tunis, and turned out Philip's client, the Hafsid Hamida. The Spanish garrison at La Goleta was thus isolated and Charles V's conquest of 1535 nearly undone. At the same time, the sultan demanded that Venice surrender Cyprus, the invasion of which by Turkish troops began in July.

The Venetians by a narrow vote decided for war rather than surrender, thus ending thirty years of lucrative peace. They began to look for allies and Pope Pius V seized the opportunity to forge a Holy League against the Turks of the Catholic Monarchy, Venice, the Papal States and the rest of Italy.

Philip II's advisers told the king that between Granada and the Netherlands he had difficulties enough. Granvelle wrote him from Rome that the Venetians could take care of themselves. But Philip, apart from his desire to assist the Holy Father at war, saw more clearly than his councillors the gains he might derive from the League. Once Cyprus was safe, the fleet of the allies could be used to recover Tunis and conquer Algiers for Spain. Philip also knew that not to join the Holy League would undermine his 'reputation' in Italy and thus impair the *Pax Hispanica*.

Philip carefully instructed his negotiators in Rome, Don Juan de Zúñiga, and the cardinals Granvelle and Pacheco, to obtain for him the right to nominate the commander-in-chief of the Holy League armada (through whom he might control its operations), and the agreement of the pope and Venice to the eventual employment of the armada against Tunis or Algiers. His plan was opposed not only by Venice, whose interests lay in the Levant, but also by the pope, whose ambitions included winning Greeks back to Rome and even the recovery of the Holy Land. Philip's stubbornness won him at least partial success: on 20 May 1571 he received the right to nominate the commander-in-chief, and agreed in his turn to contribute half the money and forces. Venice would contribute one-third; the papacy, one-sixth. Any conquests made in Barbary would fall to Philip, any made in the Levant, to Venice. The League was to be perpetual, with the present arrangements remaining in force for three years.

But by the time Philip learned of the agreement (on 6 June) he had become highly disturbed by apparent cooperation between France and England, and by the rapprochement in France between the government of the queen mother and the Huguenots, who openly aided Calvinist insurgents in the Netherlands. The French had reinforced their garrisons in Saluzzo, tried to keep Venice out of the Holy League, and encouraged Cosimo de' Medici in his defiance of Philip and Maximilian. None the less, Philip was committed to the League. He designated Don John of Austria commander-in-chief, instructing him to proceed with prudence. It had taken Philip ten years of haggling with Cortes, *parlamenti* and two successive popes to get the money to provide one hundred galleys, manned with soldiers, sailors and the wretched oarsmen, convicted by his judges, captured in battle or rounded up by press gangs (as *buenaboya*, volunteer rowers). He did not want Don John to lose all through rashness, which would throw the defences of Christendom back onto the beaches of Philip's dominions and those of his allies, until the damages could once more be laboriously repaired.

Don John, with his Spanish galleys, joined the Italians in early August at Messina, and through hard work and determination got the allied armada to sea by mid-September. Philip learned of the ensuing battle and its result while attending vespers on the eve of All Saints: the Venetian ambassador interrupted him with cries of 'victory!' Don John's armada had destroyed the Ottoman fleet at Lepanto. Of some 230 Turkish galleys and galleots only Euldj Ali's thirty-five Algerians had escaped. Over 100 Turkish vessels were captured and the Ottoman admiral, Ali Pasha, slain. The magnitude of this victory obscured, save in Venetian eyes, the fall of Famagusta, their last stronghold on Cyprus.

Lepanto, though significant in the sense that Spaniards and Italians learned that they could beat the Turks in even battle, proved, however, an empty victory. Philip (through secret orders to Don John) kept the League armada at Messina into the summer of 1572 because of his anxieties over a Huguenot incursion into the Netherlands and the overrunning of Holland and Zeeland by Dutch insurgents. He feared that the French and English would soon invade the troubled provinces in force.

The sultan in the meantime rebuilt his fleet and in the same summer of 1572, Euldj Ali sailed the Aegean with almost as many ships as had formed the fleet at Lepanto. Never was the ability of the Ottoman Empire to mobilize resources on a scale impossible for Christian rulers more clearly demonstrated, giving credibility to the claim made in the West that the sultan was the lord of slaves, while Christian kings had to contend with free subjects.

Don John objected to Philip's orders, and Pope Gregory XIII, elected in May and dedicated to the work of his late predecessor, threatened to revoke the 'Three Graces'. Neither believed that the king of France would attack the Netherlands. Before learning of the papal threat Philip gave in to Don John's request that he be allowed to sail to the Levant; but it was too late to keep the confidence of his allies or permit Don John to accomplish anything. Early in 1573 the Venetians, who were suffering from the loss of business in the Levant, saw they could gain nothing allied with Philip II and quit the League.

The St Bartholomew's Day Massacre (August 1572) temporarily

removed the threat of war with France. Philip now permitted Don John to go ahead with the Tunis plan. Late in 1573 Tunis was re-conquered and a client ruler, the Hafsid Moulay Muhammad, Hamida's brother, established. Don John, contrary to orders, then began to build a citadel in the city of Tunis itself, while seeking papal support for his desire to become king of Tunisia. Philip, caught up in the financial crisis brought about by his need to maintain a powerful armada in the Mediterranean and mobilize over 60,000 troops in the Netherlands, paid little attention to Don John's activities.

Unrest in Genoa, related to the financial crisis, forced Don John and Doria the next summer to hold their galleys off the Ligurian coast. Euldj Ali with some 250 warships attacked Tunis in July and landed 40,000 soldiers. By September Tunis, the new citadel and La Goleta had all fallen.

Without the Venetians, Don John did not have adequate forces for an effective response. In 1575, Philip declared bankruptcy; and in 1576, confronted by a mutiny of his own army in the Netherlands and the collapse there of his government, he ordered his half-brother to Brussels to try to salvage the situation. The Netherlands assumed absolute priority in his policies, and once more he sought to obtain a truce with the sultan.

The Turks in 1576 continued their advance in North Africa with the subversion of Morocco. Operating from Algiers Euldj Ali assisted two exiled Moroccan princes, Abd el-Malik and Ahmed, to overthrow their nephew, the sherif Muhammad el-Motawakkil (1574–76), who fled to Portugal. Abd el-Malik became sherif, and permitted a garrison of janissaries in Fez.

However, the death of Selim II in 1575 coincided with a shift of Turkish concerns from the Mediterranean to the frontier with Persia. The dominant army faction in the Divan was disposed towards a truce in the Mediterranean, and when Philip made a move, this time more directly than before, his agents were received. In March 1578 Giovanni Margliani, a Milanese sent by Philip, obtained a truce of two years' duration, at the price of Philip's entering into formal diplomatic relations with the sultan. Philip issued credentials to the Catalan Don Juan de Rocafull and ordered him to Constantinople. In Venice, Rocafull took sick and went no farther. Philip sent no other ambassador. The Turks, however, honoured the truce, which they needed as badly as did Philip. In 1579, an assassin struck down Mehemet Sokoli, the chief spokesman in the Divan of the faction that favoured war in the Mediterranean, composed largely of Greek seamen and exiled Iberian Jews. Euldj Ali in

Algiers was now alone in favouring the advance of Ottoman banners through Morocco to the Atlantic.

The defeat of Dom Sebastian by the Moroccans in 1578 at first seemed a triumph for Euldj Ali's design, but soon proved otherwise. His client, the sherif Ahmed el-Malik, died of apoplexy during the battle, and the deposed Muhammad el-Motawakkil fell alongside Dom Sebastian. Ahmed, Abd el-Malik's brother, was acclaimed undisputed sherif by the Moroccan warriors on the battlefield and given the name el-Mansour, 'the victorious'. He soon grew rich from the ransoms paid for the release of Portuguese fidalgos, and began to display a growing independence of Euldj Ali.

Euldj Ali wanted to invade Morocco to impose direct Ottoman rule, but the Divan, not wanting to disturb the truce with Philip, denied him sufficient forces. His intentions were, however, known to the new sherif who sought a mutual defence pact with Philip, promising him in return the Moroccan port of Larache. Philip agreed, and ordered Medina Sidonia to prepare an expedition to occupy Larache.[23]

When the sherif realized that Euldj Ali was too weak to present any real danger, he put Philip's envoys off with endless diplomatic arabesques, and the promised delivery of Larache did not take place.

The sherif's success in escaping Ottoman overlordship led to growing restlessness in Barbary, where the Turks had never been popular. In 1583, the corsair captains of Algiers gained control of the Algerian government from Euldj Ali's lieutenants. Euldj Ali, occupied in the Levant, where he – the last of the great beylerbeys – died in 1587, could do nothing about it, and effective Ottoman efforts to dominate North Africa died with him. From Philip's point of view, suffering the stings of corsairs was preferable to confronting the might of the Turks.

Essentially, the two great state complexes, the Catholic Monarchy and the Ottoman Empire, had disengaged after two generations of internecine warfare, one to turn west and north-west, the other to become a land power and fight against Persia or in the Balkans. On the whole victory had gone to the Ottomans.[24]

During Philip's reign the Catholic Monarchy had lost Tripoli and Bougie, then Tunis; only Oran, Melilla and the last Portuguese fortresses remained, and all cost more than they were worth in anything save pride. Venice had lost Cyprus. We can see several myths put to rest. Lepanto, however dramatic a victory, did not save Christendom; and Philip's truce with Constantinople did not represent a stalemate. The Turks signed it *after* they had brought North Africa, from Egypt (1516) to Morocco (1576), under their control, either directly or as client states. This is not to deny that Philip II might have stopped them if he had not been faced with so many problems elsewhere, any more than to argue that he might have crushed the revolt of the Netherlands if he had not had to contend with the Turks.

But Barbary, by the mid-1580s, was beginning to go its own way independently of the Turks although Tripoli, Tunis and Algiers accepted Ottoman governors, while Morocco did not. Morocco was indeed crucial and became a symbol of Barbary independence. The sherif (the title meant descendant of the Prophet) rejected the universalist claims of the Ottoman sultan to leadership of the Islamic world.

The 'Enemy Number One' for the Turks, as for Philip's monarchy, was distance, compounded in the case of the Turks by their Byzantine determination to run everything from Constantinople, even as in Philip's case it was compounded by the bureaucratic tendencies of his own government, which kept him and his court in Madrid. There were limits to how far a sixteenth-century state could extend from its centre, where its motivating will and monetary resources were collected, and still remain effective in the face of serious resistance. The Mediterranean world taking shape in the last years of Philip's reign ceased moving with the rhythms of the monumental struggles of the empires at its eastern and western ends.

There was a brief moment of excitement in 1596 when Philip ordered Doria to proceed with extreme caution towards the Levant with his galleys, in response to the clamours of the pope and Italy that he do something against the Turks who in 1593 had renewed the war in Hungary. Nothing much came of it: as Fernand Braudel states, from now on the Mediterranean was *hors de la grande histoire*.[25]

The North Atlantic had replaced the Mediterranean as the centre of the historical stage, and Philip II had turned his attention almost entirely towards the problems of the states and peoples of the North Atlantic seaboard of Europe. With the Castilians and Turks occupied elsewhere, the Mediterranean became more parochial, its peoples increasingly concerned with only local matters. And as the North Africans became more and more independent of Ottoman control, so the Italians grew ever more restless under the control of Madrid. Their long-distance commerce began in the meantime to pass into the hands of the English and the Dutch.

Philip II, by effectively abandoning the Mediterranean world, turned his back on the inclinations of his Spanish subjects, who still considered North Africa a field for expansion. They resented Philip's commitment

of the resources of his southern Catholic Monarchy to pursue the old
interests of Burgundy in defence of the Netherlands.

THE REVOLT OF THE NETHERLANDS

No episode in Philip's reign has been so much studied as the revolt of the
Netherlands, and rightly so. If the government the rebels established in
the provinces wrested from Philip II seems at first glance a medieval
anachronism, the motivating spirit of their republic was soon pre-
dominantly modern. Power passed from the hands of the princes, the
nobility and Church institutions, with the burghers enjoying a limited
and inferior role in its exercise, into the hands of burgher business
corporations, which proceeded to govern in the methodical, rational,
secular, competitive and exploitive fashion we associate with the
modern Western temper. The numbers of men involved in corporate
business activities, in town and country, added to the number of land-
owners, made the new regime considerably more representative of
the full life of those provinces than had been the regime of Philip II,
which was in essence one of bureaucracy, nobility and Church. But the
impulse to revolt against Philip's regime did not initially come in its
strongest form from the burghers, but rather from the nobility which
wished to be above, not collateral with, the bureaucracy and Church
institutions.

In historical literature – excepting Catholic apologies for Philip II
and traditional Spanish accounts – the myth that Philip II meant to
impose a despotic regime on the Netherlands in order to make them into
a base of operations from which he would re-Catholicize Protestant
lands by force has tended to obscure historic realities. Philip had no such
plan and the regime he had in mind, though highly centralized and
tending towards absolutism, was to be under the law in the service of
justice and right, not a despotism (or tyranny) in the contemporary sense
of arbitrary government, outside or above the law. This myth is none
the less important because many of Philip II's Protestant contemporaries
fully believed it.

Instead we find what one usually discovers in history, a complex and
interrelated series of events, in which accident plays as much a part as
design, where the result and its ramifications turn out to be distinctly
different from what anyone had foreseen. The factors involved were
many: religious convictions, political and economic interests, personal
loyalties, the wilfulness of participants and general attitudes and desires
in regard to change – 'novelties' as one would have said then. Yet

underlying these, and conditioning them, was the powerful and in-
stinctive desire of most men to maintain a predictable and familiar social
order in which their status and security were not jeopardized; and if they
found this dangerously threatened, they were willing to forgo all other
considerations to maintain it.

Those willing to risk all were few, and they succeeded largely where
they brought advantages without jeopardizing the fundamental order of
society. The republic which emerged from the revolt was not one in
which the social order had been overturned, but rather one in which the
existing society of burghers and middling gentry had been liberated
from the larger Netherlands, where a powerful high nobility, a Church
which Philip II greatly enlarged, and an entrenched class of *rentiers*
proved on the whole unsympathetic to new economic developments.
The ten 'obedient' southern provinces which remained under Philip's
sceptre did so largely because in them, the nobility, the clergy and the
rich (who were more numerous there at the outbreak of the revolt),
and many men of the middling sort feared that the social order was in
jeopardy of being overturned by the 'low people' of the numerous
manufacturing towns, led by radical Calvinists who envisioned a new,
godly order of society. They sought security in the re-establishment of
the familiar order, Roman Catholic and under Philip's sceptre, even
though they were aware that in the course of events his regime had
become increasingly directed from Madrid, not from Brussels. It was the
understanding and exploitation of this fear by Philip's most skilful
governor-general, Alexander Farnese, which made it possible to recover
ten of the seventeen provinces, including the two most turbulent
(Flanders and Brabant), which in 1577 had been united in opposition to
Philip's policies. It is hard to imagine that Farnese would have succeeded,
even with his powerful army of Flanders, against the resistance of the
entire population or even a majority of it. Too many in fact had come to
detest the rebels more than a 'Spanish' regime.

On the other hand, the provinces where the revolt succeeded, especially those which became its heart – Holland and Zeeland – had no
big manufacturing towns and were less affected by social turmoil.
Persons there who disliked the new political and religious order did not
feel dangerously threatened in their status or property. They were not
desperately awaiting the opportunity to join with Philip's forces to
bring down the rebel government. In fact in the early stages the rebels
were able to advance largely as liberators, since the particular regime of
the duke of Alba had become highly unpopular because of his attempts to
introduce an innovative and higher system of taxation. Geography,

especially the line of the great rivers (the Rhine, Maas and Waal) helped in the first desperate years of the Dutch revolt to hinder the operations of Philip II's armies, but the steady intervention of the French and English, officially and unofficially, for religious, commercial and strategic considerations, was equally important in preventing Philip's suppression of the revolt. None the less Farnese might still have reconquered Holland and Zeeland were it not for full-scale English intervention after 1585, followed five years later by Philip II's decision to give his own intervention in the civil war in France priority over operations against the rebel provinces. By the mid-1590s, the Dutch republic had developed a sense of identity, considerable maritime power and wealth and a tough, well-led army; and it had also been recognized by other powers and had thus entered the community of European states, from which Philip could no longer remove it through force of arms.

Philip had no understanding of the deeper problems of the Netherlands, but he did have some ideas for improvements in the organization of Church and government, which he had hoped to realize during his residence in the Low Countries (August 1555–August 1559). The war with France, inherited from Charles V, prevented the realization of the reforms planned; and Philip's need for money to conduct the war brought him in 1558 into an unpleasant encounter with the States General of the Netherlands. The States voted him a nine years' subsidy, but insisted on collecting the money themselves and on overseeing its disbursement. This Philip considered an infringement on his sovereign rights, though he had to accept it in order to get the money.

After the Peace of Câteau Cambrésis, Philip was in a hurry to return to Spain, where he believed he would find more money without strings than in the Netherlands. Spain also needed the presence of its reigning king. Since Charles had left in 1543, the peninsula had been governed by regents. As his governor-general of the Netherlands Philip appointed, on the advice of Granvelle and Alba, his half-sister Margaret, duchess of Parma, who, though born in the Netherlands, had spent most of her life in Italy and knew little about them. Her appointment annoyed the Netherlands magnates, led by William prince of Orange, who favoured Philip's cousin Christine, dowager duchess of Lorraine, whose son-in-law Orange hoped to become. But neither Alba nor Granvelle trusted the ambitious young prince, who would probably have controlled the government had Christine become governess-general. Orange's extensive estates, stretching from the North Sea to the Rhône valley, appeared to them another potential 'Middle Kingdom', which the arrogant prince might try to realize at Philip's expense. For this reason Philip himself blocked Orange's suit for the hand of a daughter of Lorraine.

Orange is a very important figure since his leadership of the opposition to Philip II's policies was crucial to the progress of the revolt. Born in Dillenburg in 1533 he was the eldest son of the count of Nassau, a Lutheran. In 1544 he inherited the vast estates of his cousin René, prince of Orange, converted to Catholicism for the sake of this inheritance, and joined the court of Charles V. The Emperor became extremely fond of William, who was handsome and agreeable, and at his abdication chose to lean on the young man's shoulders when walking to his place in the ceremony. William was irritated when Christine did not become governess-general, angry when he discovered that Margaret had been instructed to consult first with Granvelle, and outraged when he learnt that Philip had ruined his marriage plans. He now arranged for his marriage to Anne of Saxony, a Lutheran and daughter of Duke Moritz who in 1551 had turned against Charles V. This made Philip and Granvelle furious, but they dared not interfere for a second time in the marriage plans of the influential prince.

There clearly was a powerful personal dimension to the conflict developing between Philip, who hid behind the dignity of his office, and William, who in his *Apologia* (1580) wrote with much personal rancour against Philip. It cannot be denied that William, over the years, matured into a more compassionate and sympathetic human being than Philip. The role of each was defined by the larger issues of the age, in regard to religion, the nature of government and national awareness.

By Philip's instruction, Margaret's regime was centred upon an inner council (referred to as the *consulta*) composed of Granvelle from the council of state, Count Berlaymont, president of the council of finance, and Viglius, president of the privy council (justice department). Granvelle the cleric, whose life like that of his father was dedicated to the service of Charles V and Philip II, Berlaymont, an impoverished nobleman with many offspring to feed and place, and Viglius, Latinist and legist schooled in Roman Imperial Law, were all firm believers in the merits of a centralized princely regime.

Such regimes, their opponents, led by Orange and Count Egmont, believed, had elsewhere – Naples, Castile, France, England – reduced the nobility to vile subservience, because princes had been misguided by lawyers. They were determined to prevent this state of affairs from happening in the Netherlands, by insisting upon their birthright to counsel the prince, by holding tightly to their control of the militia and law enforcement in the provinces and by denying the government an effective armed force in time of peace, when it might be used to impose the prince's will on his own subjects. For their own reasons, including dislike of paying taxes, the burgher delegates to the States General followed the lead of the magnates, and (if Granvelle is correct) even influenced them strongly.[26]

Philip's intention to leave a garrison of 3,000 Spanish veterans in the Low Countries after his departure therefore caused an outcry during his last meeting in August 1559 with the States General at Ghent. In the face of their threat to cut off the nine years' subsidy, he agreed to remove the Spanish troops, but he did not do so until the end of 1560 when the menace of the French-supported Mary Queen of Scots to the throne of England had subsided, and when he needed the men in the Mediterranean.

Philip left the Low Countries by sea on 23 August 1559. In retrospect his departure marked the beginning of the end to the age of Burgundian glory which had opened with Philip the Bold, reached its apogee with Philip the Good, and closed with Philip the Prudent. When Charles V first sailed for Spain, the Netherlands thought that fortune had brought them an empire; when Philip II sailed, little more than forty years later, they had the sinking feeling that they had become part of a Spanish empire.

Philip had hardly left when petty infighting over patronage and appointments to office began to divide seriously the Brussels government, with Granvelle, Berlaymont and Viglius opposed to Orange and Egmont. These smaller issues were soon eclipsed by one large question, which commanded the attention of the entire population: the reform of the Netherlands episcopacy. This issue led almost inexorably to the first outbreak of revolt in 1566.

The government had long contemplated enlarging the number of bishoprics in the Netherlands from four to eighteen in order better to combat heresy and minister to the faithful. A greater Church would also give the central regime, which controlled episcopal appointments, more leverage throughout the country and – since the new bishops would take their seats in the estates – more influence in the provincial assemblies and the States General. To ensure control of the new sees by the Netherlands government, the Low Countries were to be made into a single ecclesiastical province (previously they had been divided between Rheims and Cologne), with primacy vested in the archbishop of Mechelen. In 1560 and 1562, following secret negotiations between Philip and Rome, the papacy issued the bulls necessary for the creation of fourteen new bishoprics.

Opposition was immediate and widespread. The magnates and municipal councils feared the political influence of the new bishops; the towns
designated to receive them resented the prospect of increased dues to
support them; the abbots of the ancient Netherlands abbeys disliked the
loss of part of their abbatial rents, which were assigned to help erect the
new bishoprics. Moreover, the privileges of Brabant, which by extension were considered the standard for all the Netherlands, expressly
forbade the prince to establish new bishoprics or abbacies without the
consent of the estates, lest he pack the assembly with compliant clerics.

What raised the greatest popular resentment, however, was the prospect of an enlarged Inquisition since a staff of inquisitors was to be
attached to each cathedral chapter. The existing Inquisition in the
Netherlands, established by the papacy in 1522 at Charles V's request,
acted independently of the old bishoprics. It was small and relatively
inefficient although the penalties prescribed in the placards against
heresy (issued by Charles) were severe and provided for death by drowning or the stake for a broad range of offences. On several occasions when
people had been executed under these placards there had been public
manifestations of resentment.

All opponents of the episcopal reform focused their hatred on the
Inquisition. Erasmian humanists, Jews, Christians of Jewish descent,
Lutherans and Calvinists spread terrifying tales of the cruelties and
secret proceedings of the Inquisition (which they naturally labelled
'Spanish') among the Netherlanders who (at their crossroads of shipping
and commerce) were generally tolerant of the varieties of religious
experience so long as people remained law-abiding.

Philip for his part rejected toleration as inimical to the well-being of the
individual soul and the public good and behaved as though he considered it incredible that anyone in his right mind would think otherwise.
In his strict, legalistic mind, he believed that the law-abiding and faithful
had nothing to fear, so long as they had nothing to hide. He did not see
the sinister effects of an institution which made windows into men's
souls, and was surprised that the Spanish Inquisition was held in such
horror in the Netherlands. Were not the punishments prescribed by the
Netherlands placards more severe than those prescribed in Spain?

Philip in these months, preoccupied with the Mediterranean, left the
task of establishing the bishoprics to Margaret and Granvelle, who
became archbishop of Mechelen. He heard but did not answer the
magnates who journeyed to Madrid almost annually to explain their
opposition to him. The refusal of the magnates to send troops to aid the
French government against Huguenot rebels in 1562 particularly

irritated Philip, since he had information that they had concerted their refusal with the English, who actively aided the Huguenots.[27] The opposition of the magnates and municipalities to the implementation of the bulls creating bishoprics partially succeeded. Not all were established despite repeated orders to do so. In Madrid, the duke of Alba admitted to Philip, 'Every time I read the letters of those three seigneurs of Flanders (Orange, Egmont and Count Hoorn, admiral-general of the Netherlands), I become so furious that, did I not deliberately compose myself, your Majesty would think me raving mad.' It was clear to Philip, however, that Granvelle, outvoted on the council by the magnates and ridiculed in the streets by their younger relations, could no longer function in office. At the end of 1563 he therefore gave him licence to visit his mother in Besançon (clearly a face-saving device). Two years later, he posted him to Rome.

If Philip had thought that removing Granvelle would purchase the support of the opposition to his policies, he was wrong. The magnates continued their delaying tactics by insisting that nothing could be done about the bishoprics until Philip came to the Netherlands and met with the States General to obtain their consent. They requested, moreover, through Count Egmont, who early in 1565 went to Madrid, that the placards against heresy be moderated, and that the Brussels government be reorganized so that the council of state, dominated by the magnates, should be placed above the privy and finance councils. Philip, responding to the Ottoman offensive of 1565 (Malta was attacked that May), designated Ruy Gómez, who had been notoriously friendly with the Netherlands magnates, to deal with Egmont. Working with Gonzalo Pérez, Ruy Gómez issued instructions to Egmont which permitted a board of Netherlands theologians to study the ecclesiastical matters, but gave him no answer on the proposed reorganization of the Brussels government. However Egmont, in conversations with Ruy Gómez and Philip himself, gained the impression that concessions would be made and reported this on his return to Brussels. Soon after his return a new set of instructions, drawn up by Philip's 'Flemish' secretariat of Charles de Tisnacq and Josse de Courtewille – who had not consulted with Ruy Gómez and Pérez – arrived in Brussels. These contradicted Egmont's claims, based on his impressions, and even differed from Ruy Gómez's instructions. Margaret, confused, wrote to Philip in July 1565 asking him to clarify his intentions.

What had happened in Madrid is not clear. Gonzalo Pérez suggested that Philip's tendency to give tasks to different ministers, while not telling them he had done so, lay at the root of the problem. He did not say whether Philip had some reason for this or was just absent-minded. Whatever the case, the results in this instance were unfortunate. Government in the Netherlands came to a standstill while all awaited Philip's clarification of his intentions. Religious dissenters came into the open and through their harangues excited the mobs already restless after three years of bad harvests.

Philip did not answer Margaret till October, after he had learned of the relief of Malta. He then reasserted his orders for her to establish the bishoprics, support the Inquisition and enforce the placards. He put off the reorganization of the government 'to another time', and appointed to the council of state the duke of Aarschot, a known rival of Orange and Egmont. Philip's intransigence at this point is curious since he well knew that the Netherlands magnates showed no disposition to obey him and – given developments in the Mediterranean – he did not have a free hand to use force. But his intentions were clear.

The magnates responded by in effect going on strike, refusing to carry out their offices. A band of nobles, mostly young and many of them brashly avowing their Protestantism, drew up and signed a 'Compromise of the Nobility' which called for liberty of conscience (something Egmont had never suggested to Philip), suppression of the placards and of the Inquisition. In April several hundred of these nobles, referred to by the government as 'confederates', presented their demands to Margaret. She burst into tears, and one of her councillors, trying to calm her, called them 'beggars'. Hearing his term, they took it over with relish and began shouting in the streets, 'Long live the Beggars!' Since Philip could give her no help and many of her councillors and officers were in sympathy with the Beggars, she accepted a 'moderation' of the placards worked out by the council of state. Neither side was content: the Catholics thought the concessions excessive, the Protestants called the compromise 'murderation'.

Local authorities began to take matters into their own hands. Faced with widespread and growing popular discontent in which political, religious and economic grievances were confusingly mixed, they followed the course of least resistance, which was toleration. Before huge throngs Calvinist 'hedge preachers' denounced the Church of Rome, the placards and the 'Spanish' Inquisition. The council of state sent two of its members, Baron Montigny and the marquis of Bergen, to Philip to beg him to modify his instructions of the previous October so that civil disorder should be avoided.

Philip yielded to their arguments, and agreed to certain small concessions, but he swore before a notary that these concessions were made under duress. Specifically, he ordered the papal Inquisition (which the new episcopal inquisitions were supplanting) suppressed, gave Margaret authority to relax the placards at her discretion, and promised generosity in the granting of pardons. He also agreed to come to the Netherlands in person as soon as the war against the Turks would permit.

To Pope Pius V, Philip apologized for suppressing the papal Inquisition in the Netherlands and instructed his ambassador Requesens to assure the Holy Father that, 'Before suffering the slightest damage to religion and the service of God, I would lose all my estates, and a hundred lives if I had them, because I do not propose, nor do I desire to be the ruler of heretics. If it can be, I will try to settle the matter of religion [in the Netherlands] without taking up arms, because I fear that to do so would lead to their total ruin. But if I cannot settle matters as I wish, without force, I am determined to go in person and take charge of everything, and neither the danger nor the destruction of those provinces, nor of all the rest I possess, can deter me from this end.'[28]

Before Philip's concessions became known in the Netherlands, matters got out of hand. On 3 September 1566 Philip learned that bands of young Calvinists had in mid-August gone on a rampage of image breaking, desecrating Catholic churches, molesting the Roman clergy and harassing religious processions celebrating the Assumption of the Virgin. A Calvinist-led mob had seized control of Valenciennes. Stunned Catholic officials and subjects offered no effective resistance. For the moment, order had collapsed.

Philip was profoundly shaken by the riots. He admitted to Granvelle that nothing could have given him so much grief as these offences 'against Our Lord and His images'.[29] On a digest of Granvelle's letters to him about the riots, he margined, 'They weigh on my soul, I suffer over them.'

Within a few weeks of receiving these reports, Philip learned of the death of Suleiman the Magnificent (which made an Ottoman offensive unlikely in the next year or two) and decided on firm counter-measures. After conferring with his councillors he accepted a plan, proposed by Alba, to dispatch a minister at the head of an army to ensure domestic tranquillity before he himself journeyed to the Netherlands.[30] He assigned Alba the task, made him captain-general of the Netherlands, and gave him a sweeping brief to do what was necessary to restore order. He had no confidence in news from the Netherlands that the magnates had rallied to Margaret and were restoring order. Intelligence arriving in Madrid suggested that they were merely consolidating their own position, and that Orange and the 'confederates' would overthrow the government and Catholic Church the minute they learned that Philip was on his way.[31]

Philip authorized the duke to establish a special Tribunal of Troubles to deal with the rioters and image breakers and to bring to trial Orange, Egmont, Hoorn and others who had either encouraged the riots or been derelict in their duty to carry out Philip's instructions. The duke was to renew the activities of the Inquisition and the enforcement of the placards, and to establish the bishoprics in those designated sees which resisted their introduction.

Alba's regime in the Netherlands was severe and military. Soon after his arrival in August 1567, via the 'Spanish Road', he had Egmont and Hoorn arrested. Orange had already fled to his estates in the Empire. Margaret, seeing the extent of Alba's authority, which she correctly took to show a lack of confidence in her by Philip, resigned.[32] Philip, in clear violation of the Netherlands' privileges, made Alba, a foreigner, governor-general, and excused the appointment by the emergency nature of the situation.

The Tribunal of Troubles established by Alba was soon dubbed the 'Tribunal of Blood'. Of some 18,000 persons tried by it, at least 1,000, according to surviving records, were executed. A Spanish relation of 1573 claimed that 6,000 Netherlanders were executed during Alba's regime, but of course the Tribunal of Troubles was not the only court at work.[33]

Resistance by the Beggars was soon crushed or scattered, and the counts Egmont and Hoorn, after a hasty trial, were executed in order to cow the population. (Personally, Alba had hoped the counts would acquit themselves; but by the standards by which they were judged – disobedience of direct orders – they could not.[34]) An attempt by Orange, assisted by French Huguenots and German Lutherans, to liberate the Netherlands from Alba's 'tyranny' was repulsed by the duke's generalship.

The army Alba took to the Netherlands was paid for at first by the Castilian treasury, but he was under instructions to make the Netherlands themselves take up its expenses.[35] He hectored municipal governments for money by threatening to try their magistrates for crimes of omission or commission during the 1566 riots, and in 1569 summoned the States General to present them with a plan to reform taxation in the Netherlands in order to place government finances on a firm footing and free his regime from its dependence on the States. On his own initiative, Alba proposed a tax similar to the Castilian *alcabala*, a permanent sales tax of 10 per cent on all business transactions not involving real property, a 5 per cent tax on all real estate transactions, and a one-time tax of 1 per cent on all forms of property. Known in the Netherlands as the 'Tenth Penny', this tax proposal caused an immediate and general outcry. The States objected and the duke backed down, accepting a traditional subsidy voted for one year instead, but he gave warning that he would return to his plan in the future.

The unrest fomented by Alba's attempts to obtain or impose the 'Tenth Penny' underlay the second and crucial phase of the revolt which began in 1572. After 1568 the Beggars, led by Orange, had sought aid in England, France and the Empire, and talks from 1570 onwards between Catherine de' Medici and Queen Elizabeth of Elizabeth's marriage to a Valois prince alarmed Philip. The Huguenot Admiral Coligny was in the ascendant at the French court, and by 1571, Philip's fear of an Anglo-French alliance was such that he consented to the unsuccessful Ridolfi Plot against the life of Queen Elizabeth.

Early in 1572 a Huguenot column, led by Orange's brother, Louis of Nassau, struck into the southern Netherlands and captured Mons. Alba rapidly mobilized more than 60,000 men along the French frontier, and Philip managed to keep Don John's armada in the western Mediterranean in case he should find himself at war with France and England. Then in April 1572, the Sea Beggars, expelled from England as pirates, fell on The Brill in Zeeland which was undefended since Alba had pulled his troops south. Within a few months, the Beggars had overrun Holland and Zeeland, meeting little resistance from the population which was dissatisfied with Alba's heavy-handed regime and, above all, with his 'Tenth Penny' plan. In July 1572 the estates of Holland and Zeeland, dominated by the Beggars (many of whom were Calvinist zealots), elected Orange their stadholder.

In Madrid, Alba's rivals, led by Ruy Gómez, demanded his recall, claiming that his general unpopularity, caused by his mistaken tax policies, had rendered his government ineffective. Religion, they argued, was a secondary issue. Private letters from the Low Countries confirmed this opinion. For one, Arias Montano, at first a supporter of Alba, had come to favour his removal. By this time Montano had become a Familialist, and his view of a moderate government included a less rigorous Inquisition. If, he thought, men were not disturbed in their conscience, they would gratefully conform to the prevailing religion which ought to satisfy Philip. This view was justified scripturally by reference to Nicodemus, but reckoned without the Calvinists: Calvin had already denounced *Messieurs les Nicodemites* in 1544 and the Calvinists wanted the form as well as the content of their faith.

Philip, listening to advice, decided to replace Alba with the duke of Medinaceli, whom he sent to the Low Countries with an armada which was to sweep the seas of Beggar corsairs. But the armada was instead picked apart by the Beggars, and Medinaceli was rejected by Alba who refused to step down until he had defeated the Huguenot invaders and reconquered Holland and Zeeland. Medinaceli thereupon joined the Netherlands 'loyal' opposition to Alba and sent complaints about the old duke to Madrid.

The St Bartholomew's Day massacre of August, in which Coligny and much of the Huguenot leadership perished, removed Alba's fear of a major invasion from France. In September he recaptured Mons and turned to deal with the Beggars. But the season, the terrain and above all a growing shortage of money to pay his troops worked against him. He failed to retake Holland and Zeeland and, in broken health, stepped down in November 1573, to be replaced by Don Luis de Requesens.

Requesens, who as a child had built a church of cards with Philip, had been asked by his king to restore a situation which was clearly collapsing despite Alba's victories in open battles.[36] In the winter of 1572-73 Madrid had decided that neither Alba nor Medinaceli could restore Philip's authority in the Netherlands. A policy of moderation and amnesty, in place of Alba's rigour, ought to be tried, and Requesens was the best man to implement it.[37]

Yet between February, when Requesens was designated, and autumn, when he left his governorship of Milan, Madrid could not agree on the details of the moderate policy or the extent of amnesty since everybody at court had his own ideas and few knew anything of the situation in the Low Countries first-hand. Philip himself admitted that he was thoroughly confused and confided to Requesens that he would just have to go and see for himself, not fully trusting anybody, although he should pretend to do so.[38]

Requesens therefore arrived in Brussels with inadequate authority and no clear instructions on how to proceed. Alba would not stay to advise him since he had no confidence in the policies he knew Requesens was to implement. Indeed Requesens admitted to his brother that he would have to tear Alba's regime up by the roots.[39]

Don Luis faced the same insuperable problems that Alba had faced, and learned, as Alba had learned, that religion, not taxation, as many in Madrid had argued, lay at the heart of the revolt.[40] Toleration was talked of by many, but Philip would not allow it. And the experience of Requesens and succeeding governments was that the Calvinists could not be trusted. In the provinces they controlled they did not tolerate the practice of Catholicism – although they did not, it must be added, systematically pry into private convictions.

Requesens died in March 1576 and his army, unpaid because of Philip's bankruptcy (1575), mutinied, seizing several towns and the citadel of Antwerp, scouring the countryside for food and loot and molesting the population. It was at this moment that Philip took Don John from the Mediterranean fleet and sent him to the Netherlands, hoping that his hero's laurels (and being Charles's son) would bring peace to the provinces.

Six months elapsed from Requesens's death till Don John's arrival in Luxemburg. During that time Orange's partisans purged the council of state at Brussels of Spaniards and Netherlanders who supported Philip's policies; and the States General, summoned by the estates of Brabant, assembled at Ghent to restore public order, defend themselves against Philip's mutinous army, and make peace with the rebellious provinces of Holland and Zeeland. Spurred by the 'Spanish Fury', the sack of Antwerp on 4 November* by its mutinous garrison (which felt threatened by the local militia), the States General drew up the Pacification of Ghent. In this document the seventeen provinces agreed that Philip must withdraw all foreign troops and accept the religious *status quo* (i.e. Calvinism in Holland and Zeeland, toleration in many cities, and Catholicism in most of the remaining countryside) until he came in person to settle the religious issue with the States General.

This was the high water mark of the rebellion. The States raised its own army and forced Don John to acknowledge the Pacification, before they would recognize his government. This he did through the Perpetual Edict of February 1577 and the army, loaded with loot, took the road for Italy. English diplomats openly entered into talks with the States: Elizabeth had previously refused to deal with the rebel 'Beggars', but the assembly at Ghent had in her eyes legitimized the revolt without abjuring Philip.[41]

Philip accepted the Perpetual Edict, which in fact temporized on the religious issue. He and Don John believed that the majority of the States, if put to the test, would uphold the exclusive sway of Catholicism in the Netherlands – so did the Calvinists who purged, where they had the chance, local and provincial governments of Catholics. Don John negotiated with Orange on the Calvinists' breaking of the Perpetual Edict, but to no effect. Losing his patience and fearing assassination, he seized the citadel of Namur in July 1577 and called for the return of the army.

* The city was left in shambles and 6,000 lives were lost.

Philip's task now was not the reduction of two rebel provinces, but rather the reconquest of the entire Netherlands. The army, led by Alexander Farnese (who had been at Lepanto with Don John), returned and Don John defeated the States army force at Gembloux (January 1578). Philip, still rebuilding his treasury and after August focusing his attention on the Portuguese succession, did not send him enough money to exploit his victory. In October, Don John died, and Farnese was made his successor.

Farnese achieved astonishing successes with few resources save his own military and diplomatic talents. While Philip, with his lingering hope for a peaceful solution to the revolt, sent the skilled Sicilian, the duke of Terranova,[42] to Cologne to a conference (1579) called by the Emperor Rudolf II to talk with a delegation sent by the States, Farnese captured Maastricht thus cutting the States' communications route from Germany into the southern and central Low Countries. His agents and Philip's diplomats found serious fissures in the ranks of the Netherlanders. The great Walloon nobility disliked the Calvinists and were growing frightened at social disorders instigated by Calvinist revolutionaries in the southern provinces.[43] In 1577 a popular theocracy had been established at Ghent, with the aid of German Calvinist mercenaries in the pay of the States and subsidized by Queen Elizabeth.

During the course of 1579 the son of the late Count Egmont, Philippe, and the duke of Aarschot, submitted to Philip along with other powerful nobles, their clients and militia companies. In 1580 Count Rennenberg came over, bringing Friesland with him.

Farnese argued for a policy of 'divide and conquer', and Philip came to agree. The Conference of Cologne was his last major attempt at a negotiated settlement of the revolt. There it had become clear that religion was the chief issue, and between the Catholic king, with his dependence upon Rome, Spain and Italy, and the Calvinists, there could be no compromise.

In May 1579, Farnese signed a treaty with the Union of Arras, formed by the Catholic estates of Hainault, Arras and Walloon Flanders to preserve the Catholic religion. By its terms he agreed to remove foreign troops from these provinces, and to agree to work for the appointment of a Netherlander or a legitimate Habsburg prince as governor-general.

The rebels in the meantime formed the Union of Utrecht (1579) and in 1581 abjured Philip II. They elected the duke of Anjou (formerly duke of Alençon), the younger brother of King Henri III (1574–89), as their 'Sovereign Defender'.

Orange maintained his personal sway over Holland and Zeeland, and

Anjou was left with the difficult task of holding together the tumultuous provinces of Brabant and Flanders against Farnese's advance. A Catholic, full of erratic schemes, Anjou depended upon aid from England.[44] He found the Calvinist theocracy at Ghent, and efforts to establish another in Antwerp, alarming, and early in 1583 tried to make himself master of the situation by using his French mercenaries to seize control of Antwerp and other important places. His attempted *coup* failed, he lost all credit with the powerful Calvinists and returned that summer to France, where he died a year later.

In July 1584 an assassin shot dead William of Orange, whom Philip had outlawed in 1580, putting a price on his head. Rather than breaking the rebels' will to resist, as Philip and Granvelle had hoped, the murder only stiffened their resolve. In their extremity, they sent agents to France and England seeking support.

Farnese, who in 1584 had won Philip's consent to a plan which ensured regular pay for the army, advanced victoriously from the Walloon provinces northward. By the end of 1584 he had reconquered most of Flanders; in March 1585 he received the surrender of Brussels and, on 17 August, that of Antwerp after a protracted siege. When Philip received the news in the middle of the night, the usually un-perturbable king rushed to tell the Infanta Isabel, 'Antwerp is ours!'[45]

The fall of Antwerp is by many historians considered the high water mark of Philip's reign. So, apparently, did Philip himself, even though it only meant the recovery of a town he had previously lost. None the less, its recovery brought the then chief cities of the Netherlands back under Philip's sceptre. The reconquest of Holland, Zeeland and Utrecht, it was hoped, would soon follow.

Portugal and its empire were already securely in Philip's hand, and mounting returns from the Indies permitted the steady increase of the armed forces in the Netherlands.

The other area of setback, North Africa, could be dealt with in good time, either by the recovery of Tunis and Tripoli, the conquest of Algiers and the domination of Morocco, as the Spaniards at Philip's court wished, or quarantined by naval forces and otherwise ignored, as Cardinal Granvelle thought best.

If one assumes, first, that Philip's diplomacy would be able to prevent any coalition of western European states against him – especially England and France – and second, that the Turks would remain occupied for some time to come in the East, then Merriman's comment is apt: never had Philip's monarchy seemed so majestic, so invincible; the world was apparently at his feet.[46]

What changed everything was the treaty of Nonesuch, signed three days after the fall of Antwerp, between Queen Elizabeth and the Dutch rebels. It was this treaty, not the river barrier, Charles Wilson convincingly argues in a recent study, that saved the Dutch republic.[47] The fiction maintained by Philip that the revolt was a domestic issue, despite repeated English and French intervention, usually covertly, was shattered. Philip was now forced into an open confrontation with Elizabeth, in response to which he prepared the great and costly Enterprise of England.

Farnese's army, confronting English troops alongside the Dutch rebels, made little progress in 1586, and in 1587 was ordered by Philip to stand ready to board the armada sailing from Spain for the invasion of England. The armada did not sail in 1587, and when it did in 1588, it was herded by the English and Dutch, after a thorough pounding and heavy losses, into the North Sea on course for Spain (around Scotland and Ireland), without having effected its rendezvous with Farnese's waiting army. Thus two campaigning seasons were lost, during which time the Dutch stiffened their defences and found a brilliant young commander, Maurice of Nassau, Orange's son, who was a fair match for Farnese.

When in 1589 Henri III of France was assassinated in the course of the religious civil wars, Philip ordered Farnese to intervene in France on behalf of the Catholic League to prevent the Protestant Henri of Navarre from becoming king. Farnese insisted that his first task was the recovery of the rebel provinces and acted only half-heartedly with Philip's French allies, fearing the threat of the rebels in his rear. Philip was persuaded to recall Farnese, largely by Don Cristóbal de Moura, who argued, on behalf of the Spanish treasury, that Farnese's Italian advisers were prolonging the revolt, from which they reaped immense profits. Farnese died in the field in December 1592, still in office, just as the count of Fuentes, designated to order him back to Spain, arrived in Brussels. The Brussels government, which under Farnese had ceased to be anything but a military regime, was now taken over on an interim basis by Count Peter Ernst Mansfeldt, seventy-five-years-old, councillor of state and long-time governor of Luxembourg (which he had kept obedient to Philip II). He at once fell to quarrelling with the sixty-two-year-old Fuentes over their respective powers. Little was done, apart from restarting persecution of heretics (which Farnese had not pressed). The army mutinied once more, the Dutch conquered the provinces east of the Zuider Zee, and events in France – which Philip had hoped to control – turned decisively against him.

Philip had in the meantime decided upon a new solution for the Netherlands revolt, which had become as Idiáquez put it, a voracious monster that devoured the men and treasure of Spain:[48] he would separate the Netherlands from the Catholic Monarchy, and give them in joint sovereignty to his daughter Isabel Clara Eugenia and the Archduke Ernst, whom in 1593 he designated governor-general and meant as a future husband for his daughter.

Philip had in 1553 been stubborn in defence of Don Carlos's rights to the Netherlands during the negotiations for his marriage with Mary Tudor, and he still wanted to pass the whole of his patrimony to his own heir, who after 1582 was Prince Philip. But the failure of arms, the failure of negotiations, the cost to his subjects, were things Philip had to consider. He also seems to have grasped the powerful national dimension to the revolt, which he did not understand, but accepted as a fact.

Ernst arrived in Brussels in early 1594 but died the next year. Philip then turned to his favourite nephew the Cardinal Archduke Albert, viceroy of Portugal, but at the time in Madrid, and appointed him to the Brussels government. That he sent Albert to the Netherlands, as he had Don John in 1576, underlines their importance in Philip's mind. He needed Albert's assistance in Madrid; he was growing feeble, and his heir, Prince Philip, was barely fifteen. The government, even the survival, of the monarchy might depend upon Albert until the prince became capable of ruling.

Albert arrived in the Netherlands in 1596 to find that the count of Fuentes had taken over the army and restored it to good order. In accordance with Philip's instructions it was not used for the recovery of the lost provinces, but in France. Albert's successes were mixed, but in 1597 he was driven back from Amiens in defeat. He could see clearly that continued intervention in France, where Henri of Navarre had become a Catholic and was accepted by the overwhelming majority of the French people, was as futile as it was costly. He favoured peace, and persuaded Philip to agree to let him negotiate with the French at Vervins, where in May 1598 a treaty was signed, confirming the terms of Câteau Cambrésis.

Philip arranged for Isabel's marriage to Albert, and obtained from Rome the necessary release of the bridegroom from his minor orders. He and his son Philip signed the instruments handling the Netherlands and the Franche-Comté over to the 'Archdukes', as Albert and Isabel came to be called, with the stipulation that if they had no offspring, on the death of the first of the spouses, the Netherlands and the County would revert to Prince Philip or his heirs, as in fact happened in 1621.

The hope that separating the Netherlands from the Catholic Monarchy would lead to the peaceful reunification of the provinces proved vain. The rebellion of the Dutch continued, and the 'obedient' provinces, dependent upon the money and soldiery of the monarchy, enjoyed little more than token independence.[49]

PHILIP II AND WESTERN EUROPE

Philip's II's inheritance, without the Austrian duchies and thus no opportunity to gain the Imperial crown, differed in character from that of his father. The great issues that commanded Philip's attention did not involve the affairs of central Europe to the same degree as had been the case with Charles, though they were naturally of concern, especially since the Netherlands had lingering historic ties with the Holy Roman Empire of the German Nation.

Philip's diplomacy in Germany after the Netherlands revolt concentrated on not alarming the Germans with his military activities in the Low Countries. He stressed that his armies were there to deal with rebellion, not with heresy, and requested his kinsmen, the successive Habsburg Emperors, to forbid Germans from giving aid to the rebels. The German princes, for their part, after a generation of religious strife, were anxious to avoid trouble. This desire, rather than Imperial bans, limited, though hardly stopped, aid for the Dutch.

Philip's activities in Europe thus lay largely in the West; his councillors and secretaries considered France, as always, the more significant of the monarchy's neighbours. England, however, they also had to learn to respect, since under Elizabeth it was emerging as a first-rate power, with an image of itself as champion of the Protestant cause.

ENGLAND

Philip II's relationships with England, after the death of Mary Tudor (1558), were constantly torn between the older politics of dynasty, with its respect for legitimacy, and the new politics of religious ideology. Counter Reformation Rome steadily pressured Philip to put religious considerations ahead of all others, while Elizabeth of England (whose mind, apart from being quicker, seems much like Philip's) was urged by English Protestants (above all the Calvinist-minded) to look upon every move by Philip or by the French monarchy as motivated by the Counter Reformation. In addition in England (as in Spain and the Netherlands) there were many whose motives were commercial. The Castilians claimed a monopoly in the New World; the Netherlanders enjoyed a favoured position in trading with the Castilians and, through old treaties, a lucrative reciprocal commerce with England; but the English had no advantage in Spain, except that during Philip's brief tenure as titular king of England, through licences granted to individuals, they got a taste of the possibilities of having a share of the Indies trade. Increasingly, during the latter half of the sixteenth century, they began to penetrate the Castilian monopoly, sometimes as peaceful smugglers, sometimes as piratical marauders, forcing Philip to take costly measures for the defence of Castile's New World.

In western Europe Philip wanted above all to maintain the *status quo* of Câteau Cambrésis, which was threatened in 1559–60 by the question of the English succession. During this time Philip stood as the protector of Elizabeth, whose throne was claimed by Mary Queen of Scots. In July 1559 Mary's husband became Francis II, king of France. To strengthen Mary's position to enforce her claim, her uncles, the duke of Guise and the cardinal of Lorraine, sent French troops to Scotland, where the lords of the Covenant, inspired by the Calvinist John Knox, were in rebellion against the regency government of her mother, Marie de Lorraine. Elizabeth aided the Scots rebels, and together they defeated the regency government and imposed upon Mary the Treaty of Edinburgh (July 1560), which severely curtailed Mary's power and forced the withdrawal of all French troops. This, followed by the death in December of Francis II and the consequent loss of power by Guise and Lorraine, removed the chance that Mary could gain England with French help and Philip was free to recall his 3,000 Spanish veterans from the north.

Philip's position as Elizabeth's protector began to change two years later, when she intervened in the first 'War of Religion' in France (1562–63) on the side of the Huguenots. She gave the recovery of Calais as her reason, but to Philip she appeared to support the Protestant cause. He refused Catherine de' Medici's request that he declare war on her, but Granvelle, suspecting that Elizabeth was in league with his Netherlands foes, had an embargo declared against Anglo-Netherlands commerce. Philip, responding to complaints from Seville about English smuggling in the Caribbean, followed suit. Elizabeth's intervention in France and the embargoes came to an end in 1564, and Philip's relations with her returned to normal for a time.

The great change in Philip's relations with Elizabeth came in 1567, when Alba arrived in the Netherlands at the head of a powerful army. The Counter Reformation, gaining momentum after the Council of Trent, had begun to poison relationships between the two prudent sovereigns, and Elizabeth and her councillors feared the intentions of her onetime ally, despite his insistence that Alba's mission was strictly to subdue rebels.

Elizabeth's first move against Alba is curious, and one recent historian has called it 'an act of pointless piracy',[50] since it annoyed the duke without impairing his strength. In late 1568 she seized four ships, employed by Genoese bankers under contract to Philip to carry 400,000 ducats to Alba, which storms had driven into English ports. (She kept the money eventually, and made her own arrangements with the bankers.) Alba in response ordered an embargo on Anglo-Netherlands trade: Elizabeth countered with an embargo against Philip's subjects. When Alba decided to negotiate, after the Netherlanders complained of their loss of business, Elizabeth attempted to get a treaty that would cover trade with all Philip's dominions and free English seamen from harassment by inquisitors. Alba had not the authority to negotiate such a treaty, and Philip, who linked Protestantism with the then unrest among the *moriscos*, was not forthcoming. Consequently Anglo-Netherlands trade languished, with the Netherlanders the bigger losers. Not until 1573, when Elizabeth had recoiled from her *entente* with France (1570–72), in the wake of St Bartholomew's Day, did she and Alba sign an agreement, the Convention of Nijmwegen, which restored trade and, moreover, committed Elizabeth and Philip reciprocally not to aid rebels. By then, however, the rebel Sea Beggars had overrun Holland and Zeeland, and Elizabeth had weathered the rebellion of the Northern Earls and the Ridolfi plot.

Philip suspected that Elizabeth had aided the Sea Beggars. She had given them haven, as she had many who fled Alba's persecution, and had expelled them only because her own subjects complained of their indiscriminate piracy. As for the revolt of the Northern Earls, that was an ill-timed and sorry venture, with which Philip and Alba did not get involved, though asked to by the pope. It was to have coincided with Pius V's excommunication of Elizabeth, but this was not published till January 1570, a month after the revolt had been suppressed. The failure of the revolt deprived Philip of the possibility of exploiting for his own purposes at a future and more convenient time a powerful league of great noblemen, of the sort he found in France and others found in the Netherlands.

In consequence, when he wished to stir up difficulties for the English queen, there remained only two possibilities: Ireland, which was remote and had to be reached by sea;[51] and conspiracy, which after 1568 usually involved, wittingly or otherwise, Mary Queen of Scots (a prisoner in England), isolated English Catholic magnates, and zealous or ambitious foreigners – the last two sorts were often men of no reputation. In 1571, Ridolfi, a Florentine merchant doing business in London, hatched a plot, in which the duke of Norfolk was an associate, which called for a *coup* against Elizabeth's government, her deposition (and murder, if need be), and the elevation of Mary Queen of Scots to the English throne. Alba, it was hoped, would cross the Channel with his army, and the Roman Church would be restored to England. Alba thought little of the plot and less of Ridolfi, but since the pope favoured the scheme, he sent Ridolfi to Madrid.

Philip had just ratified the Holy League and thus committed his resources to a war against the Turks. A threatened Anglo-French rapprochement, which involved Catherine de' Medici's plan to marry one of her younger sons (Henri, duke of Anjou, later Henri III; or Francis, duke of Alençon, later of Anjou) to Elizabeth, seemed to him, however, a major menace to the Netherlands. If successful, the Ridolfi plot would break the rapprochement by eliminating Elizabeth. Philip and his councillors therefore gave it their approval. The risks and costs were negligible, the possible gain immense. It was just before he learned of the victory at Lepanto that news of the plot's failure reached Philip. His ambassador to Elizabeth, Don Gerau de Spes, whose arrogance had done Philip no good in England, was expelled, and not until 1578 did Elizabeth receive another ambassador from Philip.

Before that, she had plunged deeply into the affairs of the Netherlands, sending envoys in the autumn of 1576 to the States General at Ghent. She lent them money and supported the Pacification of Ghent.[52] She suggested to Philip that he accept religious toleration: his answer was that neither she nor any other European prince did so (save under duress, as in France), nor would he.

Don John's taking up arms against the States and his victory at Gembloux changed matters. So far Elizabeth had dealt with the States as though they were Philip's government; now they were in arms against his governor-general. She therefore ceased aiding them openly, but did subsidize the mercenaries led by the Calvinist prince, John Casimir of the Rhine Palatinate, who fought on their behalf. Unwittingly she thus contributed to the breakdown of the States' unity, since John Casimir's support of the popular Calvinist theocracy of Ghent drove the Netherlands magnates and Catholics back into Philip's camp.

The last years of formal relations (1577–84) between Philip and Elizabeth were strained. She did stop aiding the Dutch rebels, but neither restrained her subjects from doing so, nor from smuggling and piracy in the Indies. Drake had royal support in his round-the-world marauding expedition (1578–81) and Elizabeth knighted him on his return. She received Dom Antonio and talked of acting in concert with Catherine de' Medici against Philip's annexation of Portugal, while entertaining

Francis of Anjou's revived suit for her hand. An English squadron took him to Antwerp in 1582 to become defender of the Netherlands.

Philip's last ambassador to England, Don Bernadino de Mendoza, soon learned that talk of Philip's might did not dissuade Elizabeth from her provocative policies. Like his predecessor, he turned to conspiracy and – implicated in the Throckmorton plot of 1583 – was expelled in January 1584.

As we have mentioned above, in 1584 the Dutch, after the assassination of Orange, sent delegations to Queen Elizabeth and Henri III, begging assistance and offering them, separately or jointly, the sovereignty of the Netherlands. Henri III refused, under considerable pressure from Philip II and the French Catholic League, led by Henri duke of Guise, with whom Philip at the end of 1584 had signed a secret treaty agreeing to subsidize the League on the condition that both parties would work for the preservation of the Roman faith in France and the Low Countries.

Elizabeth learned of this treaty in the spring of 1585 and feared that Philip and the House of Guise had united to invade England and liberate Mary of Scots, probably with the tacit approval of Henri III. At this point, convinced probably for the first time that England was in mortal danger of attack by Spain, she entered into serious negotiations with the Dutch rebels.

Was her assessment of Philip's intentions correct? The treaty itself said nothing of an invasion of England, and it is difficult to believe that Philip wanted one. Philip's main concern was that Elizabeth not aid the Dutch rebels, nor should permit depredations by her subjects against his empire. Even in these matters, he had shown himself willing to overlook English activities, so long as they did not directly threaten his 'reputation' and seriously impair his progress in the Netherlands. But he did react to her negotiations with the Dutch by ordering the arrest of all English shipping and merchandise in his ports.

In August Elizabeth signed the Treaty of Nonesuch with the rebels, agreeing to send some 6,000 soldiers to assist them against Farnese, and lending them money in return for which she received as security Flushing and The Brill. This was a direct affront to Philip. In October the Spanish port of Vigo was attacked by Drake, who then proceeded to the Caribbean (via the Cape Verde Islands), where in January he captured and held Santo Domingo for ransom, and in February stormed and sacked Cartagena, the capital of the Spanish Main.

Philip II ordered the marquis of Santa Cruz to outfit an armada of thirty-four ships to pursue and punish Drake, and requested that Farnese and Santa Cruz submit to him detailed plans for an invasion of England.

Farnese suggested a relatively minor venture, that he with his army of Flanders should take advantage of ideal conditions (for example, weather, surprise) to cross the Channel in small craft and barges. Santa Cruz proposed a vast armada, which required more shipping than Spain and Italy could probably have provided, and more money than Philip could spare, to carry a 60,000-man army from Spain against England or Ireland.

At court, Zúñiga, Granvelle, Idiáquez and Moura studied the 'Enterprise of England' plans and discussed them with Philip. Since the two former died in 1586, it was the two latter, especially Idiáquez, who were most instrumental in assisting Philip. For Moura, the Enterprise was a holy cause; to Idiáquez, it seemed a reasonable policy. Granvelle, who had strongly influenced Idiáquez, had long ago suggested an invasion of England as the best solution for the revolt of the Netherlands. Unfortunately, his thinking was out-of-date. England was no longer the confused, second-rate power of Charles V's times; it was an emerging great power, groping its way, to be sure, but by 1585 it was ready to commit itself to a course of action and persevere in it. Alba, when governor-general of the Netherlands, and his son Don Hernando, who served with him there, may have perceived this. They alone of Philip's councillors of state had serious misgivings about the Enterprise of England. The majority of ministers around Philip, however, did not, nor does it seem, did Philip. When in 1588 his battered armada limped home, he blamed the weather (God's winds) for its defeat, not the English and Dutch. In fact, Philip II seems to have hoped that his very preparation of the Enterprise might frighten Elizabeth sufficiently to withdraw her forces from the Netherlands.[53] But if she had, would not Philip eventually have launched the Enterprise for the sake of the Roman Church, as Elizabeth believed? Philip's conduct at this period seems increasingly governed by moral imperatives rather than by prudence. Aged sixty in 1587, he seems to have been in a hurry to force things his way, confident in his growing resources and in the recent successes of his arms.

The plan for the Enterprise finally agreed upon combined both Farnese's and Santa Cruz's suggestions. The marquis would outfit an armada at Lisbon, while Farnese would prepare 35,000 men of the army of Flanders to cross the Channel, when the armada, with another 10,000 men to bolster the invasion force, arrived to escort them.

In 1586 Don Bernardino de Mendoza, whom Philip in 1584 had sent to the court of France, entered into one more conspiracy (the Babington plot) against Queen Elizabeth, which if successful would have proven far cheaper than the Enterprise. The conspirators in London were soon rounded up and Mary Queen of Scots was brought to trial for her life. On 18 February 1587, convicted, she was executed.

The court of Madrid was already stepping up the tempo of its preparations for the Enterprise when the news arrived on 23 March of Mary's execution. However, Philip in his instructions to the count of Olivares, ambassador to Rome (1582–91), to seek money from Pope Sixtus V for the Enterprise, ordered the count to present the pope with a list of Philip's rights to England, including Mary of Scots' one-time letter to Mendoza in which she said she meant to will her rights in England and Scotland to Philip II, if her son James VI did not return to the Church of Rome before her death. This letter Philip did not take seriously, since it was a statement of intention, not a will, but promised in any case that he would pass his rights to the Infanta Isabel. In July Sixtus agreed to a treaty, in which he pledged Philip a gift of 1,000,000 crowns, payable when Philip's army landed in England. He did not accept Philip's claims to England, but granted him the right to nominate a king for England, subject to papal confirmation.

Philip's preparations (closely assisted by Idiáquez) for the Enterprise received a setback in April 1587 when Drake attacked the shipping assembled in Cadiz Bay, and sank or captured two dozen Indiamen. Philip still hoped to launch the Enterprise before the end of 1587, but storms damaged the armada which escorted the treasure fleets from the Azores to Spain, and Santa Cruz convinced him that 15 February 1588 would be the earliest date possible.

The delay in sailing was disastrous for Farnese's army. Famine and disease were rife in the Netherlands in 1587, and during the winter of 1587–88 his ranks were thinned by death and desertion. When spring came, he mustered fewer than half the men he had commanded the previous summer, and had to expend energy and time in recruiting more.

On 9 February 1588 Santa Cruz died in Lisbon, leaving the armada in a state of chaos. Philip, apprised of the marquis's fatal illness, had already designated his successor, the duke of Medina Sidonia. The duke, who had assisted for two years in preparing the Enterprise (and for many more in outfitting Indies fleets), tried to refuse the command. He doubted whether the Enterprise would succeed and did not care to lose his reputation, and perhaps his life. Philip reiterated his orders, and the duke capitulated. He arrived in Lisbon in mid-March and, after hard work, took the armada to sea at the end of May. Shortages in supplies and weather combined to force the armada to take harbour at La Coruña.

Despondent, the duke urged Philip to cancel the Enterprise.[54] He well knew the flaws in the plans worked out in Madrid, and thought Philip would be wiser to negotiate with the English, while keeping the armada in hand as a threat should the negotiations fail.

The chief flaw in the plan was that Farnese did not command a deep-water port where the armada might seek shelter and replenish its supplies, especially of powder and shot. The duke carried only three times as much powder as Santa Cruz had expended in one day in the Azores; and when he entered the Channel, his first request to Farnese was for more ammunition. This flaw had been pointed out to Philip on several occasions, at one of which the historian Cabrera was a witness. Philip paid no attention to the warning. One can understand why Garrett Mattingly holds that the king behaved in 1586–87 almost like a somnambulist.[55] In his correspondence for these years, Philip's rational calculations seem increasingly coloured by his religious convictions. In 1584 he had had Charles's body and the bodies of his mother and dead children, including Don Carlos, and Don John brought to the Escorial for entombment. The thought of death seems increasingly to have weighed on his mind, so that more and more desperately he wanted to settle his worldly affairs.

His commanders, driven by his orders, carried on, each according to his own lights. Medina Sidonia hoped to secure an anchorage off the Isle of Wight and wait there till he knew Farnese had embarked his army. Farnese, preparing his men and barges, however, had lost confidence in the success of the Enterprise and, after learning that the armada had anchored at La Coruña, did not expect ever to see it.

Medina Sidonia got the armada into the Channel at the end of July, where the English, contrary to his expectations, were waiting for him. He had not expected them before he reached the Straits of Dover, where in fact they had detailed a smaller squadron. When action commenced, the duke commanded sixty-five galleons and armed merchantmen, four galleasses, forty hulks carrying stores, and about twenty small craft. The English, commanded by the lord admiral Howard of Effingham mustered at first some sixty ships, but their number grew as the battle progressed. By the time the Dover squadron joined them, the English fleet had more vessels than the armada did. In addition at least forty Dutch warships stood off the Flemish coast, keeping an eye on Farnese's barges to prevent their departure.

Herded up the Channel by the swifter, better-gunned English, the armada ran into Calais, from which on the night of 8 August it was driven in confusion by English fire-ships. Its formation broken, it was

badly pounded before regrouping and escaping into the North Sea. The
duke, seeing his ammunition expended, decided not to risk the Channel,
but to return to Spain by sailing around Scotland and Ireland before
running south. Storms caught up with him off northern Ireland and
when the armada arrived off Santander on 23 September, half its ships
were lost and the survivors so battered that few put to sea again.

Philip reacted to the news with his customary equanimity. He gave
Medina Sidonia licence to retire to his estates, ordered an investigation
of the disaster, and began to build more ships to make good his losses.
Blame for the defeat was fixed not on Medina Sidonia (who had never
commanded at sea before) but rather on his chief nautical adviser, Diego
Flores de Valdés, who was briefly imprisoned. But the true blame rests
with the ageing king, his chief planning coordinator Idiáquez and his
moral supporter Moura. Philip's bureau was the central 'clearing house'
for the whole Enterprise: from it those who had to execute the plans
learned only what these three thought they should know, and sometimes,
it seems, only what Philip himself wanted to believe. The diplomatic
intrigues of Lisbon and Genoa and the court intrigues of Madrid had
not prepared Idiáquez and Moura adequately to serve as Philip's principal advisers for the largest military and naval enterprise ever launched
by a Christian state. The prior Don Hernando de Toledo, whom they
kept from Philip in order to guard the king's favour for themselves, aptly
told the Venetian ambassador that all must turn out badly if the king
insisted on seeking advice from the inexperienced.[56]

The great armada battle of 1588 was the most dramatic episode of the
war between England and Philip's monarchy, which had commenced
in 1585 and continued till after his death, ending finally in 1604. Philip
failed in his main purpose of breaking the alliance between the Dutch and
English, as well as in his secondary purpose, to conquer England itself.
The English counter-attacked the next year, hoping to break Philip by
raising Portugal in rebellion, though Drake's expedition of 1589, which
took Dom Antonio to Portugal, had no success. After that, the English
concentrated on trying to cut the treasure routes, unsuccessfully, though
causing Philip considerable inconvenience. When Philip openly intervened in the French civil wars, and in 1590 sent a *tercio* of infantry to
Brittany to conquer a base from which to renew the Enterprise of
England, Elizabeth landed troops in Brittany, successfully opposed the
Spaniards, and signed an alliance with Henri IV of France.

Philip in the meantime rebuilt his armadas. In 1591, the Ocean
armdaa drove the English blockaders, awaiting a treasure fleet, from the
Azores; and in 1594, the Indies armada began its regular sailings from

Cadiz to Tierra Firma (that is, the Spanish Main, northern South America). His new strength at sea came at a moment when Elizabeth was more interested in the affairs of France and therefore kept her navy in home waters, leaving the high seas to privateers, who were no great threat to Spanish convoys. Philip now turned his attention to growing Dutch seapower and sprung a sudden arrest on all Dutch traders in Spain, where they continued to do business and get rich despite the rebellion of their provinces against their onetime ruler. Seville claimed to Philip that the arrest hurt his loyal subjects worse than his rebels, and the duke of Medina Sidonia warned him that depriving the Dutch of business in Spain would drive them to attack Philip's overseas possessions, as the English were already doing.

While making it inconvenient for Dutchmen to do business in Spain (enforcement of such arrests was usually lax after the first few months), and driving the more adventurous to sail for the New World or Portugal's East Indies, the arrests' first result was to cause the Dutch to patch up their differences with their English allies. In the summer of 1596 a joint Anglo-Dutch expedition, commanded by the lord admiral Howard and the earl of Essex, fell upon the port of Cadiz, which they sacked and held two weeks for ransom. An Indies fleet fitting out in the bay was trapped and burnt (but by its own crews and the crewmen of the Spanish galley squadron, who had looted it, according to the consequent court martial).

Raging at Queen Elizabeth,[57] Philip ordered his new commander of the Ocean armada, the *adelantado mayor* of Castile, to sea with a hastily collected army against Ireland. The result was succinctly described by the secretary Andrés de Prada, 'God has been pleased to send a storm against the armada off Cape Finisterre. [A squadron] flagship and thirteen others are lost.'[58] A few weeks later Philip declared the third bankruptcy of his reign.

But he did not give up the Enterprise of England. In 1597, a much larger armada was fitted out and sailed for England in early autumn. It had hoved to within sight of the English coast, unopposed, when a north-easter bore down upon it, scattering its ships and forcing the *adelantado* to seek port, luckily with few losses.

In the spring of 1598, a small armada sailed the Channel to Calais (held by Philip 1596–98) with reinforcements and impressed Henri IV of France, with whom Philip had entered into negotiations for peace, with continuing Spanish strength. It thus contributed to the Peace of Vervins. England, however, persisted in the war against Philip II. Elizabeth no longer needed the French alliance, a testimony to the growth of English

confidence in its own strength, and to the imposing power on land and
sea of its other ally, the emerging Dutch republic.

FRANCE

For Philip after 1559 the threat of militant Calvinism to Catholic France,
not ancient rivalries with its kings, proved his chief concern. The menace
became evident in March 1560 when the French government, directed
by the duke of Guise and the cardinal of Lorraine, discovered the
Conspiracy of Amboise, a Huguenot plan to murder them and take
charge of the person of Francis II. Implicated in the conspiracy was Louis,
prince of Condé, the second ranking member of the powerful House of
Bourbon (after Anthony, king of Navarre), and a convinced Calvinist.

The death in December 1560 of Francis II led to the transfer of power
from Guise and Lorraine to the queen mother, Catherine de' Medici,
who obtained the regency in the name of her son, Charles IX, aged ten.
The queen mother was Philip's mother-in-law, and in his negotiations
with her he often used his own young queen, her daughter Elisabeth.
Apart from the hard political calculations which characterized his relations with France, Philip displayed a personal concern for the French
royal family, whom Henri II on his deathbed had commended to him.
But he quickly discovered, if he had not already known, that the queen
mother was hardly a widow in distress; she was rather a wily adversary,
convinced that she alone knew what was best for her children
and France (in that order), and her views differed considerably from
Philip's.

In her struggle to get and keep power in France, she was willing to
make use of all who would aid her, including the Huguenots. Her chief
aim was peace at home and abroad, which did not satisfy either the
warlike nobility or the militant Catholics and Calvinists. While Philip
was pleased that she did not intend war against him, he was far from
convinced that the policies she pursued in France would either contain
her more warlike subjects, or prevent the crown from being subverted
by the Huguenots, to whom she granted limited toleration. A Protestant
France would pose the gravest threat to the Netherlands.

To press his views upon her Philip, in addition to working through
his ambassadors, repeatedly sent extraordinary embassies, headed by his
most trusted advisers such as the prior Don Antonio de Toledo, Don
Juan Manrique de Lara, and in 1565 both the latter and the duke of Alba.[59]
However, he rejected her requests that she should meet him in person,
since Alba's private interview with her convinced both Alba and Philip

that she was determined to continue with policies they both thought mistaken.

Shortly after Alba's interview with the queen mother, Philip's relations with the French court were severely strained by the news that Philip's *adelantado* of Florida, Pedro Menéndez de Avilés, had massacred the captured defenders of a French Huguenot colony in Florida. Huguenot adventurers backed by the Calvinist admiral of France, Gaspard de Coligny, and not without the knowledge of the queen mother, had in 1562 begun to plant a colony there. In 1564, several of the colonists had been captured by the governor of Cuba while engaged in piracy. On news of this, Philip in 1565 sent the *adelantado* with a squadron to annihilate the colony. Catherine de' Medici rejected Philip's defence of the massacre, that he was protecting Castile's New World from interlopers who were also heretics. She insisted that the Huguenots had settled in the *Terre des Bretons* (the present New Jersey–New York coast), claimed in 1524 by Giovanni da Verrazanno for the French crown, a claim not recognized by Philip.

Alba's march to the Netherlands of 1567 raised apprehension in France as to Philip's designs, though more among the Huguenots than with the government. The Huguenots mobilized in defence of themselves and Geneva as Alba's column passed from the Savoyard Alps into the Franche-Comté. Clashes developed, not with Alba, but between the Huguenots and French Catholic and government forces, and two short, sharp civil wars ensued between 1567 and 1570.

Catherine's relations with Philip did not begin to change until 1568 when the period of strained understanding gave way to a return to the traditional anti-Habsburg, anti-Burgundian policies of the French Monarchy. The death in October 1568 of Philip's queen, Elisabeth de Valois, was quickly followed by his rejection of Catherine's youngest daughter Marguerite and his betrothal to Ana of Austria. Catherine, who put great stock in marriage diplomacy, was doubly wounded. Philip had not only turned down a daughter of France but by taking Ana had insulted the king of France, Charles IX, to whom Ana had been pledged. Charles had to settle for Ana's younger sister, Elisabeth. Philip promised Catherine that he would arrange a marriage for Marguerite to Dom Sebastian of Portugal, a promise he had no intention of keeping, since he hardly relished the prospect of strong French influence in Portugal.

In 1570, realizing that Philip had dissembled in regard to Portugal, Catherine opened a virtual 'cold war' against him. She disgraced the cardinal of Lorraine, who, though no friend of Philip's, had come to accept the Catholic king's leadership in defence of the Roman faith. Since the other leading Catholic ministers of Henri II's day, Montmorency (whom Philip trusted) and Francis, duke of Guise (whom Philip did not trust), had perished, the field was left to the Huguenot Coligny, who began to advise the queen mother and win the confidence of young Charles IX. Coligny believed that a war against the 'Spanish' monarchy would cause Frenchmen, both the Catholic majority and the Protestant minority, to forget their own differences and thus reconcile them. It would also give the Huguenots, as leaders in the war, a chance to make further gains in France and, as members of an international Protestant *entente*, forge an alliance against Philip II and the Counter Reformation.

An opportunity to foment war was presented by Cosimo de' Medici, who sought a French alliance to defend his new grand-ducal dignity against Philip and Maximilian II. Charles IX, wishing to be a warrior like Francis I and Henri II, was excited by the opportunity this offered, and took Coligny fully into his confidence. Coligny proposed that Charles, in the manner of his predecessors, attack Philip simultaneously in Italy and the Netherlands. French garrisons in Saluzzo were therefore reinforced, and Charles granted an interview to Louis of Nassau who planned early in 1572 to lead a Huguenot attack into the Netherlands against Alba.

Simultaneously Catherine was working to marry one of her sons to Queen Elizabeth of England, and Marguerite to the young Huguenot Henri, king of Navarre. Philip was understandably anxious as he watched his Mediterranean squadrons sail with Don John and the Holy League armada to the Levant, and upon the armada's victorious return to Messina and Naples, Philip secretly ordered his half-brother to remain there in 1572 in readiness for any attack by France.

The St Bartholomew's Day Massacre of 23/24 August 1572 removed Coligny and thousands of his Huguenot followers. Philip admitted to his ambassador in France that it was one of the most welcome pieces of news he had received in his life, and throughout Spain and Italy, *Te Deums* were offered in thanksgiving.

The legend that Alba and Catherine had planned the massacre when at Bayonne has long ago been laid to rest. Modern historians on the whole agree that Catherine perpetrated the massacre in desperation, fearing that she had lost control of Charles IX (and thus of French policy) to Coligny, who indeed intended to attack Alba as soon as the festivities in Paris attending Navarre's marriage to Marguerite (18 August) had ended. She was afraid that such an attack would lead to an open war with Philip II.

In her desire to avoid war, foreign or civil, which she saw as a threat to her son's throne and kingdom, she was consistent.

If the massacre brought temporary relief to Philip, it brought none to Catherine. The Huguenots from their strongholds in southern France took to arms and soon found a formidable leader in her new son-in-law, Henri of Navarre (who converted to Catholicism during the Massacre to save his life, but soon after recanted). Charles IX died in 1574 and Catherine's favourite son became King Henri III. Her youngest, Francis, sought his fortune by mediating between the crown and the Huguenots, whose spokesman at court he became, though he remained a Catholic. In 1576, he arranged the terms of the 'Peace of Monsieur', which ended the civil war, restored toleration to the Huguenots, and earned him his brother's former title, duke of Anjou.

The ambitious Anjou next turned his attention to the Netherlands, where, aided by adventurers and Huguenots, he aimed at advantage for himself, whether it be the governor-generalship from Philip or direct sovereignty over the Low Countries from the rebels. His sister Marguerite, his mother Catherine and Queen Elizabeth all showed sporadic interest in his intrigues, which were crowned with success in 1581 when the States of the Utrecht Union, having abjured Philip, elected him their sovereign defender. Henri III, pleased to have his restless brother outside France, gave him no official help and maintained in his relations with Philip a posture of studied neutrality.

Philip's relations with Henri III thus remained friendly, although Philip resented Catherine's claim to Portugal and protested at the queen mother's support of Dom Antonio as well as at Anjou's activities in the Netherlands. However, Santa Cruz's massacre of the French partisans of Dom Antonio in the Azores, like Menéndez's massacre of Huguenots in Florida, served to kindle in France a popular hatred of Spain.

Then in 1584 occurred another of those accidents of history that carry profound consequences in their wake. Francis of Anjou died in June 1584, making the heir-presumptive of the childless Henri III Henri de Bourbon, the Huguenot king of Navarre, who ruled French Navarre (the principality of Béarn), and had claims upon Spanish Navarra, in addition to being the head of the House of Bourbon and leader of the Huguenots.

Philip II was determined to prevent Henri of Navarre from succeeding Henri III, and despite a long history of enmity between his dynasty and the House of Guise (which had, however, begun to taper off because of their mutual concern for Catholicism), he signed with Henri, duke of

Guise, his brother Charles, duke of Mayenne, and others of their house, the secret Treaty of Joinville. Dated 31 December 1584, the treaty pledged Philip to pay the French Catholic League (La Ligue Sainte)[60] a monthly subsidy of 50,000 crowns, and both parties to assist one another in defending Roman Catholicism and suppressing heresy in France and the Netherlands, and to keep Henri of Navarre from the throne of France. As successor to Henri III, they agreed upon Navarre's elderly, celibate uncle Charles, cardinal de Bourbon.

It was with the League's aid that Philip successfully kept Henri III from negotiating with the Dutch delegates who came to offer him the sovereignty of the Low Countries. Moreover, with Philip's support, the Catholic League forced Henri III to accept the cardinal de Bourbon as his heir and outlaw Protestantism in France, an act which quickly provoked the outbreak of another civil war. The *consultas* of the council of state in Madrid reveal that such a war was hoped for since – by occupying the French – it would give Philip a free hand to deal with the Netherlands and England, the ally of the Dutch rebels after the Treaty of Nonesuch. The execution of Mary Queen of Scots in February 1587 ended Guise's plans for intervention in England, and when the armada sailed in 1588, Guise and the League, backed by Philip's ambassador to France, Mendoza, seized control of Paris, where they detained Henri III. Leaguers already controlled the rest of northern and eastern France, and Farnese's army, while waiting to embark for England, had nothing to fear from France.

But when the Spanish Enterprise failed, and Philip had to remain on the defensive in order to rebuild his forces, Henri III attempted to recover the initiative from the League. Escaping its control by flight from Paris, he summoned the Estates General of France to Blois, where in December he had Guise and his brother Louis, cardinal of Lorraine, assassinated. But Mayenne, aided by Mendoza, rallied the League and Pope Sixtus V excommunicated the king of France for the murder of a cardinal. Abandoned by most of Catholic France, Henri turned to Navarre and the Huguenots for help and acknowledged Navarre's right to succeed him. Together they laid siege to Paris, whose defence Mendoza helped organize. Henri III demanded that Philip recall Mendoza, and the prudent king, deferring to protocol, and in difficulties in his war with England, did so. Before Mendoza left Paris, however, Henri III was, on 1 August 1589, stabbed to death by a zealous friar. At the royal camp Henri of Navarre was proclaimed king of France, but in spite of his edict to respect the privileged position of the Church of Rome, many Catholic royalists pulled up their tents and withdrew to their estates and homes. Henri was soon left with his Huguenots and a handful of *politique* Catholic royalists, members of a faction which believed in toleration and unity in France, and war against France's traditional foes.

The Catholic League proclaimed the cardinal de Bourbon King Charles X, but disquietingly for Philip II, the Venetian ambassador, and soon after, the Florentine, presented their credentials to Henri IV.

Philip and his advisers determined that the struggle against Henri had to be fought in two places: on the battlefields of France, where the League would bear the brunt of the fighting, and in Rome, where Philip's ambassadors and the League's emissaries had to persuade the pope to bar Henri of Navarre (the prince of Béarn, the Spaniards called him) forever from the throne of France as a relapsed heretic, and to rally Italy against him. Sixtus V indeed raised an army in Italy to assist the League, but he negotiated at the same time with Henri's agents in hopes of reconverting Henri, and refused to excommunicate French Catholic royalists who fought on Henri's side.

On the French battlefields, Mayenne proved a feckless commander, and despite the aid of a contingent of cavalry sent him by Farnese, he lost the battle of Ivry in March 1590 to Henri IV, who promptly laid siege to Paris. Philip and his advisers now decided on direct intervention by the monarchy's own armies, in spite of objections by Farnese that such intervention would prove futile and, by exciting French xenophobia, even counter-productive. The troubles in Aragon in 1591 forced Philip to use his *tercios* from Castile there, and made it particularly urgent that his forces from the Netherlands and his ally, the duke of Savoy, who coveted Provence and the Dauphiné, invade France on behalf of the League. Most urgent was the relief of Paris.

Farnese successfully relieved Paris by outmanoeuvring Navarre, but Savoy made little headway in the Maritime Alps. Philip in the meantime was able to send a *tercio* to Brittany to assist the League (led there by the duke of Mercoeur), hoping to gain Brest, from which he could renew the Enterprise of England. As already mentioned, this led Elizabeth to dispatch 3,000 Englishmen to fight in Brittany, and sign an alliance with Henri IV. Her intervention in Brittany prevented the Spaniards from capturing Brest.

But the complexion of the war was beginning to change. The death in 1590 of the Leaguer king, Charles X, opened anew the French succession question for those Catholics who rejected Henri IV. Philip II was now ready to press the claim of his daughter, the Infanta Isabel Clara Eugenia. He instructed his agents and officers to broach discreetly the subject of the infanta's rights in France, as the eldest daughter of

Henri II's eldest daughter. Simultaneously he offered his opinion concerning the rights of others to succeed the celibate cardinal de Bourbon. He rejected the cardinal de Vendôme as a supporter of heresy, but found young Charles, duke of Guise, acceptable. (Did he find it convenient that young Guise was in Henri of Navarre's hands?) Philip held that the succession question should be settled by the staunchly Catholic and conservative Parlement of Paris, rather than by the Estates General, which might get out of control.

Philip's agents in France were divided on the infanta's chances. Some thought them *nil*, and moreover believed that open Spanish intervention would work against her and against Philip's having any say in arranging the French succession. Others were more sanguine and believed that the infanta, even should she not be accepted in her own right, would be welcomed as the bride of young Guise or whomever else the States General recognized as king, since strong Spanish support in men as well as money was vital to success against Henri IV. But most Frenchmen, including most Leaguers, rejected the infanta's claims. The Salic Law, which most Frenchmen held to be part of their constitution, barred female succession to the throne. Eminent jurists were sent to Madrid to explain the validity of the law, which Philip held to be a myth.[61] Only the Paris League, inspired by some Jesuits who saw matters from an international rather than French point of view, as well as by fanatics, favoured the infanta's candidacy.

The potential effectiveness of the religious orders, such as the Jesuits, in League affairs, was another of the reasons why Philip attached great importance to the role of the papacy in furthering his purposes. On the death of Sixtus V in August 1590 Philip was determined that his successor be more in agreement than Sixtus with those purposes, including the infanta's succession in France. Between 1590 and the end of 1591 his ambassadors, first the count of Olivares and then the fourth duke of Sessa, hectored three successive conclaves to elect popes favoured by Philip. None lived long, and in January 1592 the cardinals rejected further direction from the Catholic king and elected the independent Clement VIII, a man of proven diplomatic talents. Under him, the foreign policies of Philip II and the papacy soon began to diverge.

In 1592–93, Philip's policies for the first time became grandly imperial. He had been able to play off to his advantage the claims to France or parts of it of Leaguers and the dukes of Savoy and Lorraine, and now persuaded Mayenne to accept the infanta as his 'personal' queen and summon, as League-appointed lieutenant-general of France, the Estates General. To assist Mayenne Philip once more ordered the reluctant Farnese into

France, where he was wounded, but saved the League from defeat by Navarre. Farnese's lack of conviction in his uncle's designs had already caused the king to prepare his recall. Before being disgraced, however, he died (2/3 December 1592). The Brussels government was paralysed, and the discipline of the army of Flanders evaporated in mutiny. When the Estates General finally opened at the beginning of 1593, Philip lacked the military force to protect the League from Navarre or apply pressure to the Estates' deliberations.

None the less, the grand design was presented to the assembled delegates by Philip's ambassador extraordinary, the second duke of Feria. The Estates General should acclaim the infanta as queen of France, and allow her to select her own husband. This, Philip had decided, would be his nephew the Archduke Ernst, the heir-presumptive of his childless brother, the Emperor Rudolf II, after whom Ernst would be elected emperor. Philip would endow the infanta with the Netherlands and thus with France and eventually Austria and the Empire. Ernst and Isabel would re-establish the empire of Charlemagne. With their extensive possessions, they could subdue the Dutch rebels, bring Germany under strong rule, and restore its Protestants to the Church of Rome.

Philip realized that his grand design might not prove acceptable to the French who, 'because of excessive attachment to their own tongue',[62] might insist upon a Frenchman for a king. In this case, Feria was to work for the election of Charles, duke of Guise (who had by now escaped from Henri's camp), while making sure that he would marry the infanta.

Nothing worked out for Philip. The League-dominated Estates did insist upon a Frenchman, but could not agree upon whom, while Feria pressed the infanta's claims too long before throwing his support behind young Guise. By that time Henri of Navarre had administered another drubbing to the League army and after his reception on 25 July 1593 at St Denis into the Roman Communion, the French people began to rally to their popular and victorious king. Philip's chances to prevent him from becoming the universally recognized king of France were, in effect, finished. In May 1595, Henri received the absolution and recognition of Rome. Yet in his advanced age, committed to his stubborn League allies, who were as interested in gain for themselves as in any cause Philip hoped to promote, Philip fought on. In January 1595 Henri IV therefore formally declared war against him, and in 1596 formed a triple alliance with England and the Dutch republic against the Catholic king.

Philip was encouraged by the capture of Calais (1596) and Amiens (1597) by his forces, but Henri's recovery of Amiens that same year, following the sack of Cadiz (1596), the failure of two armadas (1596 against Ireland, 1597 against England) and his third bankruptcy (1597), finally convinced the Catholic king that he had to make peace with the king of France.

He accepted Clement VIII's mediation and entrusted his governor-general of the Netherlands, the Archduke Albert, with the negotiations with Henri. The Treaty of Vervins, not far from Câteau Cambrésis, of 2 May 1598, reaffirmed in general the *status quo* of Câteau Cambrésis, and Calais was restored to Henri IV.

The fact that France remained Catholic helped Philip accept the situation, but the question remains, had Philip's intervention been necessary to keep it so? It seems not. On the other hand, his intervention in France certainly caused the deterioration of his situation elsewhere. In the 1590s the *Pax Hispanica* in Italy had begun to break up. The Ottoman Empire took the offensive after 1593 in the Balkans and Turkish Hungary, where it consolidated its position. The Barbary corsairs, if no longer closely allied to Constantinople, continued to infest the western Mediterranean. The heretical Dutch were still in rebellion against him, and their republic had been recognized by other states. Dutch adventurers had penetrated the Castilian monopoly in the West Indies and the Portuguese in the East. The English infested the Atlantic and Caribbean, attacking shipping and towns. It would take a new regime in England and more setbacks at the hands of the Dutch before Philip's successor, Philip III, could or would make peace. From his father Philip III received in 1598 the same legacy of war and bankruptcy that Philip II had received in 1555–56 from Charles V.

Epilogue

Philip II died on 13 September 1598 at the Escorial, after a summer of steadily worsening illness and physical deterioration. He had lived seventy-one years and four months, and had reigned over his monarchy for more than forty-two years. Looking back over his long life and reign, what assessments and judgments can be made?

Taking his own standards and goals, there were both successes and failures. He meant first to conserve his patrimony, keep his dominions in the Roman faith and give them good government; but he lost the seven northern provinces of the Netherlands to Protestant rebels and, in trying to suppress their rebellion, drained the energies, resources and manpower of Spain. The rebellion caused the breakdown of the Cáteau Cambrésis settlement and the old pattern of alliances, and left Philip's monarchy upon his death at war with his rebellious subjects and England, his one-time ally. These conflicts, moreover, distracted Philip from his early goal of reforming government in his dominions for the purpose of giving his subjects better rule, especially in the dispensing of justice. He regretted that he had not done more for good government and, above all, the terrible cost of his wars to Castile, which he called the 'first' of his kingdoms, and where he resided by preference. But he died in the firm belief that these costs had been made towards a necessary and godly end.

Yet apart from the northern Netherlands, he conserved his patrimony, and save in the cases of Castile and the southern Netherlands (which was a war theatre), his policies do not seem to have been an immediate cause of the economic stagnation spreading in his monarchy.

As for religion, the Catholic Monarchy remained firmly in the Roman faith, and in the southern ('Spanish') Netherlands, the Church institutions (for example, bishoprics, clergy, universities) were streng-thened for their confrontation with the challenge of Protestantism from the rebellious northern provinces, England and Germany. The Catholicism of modern Belgium, and even the Dutch provinces of Brabant and Limburg (conquered by the republic in the seventeenth century), give proof of the success of Philip's intentions.

The acquisition of Portugal and its empire was a great triumph for Philip II, one upon which he could not have counted; but he seized the opportunity quickly and decisively when it was presented. Portugal was content under his sceptre; it was only after his death that his enemies, the Dutch rebels, began to pick apart the Portuguese empire, which helped breed discontent in the seventeenth century against 'Castilian' rule.

War Philip largely wished to avoid because of the risks entailed and the cost to his subjects. Yet the interests and extent of his monarchy made war almost inevitable during his reign. His subjects suffered the raids of Barbary corsairs, and for their sake and his (and Charles's) reputation, he wished to dominate the Barbary coast. Here he faced the Ottoman will to expand along the same coast, and thus fell into war with the Ottoman Empire. Because of the revolt of the Netherlands, he had to abandon Barbary to the Turks, though, through his diplomacy, he was able to aid the Moroccan drive for independence and thus weaken the Turkish grip over Barbary. But the corsairs of Algiers and the other Barbary states, if they ignored the sultan, did not cease to molest the coasts of Philip's dominions and harass the commerce of his subjects. The Turkish failure to subject Barbary does not therefore negate the failure of Philip's initial goal, the suppression of piracy in the western Mediterranean. The conflict continued unresolved.

Philip's other foreign wars were equally inconclusive and left the territorial *status quo* of Câteau Cambrésis intact. His war against England can be called defensive, since its prime aim was to remove the English from the Netherlands. His war with France, however, when his intervention in French affairs clearly became such in the 1590s, passed from efforts in defence of Catholicism to an attempt to bring France into the Habsburg system, Philip's grandest design. But this design was in fact doomed from the beginning, and in retrospect seems the costly folly of an old man.

Assessing Philip's reign, we can say that in general he did maintain the *status quo*, as he intended. The loss of the northern Netherlands could still be seen in 1598 as temporary, and was certainly offset by the gain of Portugal. If he achieved no grand scheme, it was in fact because, save in his last years, in the case of France, he had none.

Admittedly, he failed to achieve all the domestic reforms he intended, but the reasons for this – wars 'in defence of religion, his patrimony and reputation' – satisfied him, his court and most contemporary observers.

In regard to judgments in a moral sense, it is difficult to condone Philip's dissimulation, his willingness to persecute men for their religious convictions and to foment rebellion in the lands of his enemies and to work for the assassination of his foes. But in this he was not unique, nor was his age.

We have noted his affection for his family and his desire to give his subjects justice and honest government, a task which ultimately proved beyond him, given the realities of sixteenth-century society and the priorities, as he saw them, of his duties. During his reign his monarchy, the most impressive Christian state of his era, began, as we can see clearly in retrospect, to decline, which not only cost it its position in the power struggles among states, but consigned its subjects to demoralization and growing economic misery. If one had to single out Philip's main contribution to this decline one would have to point to his religious (ideological) intransigence in regard to the Netherlands, the most glaring shortcoming in his unimaginative conservatism. Yet in his own mind, this intransigence was right and heroic.

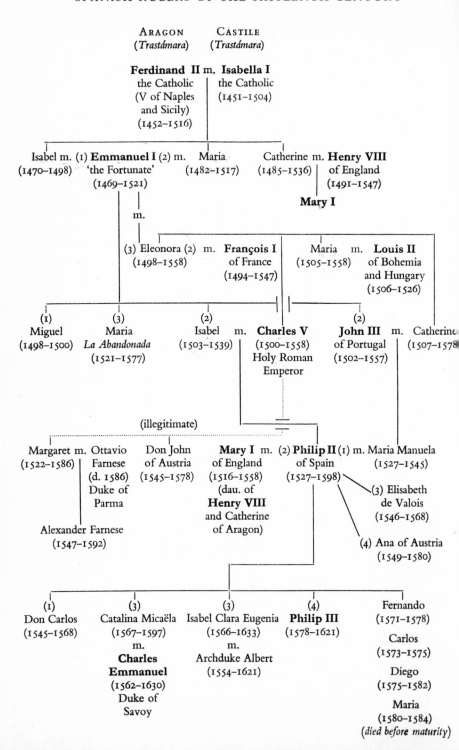

ARAGON   CASTILE
(*Trastámara*)   (*Trastámara*)

Ferdinand II m. **Isabella I**
the Catholic   the Catholic
(V of Naples   (1451–1504)
and Sicily)
(1452–1516)

Isabel m. (1) **Emmanuel I** (2) m.   Maria   Catherine m. **Henry VIII**
(1470–1498)   'the Fortunate'   (1482–1517)   (1485–1536)   of England
        (1469–1521)   (1491–1547)

                                                  Mary I

m.

(3) Eleonora (2)   m. **François I**   Maria   m.   **Louis II**
(1498–1558)   of France   (1505–1558)   of Bohemia
                  (1494–1547)   and Hungary
                                               (1506–1526)

(1)   (3)   (2)   (2)
Miguel   Maria   Isabel   m.   **Charles V**   **John III** m.   Catherine
(1498–1500)   *La Abandonada*   (1503–1539)   (1500–1558)   of Portugal   (1507–1578)
           (1521–1577)   Holy Roman   (1502–1557)
                                       Emperor

(illegitimate)

Margaret m. Ottavio   Don John   **Mary I** m.   (2) **Philip II** (1) m. Maria Manuela
(1522–1586)   Farnese   of Austria   of England   of Spain   (1527–1545)
            (d. 1586)   (1545–1578)   (1516–1558)   (1527–1598)
            Duke of   (dau. of   (3) Elisabeth
            Parma   **Henry VIII**   de Valois
                                 and Catherine   (1546–1568)
Alexander Farnese   of Aragon)
(1547–1592)   (4) Ana of Austria
                                               (1549–1580)

(1)   (3)   (3)   (4)   Fernando
Don Carlos   Catalina Micaëla   Isabel Clara Eugenia   **Philip III**   (1571–1578)
(1545–1568)   (1567–1597)   (1566–1633)   (1578–1621)
               m.   m.   Carlos
            Charles   Archduke Albert   (1573–1575)
            Emmanuel   (1554–1621)
            (1562–1630)   Diego
            Duke of   (1575–1582)
            Savoy
                                               Maria
                                               (1580–1584)
                                     (*died before maturity*)

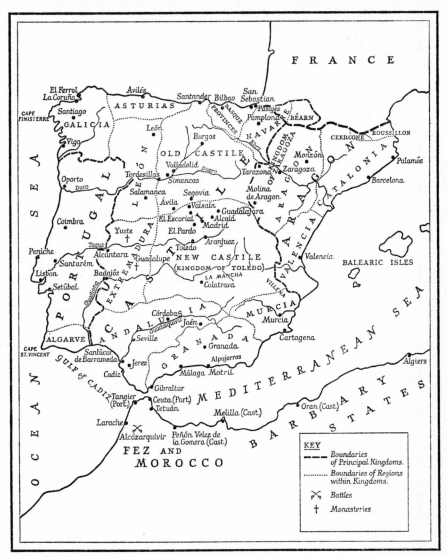

Map 1   The Iberian peninsula in the time of Philip II

Map 2   Europe in 1580

SWEDEN-FINLAND

MUSCOVY

DENMARK

BALTIC SEA

PRUSSIA

LITHUANIA

OLDENBURG

SAXONY

POLAND

BOHEMIA
Prague

Vienna

AUSTRIA

HUNGARY

STYRIA

Buda Pest

TRANSYLVANIA

OTTOMAN

Venice

Danube

BLACK SEA

DALMATIA
(Ven.)

RAGUSA

ADRIATIC SEA

TRIESTE

NAPLES

Naples

Palermo

SICILY Messina

MALTA

CORFU
(Ven.)

Lepanto

MOREA

Athens

AEGEAN SEA

EMPIRE

Constantinople

CRETE (Ven.)

Famagusta

CYPRUS
(Ven. to Turks 1571)

MEDITERRANEAN SEA

Tripoli

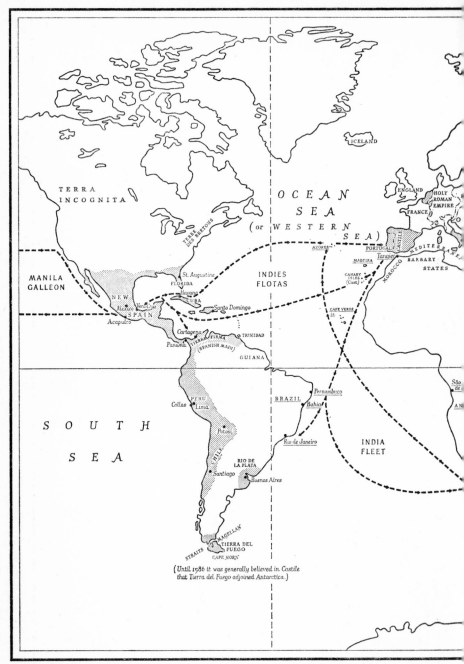

Map 3 The empire of Philip II (1580)

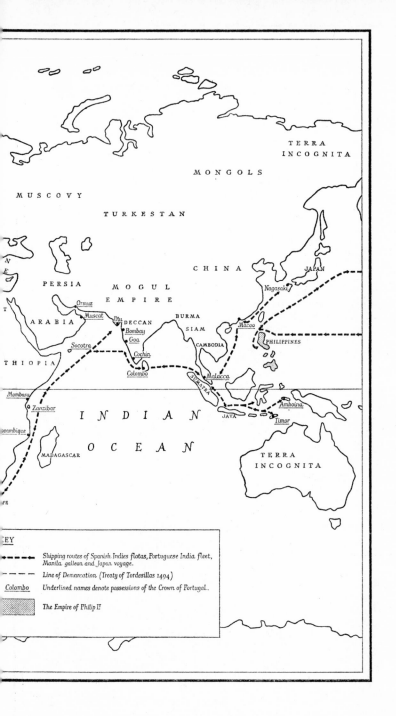

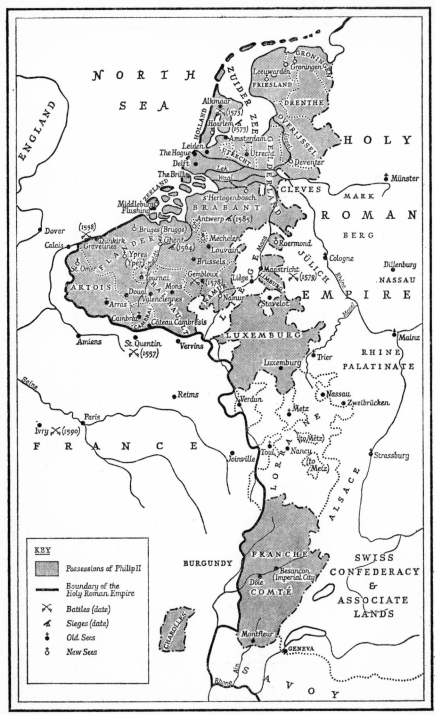

Map 4 Philip II's Burgundian inheritance (1580)

Notes to the Text

Chapter I Charles and Philip: The Education of a Christian Prince

1 Juan Ginés de Sepúlveda, *De rebus gestis Caroli Quinti et Regis Hispaniae,* in *Opera* (Madrid 1780) I–II; II, 401.

2 J. C. Davis, ed., *Pursuit of Power: Venetian Ambassadors' Reports on Turkey, France and Spain in the Age of Philip II, 1560–1600* (New York, London 1970) 67.

3 Charles and Isabel were married in March 1526. For Charles V, see Karl Brandi, *The Emperor Charles V* (English trans., London 1939); Royall Tyler, *The Emperor Charles V* (London, New York 1956); and Manuel Fernández Alvarez, *Carlos V,* XVIII of *Historia de España,* edited by R. Menéndez Pidal (Madrid 1965) and his *Charles V* (London 1975).

4 This term, used by modern Spanish historians and based on the royal title *Rey católico* (conferred by the papacy on Ferdinand and Isabella), is preferable to the 'Spanish Empire' or even the 'Spanish Monarchy' in describing Philip's Spanish and South Italian dominions taken together: all were his personal possessions, not the possessions of the Spanish nation-state.

5 *Reina proprietaria* was the title by which the Segovians acclaimed Isabella their queen in 1474, making it clear that she, not her husband Ferdinand of Aragon, ruled Castile.

6 For a sympathetic treatment of Juana, see Townsend Miller, *The Castles and the Crown; Spain 1451–1555* (New York, London 1963).

7 For the development of Charles's thinking, see Manuel Fernández Alvarez, *Política Mundial de Carlos V y Felipe II* (Madrid 1966).

8 R. B. Merriman, *The Rise of the Spanish Empire in the Old World and the New,* 4 vols. (New York 1918–34, reprinted 1962) IV, 'Philip the Prudent', 19, n. 3.

9 J. M. March, *La Niñez y juventud de Felipe II,* 2 vols. (Madrid 1941) I, 46.

10 Ibid., II, 335.

11 Ibid., I, 48.

12 Merriman, IV, 30.

13 Gregorio Marañón, *Antonio Pérez,* 2 vols. (Madrid, 7th ed. 1963).

14 March, *Niñez,* II, 175–352.

15 Ibid., II, 29–30.

16 Luis Cabrera de Córdoba, *Felipe II, Rey de España* (1619) 4 vols. (Madrid 1876–77) I, 4.

17 Claudio Sánchez Albornoz, *España: un enigma histórico*, 2 vols. (Buenos Aires 1956) II, 518–28, contests the oft-made claim that Philip II was the most typically Spanish of Spanish kings. I am inclined to accept his view.

18 For example of Philip's Latin see the Public Records Office, *Calendar of State Papers, Foreign* (reign of *Mary*) 1554, 84–85, 17 May 1554.

19 Maximilian had left for Germany on Charles's command in late 1550 to attend a Habsburg family meeting, for which see M. Fernández Alvarez, *Charles V* (London 1975).

20 See Ralph Giesey, *If Not, Not* (Princeton 1968) 203–15.

21 For scholarly edition of these two letters see March, *Niñez*, II, 7–37.

22 Henry Kamen, *The Spanish Inquisition* (New York, London 1965) 78–79.

23 A. W. Lovett, 'A New Governor for the Netherlands: the Appointment of Don Luis de Requesens, Comendador Mayor de Castilla', *European Studies Review*, I, no. 2 (April 1971) 102.

24 For Castile's economic woes, see John Elliott, *Imperial Spain* (London, Toronto 1963) ch. 5, parts 3–5; also Jaime Vicens Vives, *Manuel de Historia económica de España* (Barcelona, 3rd ed. 1964) 301–74, and Antonio Domínguez Ortiz, *The Golden Age of Spain 1516–1659*, (London 1971, translated from Spanish edition 1963) chs. 12–13.

25 For crown finances, see Ramón Carande, *Carlos V y sus banqueros*, 3 vols. (Madrid 1943–67) and Modesto Ulloa, *La Hacienda real de Castilla en el reinado de Felipe II* (Rome 1963). In this work, whatever unit of account

was used has been converted into ducats, which most often means changing the old Castilian *maravedís* into ducats, at the rate of 375 *mrs* to one ducat. In Philip's reign, the ducat was strictly a unit of account. The gold coin in circulation which approximated the ducat in worth was the *escudo*, which Philip raised in value from 350 *mrs* to 400 in 1566. The *escudo* was worth about the same as other European gold pieces, such as the French *écu*, or crown, which circulated everywhere. The English pound sterling, referred to here once or twice, was worth about four ducats. Henri Lapeyre, *Simon Ruiz et les 'asientos' de Philippe II* (Paris 1953) deals on pp. 8–9 with the currencies of most concern to Philip II.

26 See Fernández Alvarez, *Política*, 127–63.

27 Quote from Fernand Braudel, *La Méditerranée et le monde méditerranéen à l'époque de Philippe II*, 2 vols. (Paris 1949, 2nd revised ed. 1966) II, 233.

28 See E. Harris Harbison, *Rival Ambassadors at the Court of Queen Mary* (Princeton, Oxford 1940).

29 For the old alliance see Garrett Mattingly, *Renaissance Diplomacy* (London, Boston 1955) and R. B. Wernham, *Before the Armada; the Emergence of the English Nation 1485–1588* (London, New York 1966).

30 Harbison, 224, 258–59.

31 For Franco-Aragonese rivalry in Naples, see pp. 74–75.

32 See Manuel Fernández Alvarez, *Tres embajadores de Felipe II en Inglaterra* (Madrid 1951).

33 See William S. Maltby, *The Black Legend in England; the Development of Anti-Spanish Sentiment, 1558–1660* (Durham, N.C. 1971).

Chapter II Philip II: Character, Family, Interests

1 R. M. Hatton, 'Louis XIV and his Fellow Monarchs', in John C. Rule, ed., *Louis XIV and the Craft of Kingship* (Columbus, Ohio 1970) 163.

2 See María Teresa Oliveros de Castro and Eliseo Subiza Martín, *Felipe II, estudio médico-histórico* (Madrid 1956) for close attention to Philip's health; also, R. B. Merriman, IV, 21–22; and remarks in C. D. O'Malley, *Don Carlos of Spain, a Medical Portrait* (Berkeley and Los Angeles 1969).

3 Philip acknowledged no bastards; see below pp. 48–49.

4 For example see British Museum (BM) Add. Mss. 28, 363, fols. 54, 55.

5 *Calendar of State Papers, Venetian* (hereinafter *CSPV*) (P.R.O. London) IX, 13 May 1595.

6 O'Malley, *Don Carlos*, 2.

7 *CSPV*, IX, 17 May 1598.

8 Quoted in H. G. Koenigsberger, 'The Statecraft of Philip II', *European Studies Review* I, no. 1 (1971) 1–21.

9 Published in Paris, 1884.

10 See bibliographical essay, p. 221.

11 Marañón, I, 46.

12 Maurice van Durme, *El Cardenal Granvela* (Barcelona 1957, translated from the Flemish edition of 1953, Brussels) 354.

13 Cabrera de Córdoba, I, 354. Also Baltasar Porreño, *Dichos y Hechos del Rey D. Felipe II* (1628) (Madrid 1942) 293.

14 Cabrera de Córdoba, I, 337, for papers 'wilting'; dedication page for comparison.

15 Marañón, I, ch. III; also p. 217.

16 A. W. Lovett, 'Don Luis de Requesens and the Netherlands: a Spanish Problem in Government, 1573–1576' (unpublished doctoral dissertation, Cambridge 1968) quoted p. 24, 'yo me he hallado bien confuso.'

17 For example see BM Add. Mss. 28, 263, fols. 91, 424; also 28, 366, fol. 471.

18 See Marañón, bibliography, for Pérez's publications.

19 See Philip W. Powell, *The Tree of Hate* (London, New York 1971).

20 H. Wansink, ed., *The Apologie of Prince William of Orange against the Proclamation of the King of Spaine*, after the English edition of 1581 (Leiden 1969).

21 Fernández Alvarez, *Política*, discusses this and Philip's other testaments and deals with the matter of their authenticity, 205–10.

22 Ibid., 208, 211.

23 Quoted in Koenigsberger, 'Statecraft', 3.

24 For example Fernández Alvarez, *Tres embajadores*, 184.

25 Fernández Alvarez, *Política*, 210.

26 See letter of Charles V to the Regent Juana in Kamen, *The Spanish Inquisition*, 78–79.

27 Included in Wansink, ed., *Apologie*.

28 See J. H. Parry, *The Spanish Seaborne Empire* (London, New York 1966) 193–94; and Merriman, IV, 27.

29 Fernández Alvarez, *Politica*, 211.

30 Cabrera de Córdoba, II, 169.

31 Fernández Alvarez, *Política*, 214–15.

32 Ibid., 178–79.

33 BM Add. Mss. 28, 263, fol. 432, 'I am not a lawyer.'

34 Fernández Alvarez, *Política*, 212–13.

35 Ibid., 213.

36 Fernández Alvarez, *Economía*,

Sociedad, Corona (Madrid 1963) 212–14, and the author's remarks to me when I visited him in the summer of 1971 at Salamanca.

37 Fernández Alvarez, *Política*, 212.

38 Duque de Alba, ed., *Epistolario del III duque de Alba, Don Fernando Álvarez de Toledo*, 3 vols. (Madrid 1952) III, 538–42, and Cabrera de Córdoba, II, 206–207.

39 Cabrera de Córdoba, II, 588.

40 Quoted in Gabriel Maura y Gamazo, duque de Maura *El Designio de Felipe II* (Madrid 1957) 57.

41 For his relations with Queen Elizabeth see below p. 176 ff.

42 Compare Cabrera de Córdoba's claim that Philip punished and executed his greater subjects secretly so as not to give public scandal; II, 171.

43 Porreño, *Dichos*, 294.

44 For a discussion of Philip's sexual morality see González de Amezúa, *Isabel de Valois, Reina de España, 1546–1568*, 3 vols. (Madrid 1949) I, ch. X.

45 Cabrera de Córdoba, IV, 367. He admits that Doña Isabel made this claim, but implies that she had taken leave of her senses.

46 González de Amezúa, *Isabel de Valois*.

47 See Gaspar Muro, *Vida de la Princesa de Eboli* (Madrid 1877, trans. into French, Paris 1878) and the relevant chapters of Marañón, *Antonio Pérez*, I, chs. VIII–IX.

48 Ana's sister Elisabeth was not considered a suitable bride for Philip; quite apart from her young age (b. 1558) she was lower in the succession than Ana (b. 1549).

49 Fray José Sigüenza, *Historia de la Orden de San Jeronimo* (1605) (Madrid 1909) 425–30.

50 Louis-Prosper Gachard, ed., *Let-tres de Philippe II à ses filles* (Paris 1884) 187.

51 The heir to the Castilian throne carried the title prince of Asturias, and was called *el principe*. Other royal children were *infantes* and *infantas*.

52 Ulloa, *La Hacienda real*, 61.

53 See BM Add. Mss. 28, 361, *passim*.

54 For Don John of Austria see Sir Charles Petrie's *Don John of Austria* (London, New York 1967).

55 González de Amezúa, *Isabel de Valois*, III, 106–20.

56 L.-P. Gachard, *Lettres*.

57 O'Malley, *Don Carlos of Spain*; Cabrera de Córdoba (who at the time was a youngster at court with his father), I, 343–49, 426, 459, 525, 556–63, 590–92: 'I write of what I saw and heard then, with the access I had in the chambers of these princes.'

58 Fernández Alvarez, *Política*, 268.

59 Archivo General de Simancas (AGS), Estado Roma, legajo 906, 20 January 1568.

60 Ibid., Don Juan de Zúñiga (ambassador to Rome) to Philip, 5 March 1568.

61 O'Malley, *Don Carlos*, 20.

62 In the Catholic Monarchy and the Low Countries there was no legal bar to female succession, though experience taught that a male more often had a successful reign and that through women states passed to foreign houses. For examples of female succession there were: Isabella and Juana in Castile, Petronilla (1137–62) in Aragon, Constance of Sicily (1189–98), Joanna II of Naples (1414–35) and Mary of Burgundy (1477–83).

63 Cabrera de Córdoba, II, 616.

64 For further reading on the infanta, see Charles Terlinden, *L'Archiduchesse*

Isabelle (Brussels 1943); M. de Viller-mont, *L'Infante Isabelle, gouvernante des Pays-Bas*, 2 vols. (1912).
65 Archive of the dukes of Medina Sidonia, Sanlúcar de Barrameda Mss., 'Cartas de los reyes y sus secre-tarios' Juan de Ibarra to the seventh duke of Medina Sidonia, 6 December 1589. The prince, who had been under the care of the Empress Maria, did not seem very happy about the change.
66 This remark, which appears in Modesto Lafuente, *Historia General de España*, 30 vols. (Madrid 1850–67) XI, 77–78, is frequently repeated, though its origins are obscure. Moura, Philip's closest adviser in the last dozen years of his reign, was removed from court by Philip III's favourite, the duke of Lerma, and compensated with the viceroyalty of Portugal.
67 See José Fernández Montaña, *Felipe II el prudente, Rey de España en relación con artes y artistas, con ciencias y sabios* (Madrid 1912), a somewhat anecdotal approach to the subject.
68 Patrimonio nacional, *El Escorial: octava maravilla del mundo* (Madrid 1967) is a sumptuous introduction to the monument and its treasures.
69 BM Add. Mss. 28, 355, fols. 24, 43, 63, for example. Fol. 24 tells us that he read a concordance to the Bible for a while before going to bed.
70 Recordings of Victoria's works are available; for example Victoria (1548–1611) *Requiem Mass* and four *motets*, Choir of St John's College, George Guest dir. (Argo ZRG 570, London); *Music from the Chapel of Philip II of Spain*: selections by Victoria, Cristó-bal de Morales (1500–55), Antonio Cabezón (1510–66) and Alonso Mud-arra (1510–80), Roger Blanchard

Ensemble, Pierre Froidebose organ-ist (Nonesuch H71016, New York); *Pleasures of Cervantes* (Spanish popular music of the XV, XVI and XVII centuries), Polyphonic Ensemble of Barcelona, Miguel Querol Gavada dir. (Nonesuch H71116 New York).
71 See B. Rekers *Benito Arias Mon-tano 1527–1598* (London, Leiden 1972).
72 Fernández Alvarez, *La Sociedad española del Renacimiento* (Salamanca 1970) 249–50.
73 O'Malley, *Don Carlos*, 9.
74 D. C. O'Malley, *Andreas Vesalius of Brussels 1514–1564* (Berkeley and Los Angeles 1964) especially 296–308.
75 Fernández Alvarez, *Política*, 236–37, from Philip to Princesa Juana, 21 June 1559.
76 Domínguez Ortiz, *Golden Age*, 235–45. Marcelino Menéndez y Pel-ayo, *Heterodoxos españoles* (1880–82); also M. Bataillon, *Erasme et l'Espagne* (Paris 1937) and Kamen, *The Spanish Inquisition*, 82–83, 99–102 and ch. 16.
77 Richard Kagan, 'Universities in Castile 1550–1700', *Past and Present* no. 49 (1970) 44–71.

Chapter III The Catholic Monarchy of Philip II

1 Fernández Alvarez, in 'Biblioteca de Estudios Madrileños', *Madrid en el siglo XVI* (Madrid 1962) I, 1–24.
2 The old *alcázar real* was destroyed by fire early in the eighteenth cen-tury and replaced by the present Palacio Real.
3 BM Add. Mss. 28, 263, fol. 89, Gabriel de Zayas to Mateo Vázquez, 21 May 1587.
4 Cabrera de Córdoba, II, 574.
5 Population figures for the sixteenth century are all estimates. For Philip's

dominions see, Vicens Vives, *Manuel*; Braudel, *Méditerranée*, and his first chapter, *Civilisation materielle et capitalisme XVe-XVIIIe siècle* (Paris 1967).

6 J. H. Parry, *The Spanish Seaborne Empire*, ch. 3, 'Demographic Catastrophe'.

7 This term only came into common usage in the seventeenth century – in Philip's era these officers were generically referred to as governors, although different provinces had different local titles, for example in Brabant, ruward; in Hainault, grand bailiff.

8 Medina Sidonia's income is my estimate, based on reported incomes from his various holdings. For his militia, AGS, Guerra Antigua (G.A.), leg. 302, 'relación de la gente … ', *c.* 1590.

9 Both quotations in Elliott, *The Old World and New* (Cambridge, New York 1970) 76.

10 Parry, *The Spanish Seaborne Empire*, 208.

11 Pierre Vilar, '1598-1620: the Crisis of Spanish Power and Conscience', in J. Kaplow, ed., *Western Civilization: Mainstream Readings and Radical Critiques* (New York 1973) I, 373–83 (reprinted from *L'Europe*, 34, 1956); see also his 'Les Temps des Hidalgos' in *L'Espagne au temps de Philippe II* (Paris 1965).

12 AGS, Est. Roma, leg. 603, 'relación de lo que scriven los cardenales siguentes', 1566.

13 J. M. March, *El Commendador Mayor de Castilla, Don Luis de Requesens, en el gobierno de Milán 1571–1573* (Madrid, 2nd ed. 1946) 247.

14 Antonio Marongiu, *Medieval*

Parliaments (London, New York 1968) trans. from *Il Parlamento in Italia nel medioevo e nell'etá moderna* (1949, revised 1962) 148–57, especially 155–57.

15 Rosario Villari, 'Naples: the Insurrection in Naples of 1585', in Eric Cochrane, ed., *The Late Italian Renaissance* (New York, London 1970).

16 H. G. Koenigsberger, *The Practice of Empire* (Ithaca N.Y. 1970); also Marongiu, 157–70.

17 Ibid., 129 and 55.

18 Marongiu, 131–48.

19 Fernández Alvarez, *Política*, 223–28, for a discussion of the famous relation of Luis de Ortiz, an accountant of the city of Burgos of about 1560, in which he complains about the economic stagnation and suggests remedies.

20 For a recent study of its economy, set in a broad context, see H. Van der Wee, *The Growth of the Antwerp Market and the European Economy*, 3 vols. (The Hague 1963). For the Franche-Comté, Lucien Febvre, *Philippe II et la Franche-Comté* (Paris 1911, reprinted 1970).

21 Geoffrey Parker, *The Army of Flanders and the Spanish Road* (Cambridge, New York 1972) discusses arguments used by Madrid for keeping the Netherlands as a strong advance base for the monarchy, 127–35.

22 Quoted in H. R. Rowen, ed., *The Low Countries in Early Modern Times* (New York, London 1972) 27–29.

23 Orange acquired the office 1561–67, but Granvelle prevented him from exercising it until 1564; he was stripped of it in 1567. See Febvre, 243–77.

24 Cabrera de Córdoba, III, 596.

25 Carlos Riba García, ed., *Correspondencia privada de Felipe II con su* secretario Mateo Vázquez (Madrid 1959) 152.

26 Koenigsberger, *The Practice of Empire*, 48.

27 H. Wansink, ed., *Apologie of Prince William*, 71.

Chapter IV Philip II, The Court of Madrid and the Government of the Monarchy

1 Cabrera de Córdoba, I, 1–3, gives a courtier's understanding of the nature of monarchy, which seems to me more important than the theories of scholars. See Bernice Hamilton, *Political Thought in Sixteenth-Century Spain* (Oxford 1963) for these.

2 A. W. Lovett, 'A Cardinal's Papers: the Rise of Mateo Vázquez de Leca', *English Historical Review*, LXXXVIII no. 347 (April 1973) 241–61, believes that Philip usually formed *ab hoc juntas* to deal with the most important matters of state.

3 Fernández Alvarez, *Política*, 211.

4 Ibid., 217.

5 G. Parker, *Guide to the Archives of the Spanish Institutions* (Brussels 1971).

6 *CSPV*, VII, 256 (1560).

7 Cabrera de Córdoba, II, 125.

8 Ibid., II, 238–43.

9 Quoted by Luciano Serrano, *La Liga de Lepanto*, 2 vols. (Madrid 1918–20) I, 104.

10 Fernández Alvarez, *Tres embajadores*, 277, n. 49.

11 Braudel, *Méditerranée*, I, 326 (title of section).

12 Eugenio Albèri, ed., *Relazioni degli ambasciatori veneti al Senato durante il secolo decimosesto*, 15 vols. (Florence 1839–62) series 1, vol. III, 333–78.

13 Leopold von Ranke in *Die Osman-en und die Spanische Monarchie im sechszehnten und siebzehnten Jahrhundert* (Hamburg 1827). See my bibliographical essay for later editions and translations.

14 BM Add. Mss. 28, 263, fol. 129, Zayas to Mateo Vázquez, 13 August 1587.

15 *CSPV*, VIII, T. Contarini, 23 December 1589; also, H. Lippomano, 6 September 1588.

16 Alva died in 1591, and was replaced by Estéban de Ibarra.

17 See G. Parker, *Army of Flanders and the Spanish Road*, ch. 8.

18 Medina Sidonia Archives, Medina Sidonia to Philip, 17 June 1587.

19 G. Parker, 'Spain, her Enemies and the Revolt of the Netherlands', *Past and Present* no. 49 (1970) 72–95; table on 85.

20 Ulloa, *La Hacienda real*, 62–64, 533–34.

21 For example AGS Est. Flandes. leg. 530, in marginings on a résumé of Margaret of Parma's correspondence for late November 1566.

22 Koenigsberger, 'Statecraft', 7.

23 AGS Est. Flandes, leg. 569, Philip to Requesens, 23 February 1576.

24 This comment appears on a relation from an officer in Flanders, 4 December 1592, AGS Est. Flandes. leg. 603.

25 See Ulloa, *La Hacienda real*.

26 A. W. Lovett, 'Juan de Ovando and the Council of Finance (1573–1575)', *Historical Journal* XV (1972) 1, 21.

27 A. W. Lovett, 'Francisco de Lixalde: a Spanish Paymaster in the Netherlands (1567–1577)', *Tijdschrift voor Geschiedenis* (1971) 1, 14–23, p. 23.

28 Gordon Griffiths, ed., *Representative Government in Western Europe in* the *Sixteenth Century* (Oxford, New York 1968) 175, especially 4–6, 30–40.

29 Ulloa, 302.

30 Medina Sidonia Archive, Mss., Philip to the duke, 29 May 1586.

31 AGS Patronato Real, 29–36.

32 Koenigsberger, *Practice*, ch. III.

33 See Alfonso María Guilarte, *El Régimen señorial en el Siglo XVI* (Madrid 1962) 51–56.

34 See John Lynch, *Spain Under the Habsburgs*, 2 vols. (Oxford 1963–69) I, 257–70 for the best treatment of Philip's relations with the papacy.

35 Braudel, *Méditerranée*, II, 315.

36 Ulloa, chs. V, XIX–XXI for these revenues from the Church.

37 Lynch, I, 257.

38 The Conciliar Movement developed during the Papal Schism (1378–1415), and culminated in the Council of Constance (1414–17) which decreed the supremacy of the councils over the pope in certain crucial issues. The papacy, becoming more monarchical (as were secular governments), wanted to control the Church, and feared above all that without its strong central direction, the Church would become prey to powerful secular rulers, such as Philip II, who would use it for their own ends.

39 Fernández Alvarez, *Política*, 238–40.

40 Bohdan Chudoba, *Spain and the Empire 1519–1643* (Chicago 1952) 105–24.

41 Lynch, I, 266.

42 Koenigsberger, 'Statecraft', 4.

43 Medina Sidonia Archive, Zayas to duke, 27 October 1581.

44 AGS Est. Roma, leg. 906, on a letter from Zúñiga to Philip, 19 September 1568.

45 Quoted by Parker, *Guide to the Archives*, 27.

46 Cabrera de Córdoba, II, 126.

47 A. W. Lovett, 'A Cardinal's Papers: The Rise of Mateo Vázquez de Leca', *English Historical Review* 241–61.

48 Riba García, *Correspondencia Privada*, 39–41.

49 Léon van der Essen, *Alexandre Farnèse*, 5 vols. (Brussels 1933–39) V, 380.

50 Marañón, *Antonio Pérez*, ch. III, etc.

51 Alba was placed under house arrest at Uceda, near Madrid, because he assisted his son Don Fadrique in making a marriage forbidden by Philip, who demanded that he marry instead a lady of the court he had seduced.

52 See I. A. A. Thompson, 'Appointment of the Duke of Medina Sidonia to the Command of the Spanish Armada', *Historical Journal* XII, no. 2 (1969) 197–216; and Peter O'Malley Pierson, 'A Commander for the Armada', *Mariner's Mirror* 55, no. 4 (1969) 383–400.

53 *CSPV*, IX, F. Soranzo, 27 September 1598.

Chapter V Philip II, Europe and the World

1 Albèri, *Relazioni degli ambasciatori veneti al Senato durante il secolo decimosesto*, series I, vol. III, 379.

2 González de Amezúa, II, 223.

3 BM Add Mss. 28, 262, fol. 23.

4 See Mattingly, *Renaissance Diplomacy* (London, Boston 1955).

5 G. Parker, *Army of Flanders*, treats this superbly.

6 AGS Est. Castilla, leg. 178, 16 January 1598.

7 See C. R. Boxer, 'Portuguese and

Spanish Projects for the Conquest of South East Asia, 1580–1600', *Journal of Asian History*, 3, no. 2 (1969).

8 Riba García, ed., *Correspondencia privada*, 39.

9 Medina Sidonia Archive, Mss. 'Cartas', 12 August 1590.

10 Cabrera de Córdoba, II, 552, claimed that twenty-two heirs of Emanuel the Fortunate predeceased Philip – as a result Philip believed his inheritance of Portugal was the will of God.

11 Andrew C. Hess, 'The Moriscos: an Ottoman Fifth Column in Sixteenth-Century Spain', *American Historical Review*, LXXIV (1968) 1–25.

12 Quoted by Henry Kamen, *Spanish Inquisition*, 123.

13 Quoted by A. Sicroff, *Les controverses des statuts de 'Pureté de Sang' en Espagne de XVe au XVIIe siècle* (Paris 1960) 138n.

14 In addition to works cited in the bibliography, I have consulted K. Garrad, 'The Causes of the Second Rebellion of the Alpujarras' (unpublished doctoral dissertation, Cambridge 1956).

15 See Bernard Vincent, 'L'expulsion des morisques du royaume de Grenade et leur répartition en Castile (1570–1571)', *Mélanges de la casa de Velázquez* (1970) VI, 211–46.

16 Before landing at Peniche, near Lisbon, Drake had attacked La Coruña, where he hoped to destroy the remnants of the 'Invincible Armada', which in fact were at Santander. He was repulsed with heavy losses. The failure of his expedition led to his disgrace.

17 Von Ranke, *Die Osmanen und die Spanische Monarchie*.

18 *CSPV*, VIII, Contarini, 24 May 1589.

19 Braudel, II, 501.

20 See Alberto Tenenti, *Piracy and the Decline of Venice*, 1580–1615 (London, Berkeley 1967, trans. from Italian ed., Bari 1961).

21 This matter can be followed in Museo Naval, Madrid, Mss. 496, and in *CSPV*, VIII–IX, for years 1590–96.

22 Braudel, II, 319.

23 Braudel touches on this, but most of the pertinent material is in the Medina Sidonia ducal archive, 'Cartas de los Reyes y sus secretarios a los duques de Medina Sidonia y copías de unas repuestas'.

24 A. C. Hess, 'The Battle of Lepanto and its Place in Mediterranean History', *Past and Present* no. 57 (1972) 53–73, gives the Ottoman point of view.

25 Braudel, title of ch. VI, pt. 3.

26 Rowen, 27–29. Granvelle wanted Philip to give the magnates pensions and offices away from the Netherlands. What Philip did give them in 1559, according to the Venetian ambassador Tiepolo (*CSPV*, VII, 10 August 1559), left them dissatisfied, although later Don Hernando de Toledo found them ungrateful, since in his opinion Philip had not only given them handsome gifts, but also left them the government of the country. (BM Add Mss. 28, 539, fol. 279, letter to Philip, 17 December 1576).

27 See Fernández Alvarez, *Tres embajadores*, 177–212.

28 Luciano Serrano, *Correspondencia diplomática entre España y la Santa Sede*, 4 vols. (Madrid 1914) I, 316.

29 AGS Est. Roma, leg. 903, 'lo que contienen cuatro cartas de Cardenal

Granvela a su Md, de xv, xvii, xxvii, y xxix de setiembre 1566'.

30 Philip intended to journey to the Netherlands later, but by the time Alba had restored order there at the end of 1568, he had lost Don Carlos and his queen, had to make a new marriage and was faced with the revolt of the *moriscos*. The Holy League (1570–73) and the ensuing financial crisis (1573–75) intervened, then Requesens' death threw the Netherlands into total chaos. Clearly Philip was not dissembling in the sense that he never meant to go; rather, he never found the right opportunity to get away from Spain and the central government, which administered his dominions and collected its revenues.

31 For the intelligence received in Madrid, see AGS Est. Flandes, leg. 530, *passim*.

32 Margaret retired to Parma. In 1580, Philip considered appointing her governess-general of the Netherlands once more, hoping that she might restore the peace that a series of military governors had failed to achieve. But the rebellion by then had reached a point that no peaceful solution was possible, short of accepting the division of the Low Countries. The government therefore was left in the hands of her son Alexander, commander of the army of Flanders.

33 A. L. E. Verheyden, *Le Conseil des Troubles: Liste des condamnés* (Brussels 1961) gives 12,302 sentenced and 1,105 executed, 1567–73; Cabrera de Córdoba, I, 540, gives 1,700 executed; AGS, Est. Flandes, leg. 559, item 39, gives 6,000 executed.

34 *Epistolario . . . de Alba*, I, 678, 18 September 1567. In addition to

evidence of treason and dereliction of duty in regard to the troubles of 1566, Madrid had information that Egmont was in correspondence with England (Fernández Alvarez, *Tres embajadores*, 208) and the allegation of Maximilian II that 'certain great lords of the Netherlands' were accessories to a plot (the Grumbach conspiracy, 1567) in Saxony, which had wider ramifications.

35 A. W. Lovett, 'Appointment of Don Luis de Requesens', 90.

36 Alba complained (*Epistolario*, III, 538–48) that the only way to defeat the insurgents was to devastate the countryside and force the inhabitants into fortified towns. Though beaten in the field, the insurgents always reappeared as soon as the army marched away, and levied taxes on and drew supplies from the rural population.

37 For excellent treatment of this topic see A. W. Lovett's 'Appointment of Don Luis de Requesens' and his 'Francisco de Lixalde: a Spanish Paymaster'.

38 Lovett, 'Appointment', 96–97.

39 Ibid., 102.

40 Lovett continues Requesens' career with 'The Governorship of Don Luis de Requesens, 1573–1576. A Spanish View', *European Studies Review* (1972) 2, no. 3.

41 Charles Wilson, *Queen Elizabeth and the Revolt of the Netherlands* (London, Berkeley 1970) 42–62.

42 Possibly Philip sent Terranova, a Sicilian grandee, to show the Netherlanders that the monarchy was multinational.

43 See Tibor Wittman, *Les Gueux dans les 'Bonnes Villes' de Flandres* (Budapest 1969).

44 His brother, Henri III, did little for him and was chiefly pleased to have him out of France, where he had allied himself with the Huguenots to further his ambitions.

45 Merriman, IV, 514, n. 3, quoted from *CSPV*, VIII, item 284.

46 Merriman, IV, 515.

47 Charles Wilson, *Queen Elizabeth*.

48 Maura, *El Designio de Felipe II*, 167–68. Idiáquez called the revolt a *gomia* (voracious monster).

49 See Geyl's *Netherlands in the Seventeenth Century*, vol. I; and Henri Pirenne, *Histoire de Belgique*, 7 vols. (Brussels 1900–32) IV.

50 George Unwin, quoted in Charles Wilson, *Queen Elizabeth*, 25.

51 See John K. Silke, *Kinsale: the Spanish Intervention in Ireland at the End of the Elizabethan Wars* (Liverpool, New York 1970) chs. 1–2, for period of Philip II.

52 Though the situation did not permit it, Don Juan had wanted to invade England, which Elizabeth suspected from rumours rife in Rome. She thus did what she could to see that he was forced by the States to disarm. See O. de Törne, *Don Juan d'Autriche et les projets de conquête de l'Angleterre*, 2 vols. (Helsinki 1917–28).

53 I. A. A. Thompson makes this point in 'The Appointment of the Duke of Medina Sidonia to the Command of the Spanish Armada', *Historical Journal*, 200–05.

54 Maura, *El Designio*, 259–61; also Cesareo Fernández Duro, *La Armada Invencible*, 2 vols. (Madrid 1884–85) II, 134–37.

55 Mattingly, *The Defeat of the Spanish Armada* (London 1959), published in the U.S.A. as *The Armada* (Boston 1959) 81.

56 *CSPV*, VIII, Contarini, 23 December 1589.

57 *CSPV*, IX, A. Nani, 23 July 1596, reported that Philip lost his temper for the first time anyone could remember, picked up a candelabra and promised to pawn even that to avenge himself on her.

58 Medina Sidonia Archives, Mss. 'cartas', 25 December 1596.

59 On these embassies, including the Bayonne Conference, González de Amezúa, vol. II, is excellent.

60 The Catholic League first appeared in 1576, and was revived in 1584. See De Lamar Jensen, *Diplomacy and Dogmatism* (Cambridge, Mass. 1964).

61 The Salic Law was first used by the Valois kings of France in the fourteenth century to refute the claims of the English monarchs to the French throne. Philip II, like the English, believed it a Valois invention, and not a fundamental law of France.

62 L.-P. Gachard, *Lettres*, 178.

An Essay on Sources and Literature on Philip II

A proper listing of sources, archival and published, for the reign of Philip II could fill a volume this size. A fair idea of the amount of material which might be utilized is provided in the nearly sixty pages of sources in the magisterial Fernand Braudel, *La Méditerranée et le monde méditerranéen à l'epoque de Philippe II*, 2 vols. (Paris 1949, 2nd revised ed. 1966), which deals only with the Mediterranean part of his world, and mainly with the Mediterranean policies of his reign.

The fullest bibliographical aid for the reign is Benito Sánchez Alonso, *Fuentes de la historia española e hispanoamericana*, 3 vols. (Madrid, 3rd ed. 1952) which, while it does not carry critical comments, does refer the reader to pertinent reviews of works cited. Sánchez Alonso's work has been continued by the university of Barcelona in the periodical *Índice histórico español*, which reports with comments – now not so sharp as they first were – new works on Spanish history.

An interested student might best begin with R. B. Merriman, *The Rise of the Spanish Empire in the Old World and the New*, 4 vols. (New York 1918–34, reprinted 1962) IV, 'Philip the Prudent', which contains a critical guide to the literature. Such a task had first been undertaken by the Dane, Carl Bratli, who intended to revise the usual hostile view of Philip taken by Protestant historians, in his *Philippe II, Roi d'Espagne* (1911) (Paris, trans. 1912); it has been continued by Léon Halkin, 'La physionomie morale de Philippe II', *Revue Historique*, vol. 89 (1937) 355–67; R. Konetzke, 'Zur Biographie Philipps von Spanien', *Historische Zeitschrift*, vol. 164 (1941) 316–33; and Henri Lapeyre, 'Autour de Philippe II', *Bulletin Hispanique*, vol. 59 (1957) 152–75. A selection of historic views of Philip II appears in John C. Rule and John J. TePaske, eds., *The Character of Philip II: the Problem of Moral Judgements in History* (Boston 1963); this work carries a good bibliography.

An excellent introduction to archival sources, collections of documents in print and contemporary published materials is C. H. Carter, *The Western European Powers 1500–1700* (London, Ithaca N.Y. 1971). Another work, with some interesting new information is G. N. Parker, *Guide to the Archives of the Spanish Institutions in or concerned with the Netherlands, 1556–1706* (Brussels 1971).

The most obvious source of documents in print for the study of Philip II is the *Colección de documentos inéditos para la historia de España*, 112 vols. (Madrid 1842–95), with an indispensable catalogue by Julian Paz, 2 vols. (Madrid 1930–31). Several other series have appeared, with similar titles, and varied materials:

Memorial histórico español, 50 vols. (Madrid 1851 f.); *Nueva colección de documentos inéditos para la historia de España y de sus Indias*, 6 vols. (Madrid 1892–96), *Archivo histórico español: colección de documentos inéditos*. . . . 8 vols. (Madrid–Valladolid 1927–34); and since 1936/1942, a new series of *Documentos inéditos para la historia de España*. Apart from these Spanish series, there are other collections of documents, or works with considerable documentary appendices, touching on aspects or figures of the reign: J. M. March, S. J., *La Niñez y juventud de Felipe II*, 2 vols. (Madrid 1941); Carlos Riba García, *Correspondencia privada de Felipe II con su secretario Mateo Vázquez* (Madrid 1959); Luciano Serrano, *Correspondencia diplomática entre España y la Santa Sede*, 4 vols. (Madrid 1914), and his *La Liga de Lepanto*, 2 vols. (Madrid 1918–20); C. Fernández Duro, *La Armada Invencible*, 2 vols.(Madrid, 1884–85); Gabriel Maura y Gamazo, duque de Maura, *El Designio de Felipe II* (Madrid 1957), covering the king's correspondence with the duke of Medina Sidonia; and duque de Alba, ed., *Epistolario del III duque de Alba, Don Fernando Álvarez de Toledo*, 3 vols. (Madrid 1952). Published in French, but carrying the Spanish originals, is L.-P. Gachard, *Lettres de Philippe II à ses filles* (Paris 1884). Martin A. S. Hume selected and translated many documents from the archive at Simancas for *Calendar of State Papers, Spanish* (4 vols.), for the reign of *Elizabeth* (P.R.O., London). For the reign of Philip and Mary, see the printed volumes of *Calendar of State Papers*, in *Foreign, Spanish* and *Domestic* series.

A rich source are the two collections of the papers of Cardinal Granvelle: Charles Weiss, ed., *Papiers d'Etat du Cardinal de Granvelle*, 9 vols. (Paris 1841–52), which form part of the *Collection de documents inédits relatifs à l'histoire de France*; and Edmund Poullet and Charles Piot, eds., *Correspondance de Cardinal de Granvelle*, 12 vols. (Brussels 1877–96).

Few episodes of the reign have been so well documented as the revolt of the Netherlands. Best-known collections are: *Correspondance de Marguerite d'Autriche, Duchesse de Parme, avec Philippe II*, 6 vols. (Brussels, Utrecht 1867–1942), and *Correspondance de Philippe II sur les affaires des Pays-Bas* (1558–1577) 9 vols. (Brussels 1848–79/1940–53), both series begun by L.-P. Gachard; also Joseph Kervyn de Lettenhove and L. Gilliodts van Severen, *Relations politiques des Pays-Bas et de l'Angleterre sous le règne de Philippe II*, 11 vols.(Brussels 1882–1900).

Reports of foreign ambassadors provide fascinating insights into Philip and his reign; best known are the Venetians, in Albèri, ed., *Relazione degli ambasciatori veneti al Senato durante il secolo decimosesto*, 15 vols. (Florence 1839–62), and the *Calendar of State Papers, Venetian*. J. C. Davis, ed., presents an interesting translated selection, drawn from both works, in *The Pursuit of Power: Venetian Ambassadors' Reports on Turkey, France and Spain in the Age of Philip II, 1560–1600* (New York, London 1970). The correspondence of the principal French ambassadors to Philip's court appears in: A. Vitalis, ed., *L'Ambassade en Espagne de Jean Ébrard, seigneur de Saint-Sulpice* (Albi 1903); C. Douais, ed., *Dépêches de M. de Fourquevaux, ambassadeur du Roi Charles IX en Espagne, 1565–1572*, 3 vols. (Paris 1896–1904), and A. Musset, ed., *Dépêches diplomatiques de M. de Longlée* (Paris 1912). The often-overlooked interplay of interests in Morocco can be seen through de Castries, *et al.*, eds., *Les Sources inédités de l'histoire du Maroc de 1530 à 1845*, 21 vols. to date (Paris 1905 ff.).

For the relations of Philip II and the Cortes, there are the relevant volumes of *Actas de las Cortes de Castilla, 1563–1627*, 39 vols. (Madrid 1861–1925) and vol. V of *Cortes de los antiguos reinos de León y Castilla* (Madrid 1903). There are rare editions of the *Nueva Recopilación de las leyes*, the last being published in 1775; much of Philip's compilation of laws can be found in *Novísima Recopilación de las leyes de España*, 6 vols. (Madrid 1805–29). Selected documents, with commentary, concerning the Cortes of Castile and Catalonia, the Parlamento of Sicily and the States General of the Netherlands for the period of Philip II, appear in English translation, along with the originals (save for those in French or Latin, which remain in those tongues), in G. Griffiths, ed., *Representative Government in Western Europe in the Sixteenth Century* (Oxford, New York 1968).

Biographies of kings are usually also histoiies of their reigns, and thus in dealing with studies of Philip II, one must also consider the histories of Spain in his era, which most often deal with the entire monarchy. Philip looms large in the histories of his non-Spanish dominions too, but since he ruled from Spain for all but six years of his forty-three-year reign, he usually appears as some distant *deus ex machina*.

The standard study of Philip II in English is R. B. Merriman's *The Rise of the Spanish Empire in the Old World and the New*, IV, 'Philip the Prudent', which weaves the biography of the king through the history of Spain, its empire, his non-Spanish realms and Europe. Merriman's style is pedestrian, and so is his Philip, but his characterization is valid. Merriman considers Philip to have been usually 'Prudent', but narrow-minded and overly suspicious of his subordinates. However, in dealing with Philip's policies in France in 1593, Merriman admits that 'one is oppressed, from first to last, with a conviction that the king did not really believe that any of his alternatives could possibly succeed' (p. 638), which suggests that Merriman wondered whether Philip in his old age was still so prudent. Merriman's Philip, in my mind, is too commanding, primarily because Merriman did not give enough attention to Philip's collaborators, who assisted him in making policy.

A fine, moving portrait of Philip is presented by Garrett Mattingly, a student of Merriman's, in *The Armada* (Boston 1959), in the U.K. entitled *The Defeat of the Spanish Armada* (London 1959). Mattingly's Philip is not very different from Merriman's (see p. 409), but Mattingly delineates far more lucidly the king's personality; the hesitancy to which his prudence gave rise; the partial escape he found among his papers. Mattingly finds Philip in 1587–88, however, an ascetic with a commanding vision, a man who usually held that in undertaking great enterprises, one should walk with feet of lead (79), moving ahead like a somnambulist (81).

The specialist on Philip and his Spain needs to read carefully Luis Cabrera de Córdoba, *Felipe II, Rey de España* (1619) 4 vols (Madrid 1876–77). Anyone who has spent time in the Spanish archives will quickly see that Cabrera, who served as secretary to the duke of Osuna in Naples and to Alexander Farnese in the Netherlands before serving at court, had access to state papers, which he often used in his work. He was sent by both Osuna and Farnese on important missions to Philip, and dealt directly with the king on at least two occasions. He was party to the views held at court, and the excellent intelligence gathered by Spanish agents about European affairs. When I have at random subjected his statements to verification, by checking them with other evidence, I have found him essentially correct. Cabrera leaves no doubt that Philip always sought advice and worked closely with his collaborators, though in Cabrera's opinion, not always with the best of them. Philip does not dominate Cabrera's history, though he is at the centre of it. Cabrera places Philip in the context of his court, portraying the views and opinions shared by those around the king, which affected him, and reflected him.

A rich modern study which gives the court its due is Agustín González de Amezúa, *Isabel de Valois, Reina de España, 1546–1568*, 3 vols. (Madrid 1949). Traditional court and diplomatic history at its best, the work carries a considerable documentary appendix that elucidates Philip's relations with France in the 1560s.

A study of the reign which Merriman correctly called indispensable, though flawed by frequent minor errors, is Henri Forneron, *Histoire de Philippe II*, 4 vols. (Paris 1881–82), whose treatment of the complexities of Philip's foreign relations is better than Merriman's. Forneron's Philip, however, is always seen as the Machiavellian enemy of France.

Of the major recent studies of Philip's reign, the finest is Fernand Braudel's *Méditerranée*, which portrays the king in the context of the splendidly delineated Mediterranean world of his age, dealing with complexities neither he nor his contemporaries could fully grasp, since they had to react to events in the light of their own values and perceptions. Braudel's Philip is a man quietly trying to do his best under difficult circumstances with imperfect means: he is neither good nor evil, just alive and striving. But the protagonist of Braudel's work, as the Spanish scholar Manuel Fernández Alvarez has pointed out, is not Philip, but the Mediterranean. Fernández Alvarez has written two important studies of Philip, one 'Felipe II, Semblanza de Rey Prudente', in his *Economía, Sociedad, Corona* (Madrid 1963), the other, *Política Mundial de Carlos V y Felipe II* (Madrid 1966). The latter work, concentrating chiefly on Charles, shows the continuity in the ideas of the two men, and presents material from the little-known political testaments of Philip.

A fascinating portrait of Philip appears in Gregorio Marañón, *Antonio Pérez*, 2 vols. (Madrid, 7th ed. 1963). To Marañón, as has been mentioned in the text, Philip was basically a weak, insecure man of mediocre intelligence, who feared that he could never reach his father's stature. A less sophisticated view, of the same school, is Rafael Altamira, *Felipe II, Hombre de Estado* (Mexico 1950). Both authors were Spanish liberals, but Marañón had the advantage of medical training. Steering between Marañón's Philip and Merriman's is John H. Elliott, in his excellent *Imperial Spain* (London, Toronto 1963). For Elliott, Philip was pulled between an inclination to procrastinate and an iron sense of duty; successfully suppressing his feelings, he became an accomplished professional ruler. But like most others, Elliott only deals with Philip's mature character, not with its development from childhood to old age. In another good study, John Lynch, *Spain under the Habsburgs*, 2 vols. (Oxford 1963–69), we get essentially Merriman's

Philip, combined with a more sophisticated, if less detailed, study of the reign. A fine brief history of Habsburg Spain is Antonio Domínguez Ortiz, *The Golden Age of Spain 1516–1659* (1963) (London, trans. 1971) which concentrates chiefly on institutional, social and economic history. Domínguez sees Philip II as a ruler whose interests were largely in the area of foreign policy, which he treats quickly, if accurately, since it is not his chief interests. Brief, provocative and convincing is a more recent essay, H. G. Koenigsberger, 'The Statecraft of Philip II', *European Studies Review*, I, no. 1 (1971) 1–21. Koenigsberger, like Elliott, is sensitive to Philip's humanity, but delves more deeply into Philip's thinking. Like most who attempt to do this, he finds much evidence of the king's attitudes, but little of his calculations. While many call Philip's reign a failure, Koenigsberger, considering Philip's aims, calls it a qualified success.

Two views of Philip by modern Spanish historians, revealing differing judgments are: Antonio Ballesteros y Beretta, *Historia de España*, 12 vols. (Barcelona, 2nd ed.) vols. VI (1950) and VII (1953), whose Philip is a prudent Spanish king; and Ferand Soldevila, *Historia de España*, 8 vols. (Barcelona, 2nd ed. 1963), writing from a Catalan point of view, whose Philip is a narrow-minded Castilian king. Interesting, too, is the brief portrait of Philip by the Mexican historian, José Miranda, in *España y Nueva España en la época de Felipe II* (Mexico 1962), whose conclusions approximate those of Elliott but pay more attention to Philip's intellectual interests. *L'Espagne au temps de Philippe II* (Paris 1965), published by Hachette with a preface by Fernand Braudel, presents a collection of essays by distinguished French scholars on various aspects of Philip's Spain. Pierre Chaunu contributes a good essay on the Indies, and Henri Lapeyre on 'La dernière croisade' in the Mediterranean. Michel Devèze's treatment of Philip's policies in northern Europe is straightforward.

In a separate category are the polemics of those who try to brand Philip as a saint or an immoral tyrant. J. C. Rule and J. TePaske, eds., *The Character of Philip II*, deals well with the problem, but several works deserve special mention. C. J. Cadoux, *Philip of Spain and the Netherlands* (London 1947) portrays Philip as a monstrous tyrant, and takes to task W. T. Walsh, *Philip II* (Camden N. J., London 1937) and R. Trevor Davies, *The Golden Century of Spain* (London, Toronto 1937) for defending the king. Trevor Davies can be excused as he was trying to write a balanced history of Spain, free from polemics; his work has by now been superseded by those of J. H. Elliott and John Lynch, cited above. But W. T. Walsh, whose only merit is that he mimes Cabrera de Córdoba, lacks historical objectivity and judgment. The two-volume work by P. Luis Fernández y Fernández de Retana, *Historia de España en el tiempo de Felipe II*, vol. XIX of the general history of Spain directed by the late Don Ramon Menéndez Pidal, is the worst work in the series, a tedious compendium of well-known anecdotal detail.

Of all the larger works dealing with Philip, the one which seems to me most successful in relating the policies of the king to the composition of his ministries is Leopold von Ranke's superb *Die Osmanen und die spanische Monarchie im sechszehnten und siebzehnten Jahrhundert* (Hamburg 1827; revised eds., Berlin 1857 and Leipzig 1887): an English translation by W. K. Kelly, not easy to come by, exists, *The Ottoman and Spanish Empires in the Sixteenth and Seventeenth Centuries*

(London 1843); the part dealing with Spain has been translated into Spanish (Mexico 1946) and French (Abbéville, 2nd ed. 1873).

The best study, I think, showing Philip at work with his ministers is a brief article, A. W. Lovett, 'A New Governor for the Netherlands: the Appointment of Don Luis de Requesens, Comendador Mayor de Castilla', *European Studies Review*, I, no. 2 (1971) 89–103. Lovett minutely examines Philip's reactions to certain events and his role in decision making, surrounded by councillors who had their own reactions and opinions, and therefore presents a more plausible and human Philip than any other scholar, save for Mattingly and Marañón. Lovett portrays Philip as uncertain and hesitant, considering alternative courses of action: with Philip, Lovett remarks, 'Indecision became an instrument of statecraft' (p. 95).

Good popular biographies of Philip include Sir Charles Petrie, *Philip II of Spain* (London 1963), a traditional study, sympathetic to Philip; and Orestes Ferrara, *Philippe II* (Paris 1961, translated from the Spanish edition, Mexico), which places a balanced perspective on the reign, giving Philip's Church, Italian and Mediterranean policies their due. Ludwig Pfandl, *Philipp II: Gemälde eines Lebens und einer Zeit* (Munich 1938) and Reinhold Schneider, *Philipp der Zweite: oder Religion und Macht* (Cologne 1957) are both works in the Romantic tradition of Schiller, though much more sympathetic to Philip than was the author of Don Carlos, and certainly more reliable.

Biographies of Philip's collaborators remain scarce, which is one reason Philip so dominates histories of his reign. Recommended are: Gregorio Marañón, *Antonio Peréz*; Maurice van Durme, *El Cardenal Granvela* (Barcelona 1957, translated from the Flemish edition of 1953, Brussels) and Martin Philippson, *Ein Ministerium unter Philipp II: Kardinal Granvella am spanische Hofe 1579–1586* (Berlin 1895); Sir Charles Petrie, *Don John of Austria* (London, New York 1967), a better book than his *Philip II;* Léon van der Essen, *Alexandre Farnèse, prince de Parme, gouverneur général des Pays-Bas 1545–1592*, 5 vols. (Brussels 1933–37); Francisco Caeiro, *O Arquiduque Alberto de Austria* (Lisbon 1961); Alfonso Dánvila y Burguero, *Don Cristóbal de Moura* (Madrid 1900); A. González Palencia, *Gonzalo Pérez, secretario de Felipe II*, 2 vols. (Madrid 1946); J. M. March, *El Comendador Mayor de Castilla, Don Luis de Requesens, en el Gobierno de Milán 1571–1573* (Madrid 1943, 2nd ed. 1946) and for the Netherlands, A. W. Lovett, 'Appointment', and 'The Governorship of Don Luis de Requesens, 1573–1576. A Spanish View', *European Studies Review*, II, no. 3 (1972). Neither the duke of Alba nor Ruy Gómez de Silva have biographies worthy of them; and Fidel Pérez Mínguez's *Don Juan de Idiáquez* (San Sebastian 1935) is a thin study of a most important figure. A provocative article is A. W. Lovett's 'A Cardinal's Papers: the Rise of Mateo Váquez de Leca', *English Historical Review*, LXXXVIII, no. 347 (April 1973), which assigns the 'arch secretary' a somewhat larger role in policy making than I am willing to accept. J. A. Escudero, *Los Secretarios de Estado y del Despacho 1474–1724*, 4 vols. (Madrid 1969) gives vital data on Philip's leading secretaries.

Works not yet cited on particular aspects of Philip's monarchy include Modesto Ulloa, *La Hacienda real de Castilla en el reinado de Felipe II* (Rome 1963);

J. Caro Baroja, *Los Moriscos del Reino de Granada* (Madrid 1957); Henri Lapeyre's *Simon Ruiz et les 'asientos' de Philippe II* (Paris 1953), and his *Géographie de l'Espagne morisque* (Paris 1959). A good summary of studies on the *moriscos* is in Bernard Vincent, 'L'Expulsion des morisques du royaume de Grenade et leur repartition en Castille', *Mélanges de la casa de Velázquez*, VI (1970) 211–46; E. Schäfer, *El Consejo Real y Supremo de las Indias*, 2 vols. (Seville 1935); Carlos Riba García, *El Consejo supremo de Aragón en el reinado de Felipe II* (Valencia 1914); J. Reglá Campistol, *Felip II y Catalunya* (Barcelona 1956); Ralph Giesey, *If Not, Not* (Princeton 1968), on the oath of the Aragonese; Henry Kamen, *The Spanish Inquisition* (London, New York 1965), an up-to-date and judicious survey; I. A. A. Thompson, 'The Armada and Administrative Reform: the Spanish Council of War in the reign of Philip II', *English Historical Review*, LXXXII, no. 325 (1967) 698–725; and his 'Appointment of the Duke of Medina Sidonia to the Command of the Spanish Armada', *Historical Journal*, 12, no. 2 (1969) 197–216; and P. O'M. Pierson, 'A Commander for the Armada', *Mariner's Mirror*, 55, no. 4 (1969) 383–400. For the annexation of Portugal, see Alfonso Dánvila, *Felipe II y el Rey Don Sebastián de Portugal* (Madrid 1954) and his *Felipe II y la sucesión de Portugal* (Madrid 1956). For Philip's rule, L. A. Rebello da Silva, *Historia de Portugal nos seclos XVII e. XVIII* (Lisbon 1862), vol. I.

An excellent recent survey dealing with Philip's overseas possessions is J. H. Parry, *The Spanish Seaborne Empire* (London, New York 1966). A stimulating, well-written essay is J. H. Elliott, *The Old World and the New* (Cambridge, New York 1970). See also, J. Miranda, *España y Nueva España;* C. H. Haring, *Th Spanish Empire in America* (New York, Oxford 1947); J. H. Parry, *The Spanish Theory of Empire in the Sixteenth Century* (Cambridge, Toronto 1940); and A. P. Newton, *The European Nations in the West Indies 1492–1688* (London, Toronto 1933). The histories of Spain by Merriman, Ballesteros, Elliott and Lynch all have good chapters on the New World; also see Pierre Chaunu's contribution to *L'Espagne aux temps de Philippe II*. For the Portuguese overseas possessions, see C. R. Boxer, *The Portuguese Seaborne Empire* (London 1969, New York 1970).

For Italy, see especially H. G. Koenigsberger, *The Practice of Empire* (Ithaca, N.Y. 1969), an 'emended' edition of *The Government of Sicily under Philip II* (London 1951). B. Croce, *Storia del regno di Napoli* (Bari 1925, 6th ed. 1965) breaks from the anti-Spanish bias of Italian historiography to portray the reality of Philip's reign in Naples, which was generally acceptable to the population; Croce's essay asserting that the age of Philip II in Italy was still a vital period appears in translation in Eric Cochrane, ed., *The Late Italian Renaissance* (New York, London 1970), which also carries Rosario Villari's, 'Insurrection in Naples of 1585'. For the Franche-Comté see Lucien Febvre, *Philippe II et la Franche-Comté* (Paris 1911, reprinted 1970). This work established the method, brought to fruition by Braudel in his *Méditerranée*, of dealing with geography and the economy, social and mental structures, political and religious institutions and attitudes, before discussing the leading figures and great events, in such a fashion that the latter emanate, in a nearly deterministic manner, from the total ambience.

A good, brief bibliography for the Netherlands revolt can be found in H. R.

Rowen, ed., *The Low Countries in Early Modern Times* (New York, London 1972). Pieter Geyl, *The Revolt of the Netherlands* (London, 2nd corrected ed. 1962) is the standard introduction to the topic. New insights have been offered by Charles Wilson, *Queen Elizabeth and the Revolt of the Netherlands* (London, Berkeley 1970), who claims that without English intervention, the Netherlands revolt would have been subdued by Philip, regardless of how many rivers Geyl found between the rebels and Philip's armies. His portrait of the queen as a woman swayed by prejudice and passion, given to procrastination and hysteria, as well as capable of statecraft, is a welcome relief from the fulsome praise she is usually accorded. Wilson's Elizabeth is a much more believable contemporary of Philip II than most others. G. N. Parker, 'Spain, her Enemies and the Revolt of the Netherlands', *Past and Present*, no. 49 (1970) 72–95, intelligently takes on Pierre Chaunu's contention, in 'Seville and la Belgique', *Revue du Nord*, no. 42 (1960) 259–92, that Philip's war effort was proportional to the amount of treasure arriving in Seville; Parker argues, rightly I think, that the war effort was much more closely related to the Turkish threat in the Mediterranean. G. Parker's *Army of Flanders and the Spanish Road 1567–1659* (Cambridge, New York 1972) is a brilliant work which, though monographic in format, becomes immediately essential for studies not only of Dutch revolt and Spain, but for warfare and military organization in the sixteenth and seventeenth centuries in general, and their impact on governments and society. Its 'Conclusion' presents much the same argument as his article mentioned above, but the article is in some ways more satisfying, and not supplanted by the appearance of the book.

An interesting study of Netherlands society, from a Marxist point of view, is Tibor Wittman, *Les Gueux dans les 'Bonnes Villes' de Flandre* (Budapest 1969); he also published, in Magyar, a biography of Philip II, which I unfortunately have not seen.

All the above works presuppose some knowledge of the revolt: English-speaking readers, wanting background, can read with profit and pleasure J. L. Motley's classics, *The Rise of the Dutch Republic*, 3 vols. (New York, London 1855) and the *United Netherlands*, 4 vols. (New York, London 1860–68, and many subsequent editions). Though strongly biased towards the Protestant and rebel side, Motley was thorough in his research, and many of what later historians claim to be new insights into the revolt can be found, lying in a matter-of-fact fashion, in his splendid narrative.

For interesting aspects of Philip's relations with England: Manuel Fernández Alvarez, *Tres embajadores de Felipe II en Inglaterra* (Madrid 1951); with France, De Lamar Jensen, *Diplomacy and Dogmatism* (Cambridge, Mass. 1964), on the embassy of Don Bernardino de Mendoza; and Bhodan Chudoba, *Spain and the Empire 1519–1643* (Chicago 1952).

Recent general histories of Europe which deal intelligently with Philip II include: *New Cambridge Modern History*, vol. III, 'Western Europe and the Power of Spain' by H. G. Koenigsberger. The chapter also appears in Koenigsberger's *The Habsburgs in Europe, 1516–1660* (Ithaca, N.Y., London 1971); J. H. Elliott, *Europe Divided 1559–1598* (London, New York 1968); and Henri Lapeyre, *Les monarchies européennes du XVIe siècle* (Paris 1967).

List of Illustrations

Index

Topics clearly indicated in chapter and section headings have not invariably been included in the index. Dates
birth, death, the grant of titles and appointment to important positions are given when known. If only one da
for an office is given, the office was held for life; otherwise the date of departure from office is given. Fo
offices not usually held for life, such as governorships and viceroyalties, a terminal date is given even when th
holder died in office. Don is abbreviated to D. Titles of paintings and works of scholarship or literature hav
not been included in the index.